The Teacher's Reflective Practice Handbook

What do we mean by reflective practice?
What does it involve?
How can it help you develop as a teacher?

The Teacher's Reflective Practice Handbook is an essential source of advice, guidance and ideas for both students and practising teachers. Helping you to translate pedagogical knowledge into practice, this handbook guides you through studying your own teaching for personal development, evaluating your lessons through classroom research, and enhancing the quality of pupil learning. It offers an innovative framework which serves to prepare you for the challenges and complexities of the classroom environment, and supports the continuing improvement of your teaching.

Underpinned by key theoretical concepts and contemporary research within the field of education, chapters help you to:

*   systematically evaluate your teaching through classroom research procedures
*   question personal theories and beliefs, and consider alternative perspectives and possibilities
*   try out new strategies and ideas to maximise the learning potential of all students
*   enhance the quality of, and continue to improve, your teaching.

Including a range of reflective tasks, links to online resources, exemplification material and further reading to help you develop your own thinking, *The Teacher's Reflective Practice Handbook* is an accessible guide which supports the facilitation of reflective practice through self- and peer-assessment, problem-based learning and personal development planning. The multi-dimensional framework enables you to build a meaningful, personally relevant portfolio of evidence-informed practice.

Paula Zwozdiak-Myers is Course Director for the Secondary Postgraduate Certificate in Education at Brunel University, UK.

The Teacher's Reflective Practice Handbook

Becoming an extended professional through capturing evidence-informed practice

Paula Zwozdiak-Myers

Routledge
Taylor & Francis Group

LONDON AND NEW YORK

First published 2012
by Routledge
2 Park Square, Milton Park, Abingdon, Oxon OX14 4RN

Simultaneously published in the USA and Canada
by Routledge
711 Third Avenue, New York, NY 10017

Routledge is an imprint of the Taylor & Francis Group, an informa business

British Library Cataloguing in Publication Data
A catalogue record for this book is available from the British Library

Library of Congress Cataloging in Publication Data
Zwozdiak-Myers, Paula.
The teacher's reflective practice handbook : how to engage effectively
in professional development and build a portfolio of practice / Paula
Zwozdiak-Myers.
    p. cm.
    Includes index.
    1. Reflective teaching–Handbooks, manuals, etc. 2. Teachers–In-
service training–Handbooks, manuals, etc. 3. Portfolios in education–
Handbooks, manuals, etc. I. Title.
    LB1025.3.Z86 2012
    371.102–dc23   2011048688

ISBN: 978-0-415-59757-9 (hbk)
ISBN: 978-0-415-59758-6 (pbk)
ISBN: 978-0-203-11873-3 (ebk)

Typeset in Galliard
by HWA Text and Data Management, London

MIX
Paper from
responsible sources
FSC® C004839
www.fsc.org

Printed and bound in Great Britain by
TJ International Ltd, Padstow, Cornwall

For Jonathan and Rosanna, my pigeon pair
And with fondest memories of the most remarkable friend and mentor,
my beloved husband Coleman Everett Myers

Contents

Figures

Tables

Preface

In past decades, reflective practice has been recognised by eminent scholars, researchers and practitioners within the field of education, as an important core component for the professional development of teachers. Currently, reflective practice is in the foreground of key drivers advanced by governments and education departments worldwide, to raise educational standards and maximise the learning potential of all pupils. The broad consensus arising from recent national and international large-scale surveys is that *teacher quality* is the 'single most important school variable influencing student achievement' (OECD, 2005: 2), and characteristics which mark teachers at different career stages should be built 'on a concept of teaching as praxis in which theory, practice and the ability to reflect critically on one's own and others' practice illuminate each other' (ETUCE, 2008: 26). This requires teachers who can determine the relevance of new knowledge; are flexible, creative and adaptive to change, innately curious and capable of 'asking intelligent questions about the world in which they live and work' (AGQTP, 2008: 7).

There can be no doubt that learning to teach and striving to improve the quality of practice in the twenty-first century is a major global challenge, particularly within the culture of schooling 'envisioned for an increasingly pluralistic society' (ETUCE, 2008: 58). Schools are expected to: effectively accommodate pupils from diverse backgrounds and with different languages; be sensitive to gender and cultural issues; promote social cohesion and tolerance; respond to disadvantaged pupils and those with learning and behavioural difficulties; use new technologies; and keep pace with rapidly developing fields of knowledge and approaches to pupil assessment. Teachers must be capable of preparing pupils for a society and economy in which they 'will be expected to be self-directed learners, able and motivated to keep learning over a lifetime' (OECD, 2005: 2).

Performance management has also become an important focal point for professionals working within educational contexts. Teachers are expected to assume responsibility for their professional development planning at each career stage and to gather evidence of that development in relation to prescribed performance criteria, which places an emphasis on performativity and accountability in relation to measurable, instrumental outcomes. Progression is regularly audited, assessed and rewarded through various internal and external appraisal and evaluative systems. For example, the vision of professional development portrayed in the *Five Year Strategy for Children and Learners* (DfES, 2004a, para 39) champions:

a new professionalism for teachers in which career progression and financial rewards will go to those who are making the biggest contributions to improving pupil attainment, those who are continually developing their own expertise, and those who help to develop expertise in other teachers.

This highlights the need for teachers to become very active agents in analysing their own practice both 'in the light of professional standards and their own students' progress in the light of standards for student learning' (OECD, 2005: 11). A cautionary note however is that although a number of standards might serve to identify the professional attributes, skills, knowledge and understanding teachers must acquire and develop to demonstrate effectiveness, these cannot be applied in a purely prescriptive manner to guide practice. Characteristics that are difficult to measure yet which can be vital to pupil learning include the capability to convey ideas in clear and convincing ways; be creative and enthusiastic; provide positive learning environments for different types of pupils; foster productive teacher–pupil relationships; and 'work effectively with colleagues and parents' (ibid.: 2).

Terms associated with reflective practice such as *critical thinking, metacognition, reflective judgement, reflective thought,* and *reflexivity* have been introduced into teacher education and classroom contexts based on the assumption that acquiring skills associated with reflective practice should enable teachers to become effective practitioners. Yet, as Furlong and Maynard (1995) persuasively argue, the concepts and theories which underpin such terms reveal a number of variations: debate concerning the development of reflective practice stems, in part, from different discourses within the process of learning to teach which writers have focused on to examine the complex relationship between the process of theorising and other forms of propositional knowledge – those derived from Dewey (1933) and from Schon (1987). A further dilemma concerns their widespread usage and common currency in educational discourse, performance management, research publications and textbooks wherein little or no reference is made to how these terms are being used or what they explicitly mean; an assumption of shared meanings seems to be prevalent.

The development of reflective practice is a vitally important core component of professional development, which serves to prepare teachers for the challenges and complexities of the twenty-first-century classroom and to become effective decision makers with an understanding of how to translate pedagogical knowledge into their own practice. The ability to question *why* a teacher does what she does has been linked to the development of *contextual knowing, professional artistry* and *reflective reasoning.* Scholars have also argued that reflective practice is characteristically associated with *autonomy, empowerment* and *effective teaching.*

In light of numerous claims advanced concerning the values inherent in reflective practice for professional development – and we have merely begun to scratch the surface here – what becomes readily apparent is that reflective practice is a complex, multifaceted phenomenon; and, if the goal to raise *teacher quality* is to be realised, then how we conceptualise reflective practice must be unpacked so that its core components can be recognised, enacted and understood. On the one hand, we need to address such questions as: What do we mean by reflective practice? What are its core components? How might we recognise it? What can we learn from doing it? On the other: How do we define professional development? What criteria might we use to distinguish between *restricted* and *extended* professionals? What links can be drawn between reflective practice and professional development? Are the two phenomena synonymous, interdependent or mutually exclusive? An important goal, which permeates through this book, is that of enabling you to respond to such searching questions from a knowledgeable, experiential and well-informed platform.

The *Framework of Reflective Practice* presented in this book has been designed to capture the somewhat elusive boundaries of reflective practice within nine discrete, yet interrelated dimensions so that you understand how to: effectively engage in reflective practice; plan for and structure your own professional development as you acquire the art of self-study; and build a reflective portfolio to evidence your journey of professional growth and development.

In addition to the nine dimensions which provide specific focal points to guide and structure evidence of reflective practice, different types of discourse can highlight qualitative distinctions between ways of thinking and speaking about aspects of teaching and learning, as well as of practising teaching. Three particular types of discourse are captured within the Framework of Reflective Practice – *descriptive, comparative* and *critical reflective conversations* – to exemplify and signal the transition from *surface* to *deep* to *transformative learning*.

An increased awareness of how to meaningfully engage with the core components embedded within this 9 × 3 Framework of Reflective Practice, should help you to improve the quality and effectiveness of your teaching, as the focus and content of reflective practice and types of discourse you engage in can be clarified with a specific purpose in mind. As you explore the connections and interrelationships between them and assume a critical stance to your professional work, you will come to exemplify the attributes associated with a *critical being* (Barnett, 1997), an *extended professional* (Hoyle, 1974; Stenhouse, 1975) and a *reflective practitioner* (Schon, 1987).

This Framework of Reflective Practice is soundly underpinned by the concepts and theories advanced over many decades by key scholars, researchers and practitioners who have contributed important insights into this field of study.

The structure of this book

Eleven chapters are presented in two main parts:

Part I – Reflective practice for professional development: Framing the construct

Chapter 1 introduces the Framework of Reflective Practice which has been designed to capture nine dimensions of reflective practice in which teachers can demonstrate capacity and commitment as they study their own teaching for personal improvement. Chapter 2 presents three types of discourse which can be used in conjunction with each dimension of reflective practice to highlight qualitative distinctions between descriptive, comparative and critical reflective conversations teachers can engage in.

Part 2 – Dimensions of reflective practice: Key features and processes

Chapters 3 through 11 take each of the nine dimensions of reflective practice in turn, and explore the key features and processes embedded within the nature of their reflective activity and translation into professional practice. The attributes associated with the teacher as researcher as well as the qualities and characteristics associated with striving toward becoming an extended professional are interrogated in depth to help you structure and evidence your professional growth and development from a well-focused and purposeful platform.

Each chapter is organised as follows:

- Learning objectives
- Introduction
- The content presents theoretical underpinnings of the major concepts drawn upon, which are interwoven with a diverse range of reflective tasks
- Summary of key points
- Recommendations for further reading.

Reflective portfolio

Reflective tasks accompany each chapter and invite you to explore the relationships between academic debate, policy, rhetoric, theory and practice. They aim to provide an enquiry-led, research-informed and critical approach to teaching and learning. As you complete these tasks you are encouraged to keep a reflective portfolio to record evidence of your professional growth and development. The portfolio also provides a vehicle through which you can articulate and give voice to your personal philosophy and thoughts about factors that shape and influence teaching and learning as they emerge. In so doing, your portfolio becomes an iterative and dynamic working document to exemplify your journey of discovery and enlightenment. Several tasks ask you to set SMART targets or goals, interpreted as follows:

- Specific – the goal has a clear purpose and defined outcome
- Measureable – it will be clear when the goal has been met
- Achievable – the goal is realistic and sustainable within existing resources
- Relevant – the goal adds value to professional development and reflects identified needs
- Time-bound – a deadline for achieving the goal has been established.

Appendices

Although Chapter 10 explicitly invites you to explore criteria against which the quality and standards of teaching can be judged, you will find it beneficial to familiarise yourself with Appendix A: Standards for teachers (DfE, 2011) effective 1 September 2012 and which apply to all teachers in England, and Appendix B: Criteria to determine 'outstanding' trainee teachers (Ofsted, 2008) from the outset. This enables you to align and cross-reference reflective tasks from each chapter, as appropriate, with criteria currently in use.

Use of terminology

Throughout this text the terms *he* and *she* or *his* and *her* are used in a balanced way so as to avoid gender bias and unduly lengthy terminology, which enables you to access key messages embedded within the narrative in a more cogent, fluent manner. School children are referred to as *pupils* rather than students: other than when school children are referred to as students within a direct quote. The expression *student teachers* relates to individuals following initial teacher education (ITE) or pre-service teacher education courses, e.g. undergraduate and postgraduate students working toward a qualified teacher status (QTS) award.

Paula Zwozdiak-Myers
August 2011

Part I

Reflective practice for professional development

Framing the construct

Chapter 1

Reflective practice

Captured, framed and defined

Learning objectives

In this chapter you will consider:

- how reflective practice as a *disposition to enquiry* and a *process* has been interpreted within the Framework of Reflective Practice;
- how *reflective attitudes* can influence your approach to teaching;
- key characteristics and attributes used to describe *extended professionals*;
- central concepts associated with defining the *teacher as a professional*;
- how *emotional intelligence* and *professional values* may be reflected in your teaching.

Introduction

In recent decades, reflective practice has increasingly become embedded within discourse concerning teacher professional development, particularly in relation to raising educational standards, performance management and whole-school improvement planning. Teachers who ask searching questions about educational practice that arise from their own contexts and professional concerns demonstrate a commitment to continuous learning by seeking new ideas, evaluating and reflecting on their impact, and trying out new ways of working to improve their effectiveness. This approach to professional development underpins concepts of the teacher as a *reflective practitioner,* a *researcher* and an *extended professional.* These concepts are interrelated as Stenhouse (1975) argues, the outstanding feature of extended professionals is their capacity and commitment to engage in autonomous self-development through systematic self-study, reflection and research.

Central to your development as a teacher is your commitment and capacity to analyse and evaluate what is happening in your own lessons and to use your professional judgement both to *reflect* and *act* upon these analyses and evaluations to improve pupil learning and the quality of your teaching. This enables you to make informed judgements derived from an evidence base about the effectiveness of both.

Although reflective practice is a complex, multifaceted phenomenon, it is important that you gain an insight and understanding of its core components as each component plays a significant role in your on-going professional development. The purpose of this chapter is to demystify this phenomenon and, in so doing, open your eyes to the numerous factors and variables that may influence and impact the quality of your teaching. This should enable you to exercise greater discernment in making professional judgements about how and in what areas you need further development so as to maximise the learning opportunities you provide for all your pupils from a well-informed platform.

To that end, the Framework of Reflective Practice, designed to capture nine dimensions of reflective practice in which teachers can demonstrate capacity and commitment as they engage in research to study and improve their own teaching, is presented here. The Framework, with its definition and associated dimensions of reflective practice, provides you with specific focal points to guide and structure evidence-informed practice.

Reflective practice for professional development

Figure 1.1 illustrates the *Framework of Reflective Practice* (Zwozdiak-Myers, 2010) based around nine dimensions, which have been identified through a synthesis of the literature on reflective practice advanced by eminent scholars, researchers and practitioners within the field. The key attributes associated with *reflective attitudes* (Dewey, 1933), *extended professionals* (Hoyle, 1974; Stenhouse, 1975) and the *teacher as a professional* (Day, 1999; Eraut, 1994; Hoyle and John, 1995) are particularly significant as these have resonance with the central features used to characterise the *teacher as researcher* (Hopkins, 2002; Stenhouse, 1975). This construct supports Moore's (2000: 146) proposition that teachers should perceive themselves 'as researchers and theorists as well as practitioners' as the pursuit of becoming a reflective practitioner is not so much about the *acquisition* or development *per se* of the skills and areas of knowledge required for successful teaching, but rather concerns 'the particular skills needed to *reflect constructively* upon on-going experience as a way of developing those skills and knowledge and improving the effectiveness of one's work' (ibid.: 128).

Although the dimensions presented in Figure 1.1 might not appear to have well-defined boundaries given the complex, interdependent nature of variables that abound within the context of teaching and learning, they have been separated out to map the salient features embedded within each, in relation to the development of reflective practice. It is important to note that although the dimensions are presented in a linear, sequential manner from 1 through 9, any one dimension can provide the initial catalyst for reflective practice. For example, a debriefing session with a mentor or professional tutor following an observation of your lesson might through discussion provide the springboard from which you *consider alternative perspectives and possibilities* (dimension 5) for future lessons, or you might decide to attend a specific training session offered by your local authority or subject association to *continue to improve your own teaching* (dimension 9). Following the initial impetus to engage in reflective activity, other dimensions will come into play; ultimately they all interrelate and each forms an integral part of the construct. The picture should begin to emerge as a coherent whole.

Situated at the core of this framework, reflective practice is defined as:

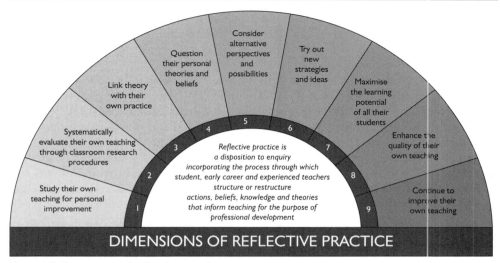

Figure 1.1 Framework of reflective practice

a disposition to enquiry incorporating the process through which student, early career and experienced teachers structure or restructure actions, beliefs, knowledge and theories that inform teaching for the purpose of professional development.

Two very broad, interrelated strands – a *disposition to enquiry* and a *process* – are embedded within this definition. Ways in which the work of key proponents within the field contribute toward an understanding of the characteristic features associated with the first strand are identified in the following sub-sections of this chapter.

The second strand, which captures reflective practice as a *process*, incorporates numerous concepts advanced by theorists over past decades, particularly in relation to the nature of reflective activity and its translation into professional practice. The seminal work of Schon (1987) and his concepts of *reflection in action* and *reflection on action* along with Kolb's (1984) model of *experiential learning* are but two examples. Although some of these processes are inextricably linked to a disposition to enquiry and are briefly touched upon here, Chapters 3 through 11 explore the main concepts and theories used to clarify the range of processes embedded within each dimension of reflective practice highlighted in Figure 1.1.

Reflective practice as a disposition to enquiry

Reflective attitudes

Reflective practice as a *disposition to enquiry* has at its roots the early work of Dewey (1933), specifically in relation to the reflective attitudes of *open-mindedness, responsibility* and *wholeheartedness*, which he considers to be both prerequisite and integral to reflective action.

Open-mindedness refers to the willingness to consider more than one side of an argument and fully embrace and attend to alternative possibilities, which requires an active desire to listen to more than one side and recognise that formerly held views and beliefs could be misconceived. Reflective teachers question and challenge why they do as they do (Zeichner and Liston, 1996) by interrogating assumptions, beliefs and personal theories from a range of perspectives or *lenses* (Brookfield, 1995), which can be evidenced in those who are open to scrutiny and change.

Responsibility refers to the disposition to carefully consider the consequences of actions and willingness to accept those consequences. Dewey (1933: 32) argues that misconceptions and confusion can arise when individuals 'profess certain beliefs [yet] are unwilling to commit themselves to the consequences that flow from them'. Teachers who evaluate their own practice and question whether the outcomes are effective, for whom and in what ways, as opposed to those who merely question whether their objectives have been met (Zeichner and Liston, 1996), demonstrate responsibility.

Wholeheartedness refers to the way in which open-mindedness and responsibility come together, through an interest in and enthusiasm for some situation or event. Whole-hearted teachers examine their assumptions, beliefs and the consequences of their actions regularly and approach each situation with a view to learning something new (Zeichner and Liston, 1996). As Dewey (1933: 30) writes:

> a genuine enthusiasm is an attitude that operates as an intellectual force. When a person is absorbed, the subject carries him on. Questions occur to him spontaneously; a flood of suggestions … further inquiries and readings are indicated and followed … the material holds and buoys his mind up and gives an onward impetus to thinking.

Very clear links can be drawn between Dewey's exposition of reflective attitudes and assuming responsibility for your own professional development, which has been positioned as a central feature in Zeichner and Liston's (1996: 6) idea of a reflective teacher: 'when embracing the concept of reflective teaching, there is often a commitment by teachers to internalise the disposition and skills to study their teaching and become better at teaching over time, a commitment to take responsibility for their own professional development'.

Extended professionals

Several theorists built upon Dewey's discourse of reflective attitudes. The early work of Hoyle (1974) gave rise to the distinction between *restricted* and *extended* professionals. Characteristics used to describe restricted professionals include: a high level of skill in classroom practice; an ability to understand, establish and enjoy positive working relationships with children by adopting a child-centred approach; the use of personal perceptions of change in pupil behaviour and achievement to evaluate performance; and short-term practical course attendance. Characteristics used to describe extended professionals incorporate all those associated with restricted professionals in addition to the following:

- contextualising classroom practice by relating it to the wider contexts of school, community and society;
- participating in a wide range of professional development activities such as conferences, subject panels and in-service educational training;
- an active concern to link theory and practice;
- engagement in peer observation and small-scale collaborative research studies.

Reflective task 1.1 **Reflective attitudes**

Distinctions drawn by Gore (1993) between *recalcitrant, acquiescent* and *committed* student teachers in terms of their disposition to think, talk and write about their experiences as learners and as teachers, illustrate the significance of Dewey's reflective attitudes. Similarly, based upon evidence of student teachers' proclivity to explore pedagogical thinking, LaBoskey (1993: 30) categorises *alert novices* as those who appear to be driven by the desire to continuously look out for something better, who possess the will to know, for which she introduces the metaphor *passionate creed*.

* Research these literary sources and compare and contrast the basis upon which their distinctions between student teachers have been made.
* Reflect on how your approach to professional learning might be categorised and judged when using their criteria.
* What have you learned about yourself in terms of how your reflective attitudes may impact your teaching and pupil learning?

Reflective task 1.2 **Becoming an extended professional**

* Take each characteristic identified by Hoyle to describe both restricted and extended professionals in turn and reflect upon *how, when* and *why* you have demonstrated and/or engaged in them.
* On the basis of your overall response to this task, would you describe yourself as a restricted or an extended professional? Explain why you have reached this conclusion.
* Are there any characteristics for which you would welcome further developmental and experiential opportunities?
* Select three SMART targets and devise an action plan to gain this development and experience.

Building on Hoyle's work, focusing particularly on the *teacher as researcher*, Stenhouse (1975: 143–144) identifies five key attributes to characterise extended professionals as they research their own practice; notably, extended professionals:

* have a commitment to question their practice as the basis for teacher development;
* reflect critically and systematically on their own practice;
* have a concern to question and test theory in practice;
* appreciate the benefit of having their teaching observed by others and discussing their teaching with others in an open and honest manner;
* have the commitment and skills to study their own teaching and in so doing develop the art of self-study.

Reflective task 1.3 **Comparing theories of an extended professional**

- Examine the focus of each dimension of reflective practice presented in Figure 1.1 very closely and map out where Hoyle's characteristics and Stenhouse's attributes of an extended professional can be situated.
- Research the work of these theorists and make notes on ways in which their respective concepts of an extended professional are similar and how they differ.
- Discuss the main points of your argument with a critical friend.

These attributes are significantly led by the teacher's personal interest and desire to become increasingly more effective in promoting pupil learning. At the heart of reflecting on teaching and of research into teaching is a concern to ensure that all pupils learn as a result of your teaching. Genuine commitment to teacher development arises from critically constructive self-reflection and considered response, which has the potential to develop into more systematic research into teaching.

The teacher as a professional

Teaching and learning about how to become an effective teacher centre on complex, interrelated sets of thoughts and actions. They can be perceived as demanding tasks, which might be approached in a number of different ways. As teachers gain proficiency in the basic knowledge and skills of teaching, 'the more an understanding of the relationship between teaching and learning may influence practice, and the more deliberately a teacher considers his or her actions the more difficult it is to be sure that there is one right approach to teaching, or teaching about teaching' (Loughran, 1996: 3).

While reflective practice is very much part of what is currently expected of teachers, there has long been concern for teachers to take responsibility for their own professional learning and development. During the 1990s there was considerable debate amongst theorists about how to conceptualise the teacher as a professional, which builds further on the work advanced by Dewey and Stenhouse. Some distinctive qualities about the nature of the teacher as a professional are highlighted in Day's (1999: 4) description of professional development as:

> All natural learning experiences and those conscious and planned activities which are intended to be of direct or indirect benefit to the individual, group or school, which contribute, through these, to the quality of education in the classroom. It is the process by which, alone and with others, teachers review, renew and extend their commitment as change agents to the moral purposes of teaching: and by which they acquire and develop critically the knowledge, skills and emotional intelligence essential to good professional thinking, planning and practice with children, young people and colleagues throughout each phase of their teaching lives.

Embedded within this interpretation are factors associated with the nature of teachers' autonomy, knowledge and responsibility, along with suggestions as to how

---

Reflective task 1.4 **Emotional intelligence**

Table 1.1 identifies 18 competencies associated with emotional intelligence.

- Reflect upon how well you demonstrate these competencies using the rating scale in the right-hand column and provide examples of how, when and why you demonstrated these competencies.
- Ask a colleague/peer or tutor who knows you well to record their perceptions of you in relation to these competencies.
- Compare your responses and discuss any differences that may have emerged. Did anything surprise you? Have you learned anything new about yourself? Have you discovered areas in need of development? For each area, identify three steps you can take to improve in this area.
- Write a 2,000-word reflective narrative on how your emotional intelligence enhances and/or inhibits your capacity to create a positive learning environment for your pupils and establish effective working relationships with your colleagues.

In seeking relevant literature the following provide a useful springboard: Boyatzis, Goleman and Rhee (2000) *Clustering Competence in Emotional Intelligence*; Druskat, Sala and Mount (2006) *Linking Emotional Intelligence and Performance Management at Work*; and Mayer and Salovey (1997) *What is Emotional Intelligence?*

---

they might acquire the knowledge, skills and emotional intelligence which underpin effective practice. It also embraces the development of the individual teacher, the pupils and the school, affective aspects of personal growth and development driven by intrinsic motivations and explicitly makes reference to continuing professional development. Day endorses the view that teachers should stay abreast of developments in subject knowledge and not 'overly rely on knowledge gleaned during their previous educational experiences' (Moore, 2000: 125) and importantly, the view of Hargreaves (2003: 16) who cautions that 'teachers who do not keep learning by more than trial and error are a liability to their pupils'.

Day makes reference to a relatively new and under-researched construct within the field of education, which has important implications in the context of teaching and learning – that of emotional intelligence. Reflective task 1.4 enables you to learn more about the multifaceted nature of this construct and contemplate how your emotional intelligence may be reflected in and through your own practice.

In writing about the teacher as a professional, Eraut (1994: 232) suggests *accountability* is exemplified when professionals demonstrate:

- a *moral commitment* to serve the interests of pupils by reflecting on their well-being and progress and deciding how best it can be fostered or promoted;
- a *professional obligation* to review periodically the nature and effectiveness of one's practice to improve the quality of one's management, pedagogy and decision-making;
- a *professional obligation* to continue to develop one's practical knowledge both by personal reflection and through interaction with others.

Table 1.1 Emotional intelligence competencies, adapted from Boyatzis, Goleman and Rhee (2000)

Cluster	Competencies	Description	Rating Low 1	2	3	4	High 5
Self awareness	Emotional self awareness	Recognise how your emotions affect performance					
	Accurate self assessment	Know your inner resources, abilities and limits					
	Self confidence	Strong sense of self-worth and capabilities					
Self management	Self control	Keeping disruptive impulses and emotions in check					
	Transparency	Maintaining integrity, acting congruently with your values					
	Optimism	Persistence in pursuing goals despite obstacles and setbacks					
	Adaptability	Flexibility in handling change					
	Achievement orientation	Striving to improve or meeting a standard of excellence					
	Initiative	Readiness to act on opportunities					
Social awareness	Empathy	Sensing others' feelings and perspectives and taking an active interest in their concerns					
	Organisational awareness	Reading a group's emotional currents and power relationships					
	Service orientation	Anticipating, recognising and meeting customer/client needs					
Social skills	Developing others	Sensing others' development needs and bolstering their abilities					
	Inspirational leadership	Inspiring and guiding individuals and groups					
	Influence	Having an impact on others					
	Change catalyst	Initiating or managing change					
	Conflict management	Negotiating and resolving disagreements					
	Teamwork and collaboration	Working with others toward a shared goal, creating group synergy in pursuing collective goals					

This has resonance with Hoyle and John's (1995) exposition of *Professional Knowledge and Professional Practice*, in which they identify *knowledge, autonomy* and *responsibility* as central concepts in defining the teacher as a professional. The interrelationship between these concepts has been summarised by Furlong, Barton, Miles, Whiting and Whitty (2000: 5) as follows:

> It is because professionals face complex and unpredictable situations that they need a specialised form of knowledge; if they are to apply that knowledge, it is argued that they need the autonomy to make their own judgements. Given that they have that autonomy, it is essential that they act with responsibility – collectively they need to develop appropriate professional values.

This highlights not only the importance for practitioners to clearly express and frequently review their own professional values but also that these values need to derive from an understanding of what constitutes appropriate ethical practice in educational contexts. To realise this aim teachers must justify how their own values are underpinned by the expectations of what those within the profession regard as appropriate, legitimate rules of engagement.

The *Code of Professional Values and Professional Practice for Teachers* (GTCE, 2006a) provides a framework to illustrate what aspects of teachers' professional behaviour must conform to specific rules when conducting their duties. Thus, an important task for teachers is to 'work out their educational values, not in isolation and abstraction but in collaboration with colleagues and amid the complexities of school life' (Nixon, 1995: 220). This can, in part, be accomplished by reflecting critically on what it is that you do and importantly, justifying *why* it is that you are doing it, in relation to what is happening around you in your own classroom and the wider context of your school.

This said, a number of teachers within the same school context may have different backgrounds, different career aspirations, different expectations and different priorities along with divergent perspectives as to the nature, goals and purposes of education and schooling, which may lead to differences in their respective values. Haydon (1997: 11) argues that the difficulty often faced by teachers 'lies not in outlining the values which a school stands for, but in recognising what this endorsement will mean in practice, particularly if some of the values do not sit comfortably together'. This line of argument suggests some teachers' experience within the context of schools could be incongruent, as values expressed in principle might not necessarily be demonstrated in practice (Ghaye and Ghaye, 1998).

Carr (1992: 244) uses the phrase *principled preferences* to describe values as 'a consequence of something approaching intelligent deliberation', which are thus, in principle, 'susceptible of rational appraisal and re-appraisal'. As you gain experience and critically reflect on and discuss your actions, feelings and thoughts about different aspects of teaching and learning with your colleagues/peers and pupils, the professional judgements and decisions you make will be based on educational goals and values, which in turn, can reflect the kind of teacher you aspire to be. When you experience *autonomy* in terms of exercising professional judgement and making decisions about the learning objectives, content, pedagogical strategies/approaches and assessment procedures you plan to use with pupils in the context

---

Reflective task 1.5 **Professional values and attributes**

The Code of Professional Values and Practice for Teachers (GTCE, 2006a) clearly articulates the values you are expected to uphold in your work as a professional. The *Teachers' Standards* (DfE, 2011) (which apply to teachers at all career stages) also underpin this fundamental aspect of your teaching practice.

- Access copies of these documents and read them thoroughly to ensure you are fully aware of your professional responsibilities and obligations as a teacher.
- Consider how the concepts advanced by Dewey, Hoyle, Stenhouse and Eraut relate to the professional values expressed in these documents.
- Select three standards (see Appendix A) and reflect upon *how, when* and *why* you demonstrated these within your own practice.
- Discuss the outcomes of this activity with a colleague/peer or your professional tutor and consider how the values which underpin your own practice are reflected in those upheld within your school and the wider teaching profession.

---

of your own classroom, you should as Whitehead (1993) notes, begin to more fully realise personal educational values within your own teaching.

Summary of key points

This chapter has introduced the Framework of Reflective Practice, which defines and captures this elusive phenomenon within nine dimensions of reflective practice. The reflective attitudes of *open-mindedness, responsibility* and *wholeheartedness*, characteristics and key attributes of *extended professionals*; and qualities associated with the *teacher as a professional* signpost how reflective practice as a *disposition to enquiry* has been interpreted within this construct. It has also invited you to explore how your emotional intelligence may influence and be reflected in your approach to teaching and learning.

Although articulated some years ago, these same concepts and theories remain highly significant for teachers working within the context of twenty-first-century schools and permeate through the professional standards teachers must evidence in addition to the code of professional values and practice they must uphold to demonstrate personal effectiveness, across the national and international landscape.

Recommended reading

Day, C., Kington, A., Stobart, G. and Sammons, P. (2006) The personal and professional selves of teachers: stable and unstable identities, *British Educational Research Journal*, 32, (4): 601–616.

Based on findings of a large-scale, 4-year research project in England to investigate variations in teachers' work and lives and their effect on pupils, this article addresses the issue of teacher identities, which may be 'more, or less, stable and more or less fragmented at different times and in different ways according to a number of life, career and situational factors' (ibid.: 601).

European Trade Union Committee for Education (ETUCE) (2008) *Teacher Education in Europe: An ETUCE Policy Paper,* Brussels: ETUCE.
This policy paper, involving 46 participating countries, sets out the ETUCE's vision on teacher education for today's society and explores how a highly qualified profession can ensure a good balance between the professional autonomy of teachers and their public and social accountability.

Organisation for Economic Cooperation and Development (OECD) (2005) *Teachers Matter: Attracting, Developing and Retaining Effective Teachers: An Overview,* Paris: OECD. Available online: www.oecd.org (accessed June 2010).
This research-based international comparative analysis of 25 countries draws a number of conclusions relating to how teachers' roles are changing in light of the complex demands placed upon schools and teachers working in the twenty-first century, and explores diverse variables that can influence pupil learning.

When viewed collectively these sources provide a global perspective of how the professional landscape of teaching is and has been changing, particularly since the turn of the twenty-first century, in response to broader changes within society and the significant challenges facing teachers, education and training systems in the world today.

Chapter 2

Qualitative distinctions in reflective practice

Learning objectives

In this chapter you will consider:

*   how qualitative distinctions between descriptive, comparative and critical reflective conversations are interpreted within the Framework of Reflective Practice;
*   reflective conversations and narrative enquiry as different types of discourse and patterns of thinking to question particular aspects of teaching and learning;
*   some key theorists' distinctions between dualism and relativism and between reflective and routine practice;
*   how critical thinking and metacognition can inform teaching and learning.

Introduction

Numerous scholars, researchers and practitioners within the field of education have sought to capture and explain qualitative distinctions exemplified by professionals in their reflective practice. A common thread permeating through many of the concepts and theories proposed is that the types of discourse or reflective conversations teachers engage in, may be indicative of their development from *surface* to *deep* to *transformative learning* (Moon, 1999); progressive stages of *epistemological cognition* (Baxter Magolda, 1999); and different stages of *reflective reasoning* (King and Kitchener, 1994).

Table 2.1 highlights some key proponents who have worked extensively in this field and identifies the focus and themes underpinning their respective theories. This chapter explores the nature of these qualitative distinctions by introducing three broad types of discourse: *descriptive, comparative* and *critical* reflective conversations.

Figure 2.1 illustrates how these reflective conversations can be mapped onto and used in conjunction with the Framework of Reflective Practice presented in Figure 1.1, and which gives rise to a 9 × 3 two-dimensional construct.

The terms discourse and reflective conversation are used interchangeably to denote ways of thinking and speaking about teaching as well as of practising teaching (Fairclough, 1998). Within any discourse it is important to note that more than one

Table 2.1 Concepts and theories related to qualitative distinctions in reflective practice

Proponent	Focus	Themes
Barnett (1997)	Critical reflection: political-social dimensions	Action, self-reflection and understanding Critical being
Baxter Magolda (1999)	Epistemological cognition	Dualist – relativist position
Ghaye and Ghaye (1998)	Reflective conversations	Descriptive, perceptive, receptive, interpretive, critical
Grimmett, MacKinnon, Erickson & Riechen (1990)	Levels of reflective teaching	Technical: instrumental mediation of actions Deliberative: deliberation among competing views Dialectical: reconstruction of experience
Habermas (1971)	Knowledge constitutive interests	Instrumental – Interpretive – Emancipatory
Hatton and Smith (1995)	Forms of reflection	Descriptive writing, descriptive reflection, dialogic reflection, critical reflection
Jay and Johnson (2002)	Dimensions of reflection	Descriptive, comparative, critical
King and Kitchener (1994)	Reflective judgement model	Pre-reflective reasoning (stages 1–3) Quasi-reflective reasoning (stages 4 & 5) Reflective reasoning (stages 6 & 7)
Lee (2005)	Depth of reflective thinking	Recall – Rationalisation – Reflectivity
Mezirow (1990)	Adult learning theory	Habitual action; thoughtful action/understanding; reflection; critical reflection
Moon (1999, 2005)	Critical thinking – metacognition	Surface to deep to transformative learning Dualist – relativist position
Sparks-Langer (1992)	Orientations to reflective thinking	Cognitive – narrative – critical
Valli (1992)	Forms of reflection	Behavioural [non-reflective] Technical reflection Reflection in action and reflection on action Deliberative reflection Personalistic reflection Critical reflection
Van Manen (1977)	Forms of rationalisation	Technical rationality: methodology and theory development to achieve objectives Practical rationality: pragmatic placement of theory into practice Critical rationality: value commitment toward educational process

type of reflective conversation may be evident as the discourse unfolds, moving from *descriptive* through *comparative* toward *critical* reflective conversations. Thus, each type of discourse should not be viewed as mutually exclusive as reflective conversations can be 'dynamic and fluid' phenomena (Ghaye and Ghaye, 1998: 25) and 'intimately intertwined to compose a composite concept' (Jay and Johnson, 2002: 80).

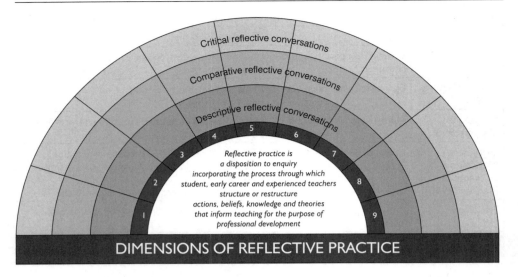

Figure 2.1 Qualitative distinctions between reflective conversations

Reflective conversations

As a form of discourse, the *reflective conversation* (Loughran, 1996; Schon, 1987; Yinger, 1990) is recognised as the responsive interchange between acting and thinking and an insight into the data of reflective practice. Described by Schon (1987) as having a conversation with the situation, it provides a vehicle through which teachers can interrogate what they do, question the educational values and goals which give 'shape, form and purpose' (Ghaye and Ghaye, 1998: 19) to what they do and learn from their experiences. As such, the reflective conversation can be positioned at the very heart of the improvement process and has potential on the one hand, to challenge and disturb those educational values and goals teachers perceive to be important and on the other, to reaffirm those values and goals they perceive as important in defining the kind of teacher they aspire to be.

If you are to recognise factors, which either serve to improve or constrain your own practice, Smyth (1992: 295) claims you will need to engage with some very fundamental questions:

- *Describe* – What do I do?
- *Inform* – What does this mean?
- *Confront* – How did I come to be like this?
- *Reconstruct* – How might I do things differently?

Different types of question may lead to different patterns of thinking. The question, 'What do I do?' for example, requires a reflective process-analysis of the approach that has been followed. It is formative in nature and aims to develop your skills and capabilities. Analysis questions enable you to break down what you already know and reassemble this knowledge to help you solve a problem. Such questions can be linked to more abstract, conceptual thinking which is central to the process of enquiry. The

---

Reflective task 2.1 **Having a conversation with the situation**

The questions framed by Smyth typify those you might ask when evaluating the effectiveness of your own teaching.

- Select a lesson you have recently planned and taught and work through these four questions systematically.
- What links can you detect between your analytical and evaluative reflection, particularly in relation to pupil learning outcomes?
- What additional questions can you ask yourself about this particular lesson?
- Reflect upon how your use of different types of questions may have shaped your patterns of thinking.
- Research how Bloom's (1956) *Taxonomy of Educational Objectives* has been linked to the development of higher-order thinking skills through the use of higher-level questions (see Table 8.2, p. 118).
- How might this classification influence your future use of questioning?

---

question, 'How might I do things differently?' requires a reflective self-evaluation of a particular type of performance using criteria against which judgements can be made. This is summative in nature and aims to develop the goals and standards you have set for yourself. Evaluative questions enable you to use your knowledge to form judgements and to justify and defend those judgements. Such questions involve more complex thinking and reasoning skills. The terms *analytical reflection* and *evaluative reflection* are used by Cowan (1998) to distinguish between these two types of discourse. The question 'How did I come to be like this?' appeals to the affective aspect of a teacher's practice, and discourse arising from this question can reveal insights into your disposition to enquiry. What should become apparent is that you will need to engage in different types of questioning as you interrogate why you do what you do in a given context if you are to learn from your experiences.

Narrative enquiry

A body of literature has emerged in recent decades, which captures the stories of teachers as they strive to become more effective practitioners. Through narrative enquiry, their voices can be heard as they speak of ways in which they experience their own professional learning and professional lives in education (e.g. Connelly and Clandinin, 1990; Sparks-Langer, 1992; Witherall and Noddings, 1991). These researchers challenge the traditional view of teacher education as 'training', where gaining proficiency in specified techniques or strategies from theory externally produced is privileged over theory grounded in personal experience (Elliott, 2005a; Glaser and Strauss, 1967; McKernan, 1996).

Beattie (2000: 18), for example, reports the narrative accounts of three prospective teachers to illustrate their increased understanding of teaching as 'moral, ethical and socially responsible work ... a willingness to review choices available ... question the "status quo" ... engage in critical and creative thinking, and re-script the stories of their current and future professional lives'. Through the process of reflection and enquiry

---

Reflective task 2.2 **The impact of narrative enquiry**

- Read Beattie's article and trace how the teachers increased their personal awareness of teaching as a moral, ethical and socially responsible way of working.
- Compare and contrast the similarities and differences between them.
- Consider how these similarities and differences may be interpreted in *The Code of Professional Values and Practice for Teachers* (GTCE, 2006a) (see task 1.5).
- Revisit your response to task 2.1 and think about *how, when* and *where* you may have exemplified a moral, ethical and socially responsible way of working during the lesson.
- Explain how this task may have increased your awareness of the potential narrative enquiry has for improving your practice.

Discuss your response to these activities with a colleague/peer or your professional tutor.

---

they were able to question their 'life histories, socialisation and the ideologies and "official stories" being enacted around them' (ibid.).

When characterised as a discourse, it should become evident through the way in which you frame questions and use language to explore your teaching and learning experiences, that different types of reflective conversation can be identified. Each type serves a particular purpose and may be used to shape the way in which you express and make sense of your own practice. Underpinning the direction of reflective conversations you can engage in with self, others and theoretical literature are the different types of question you might ask.

Moving from dualism toward relativism

Early qualitative research on student learning (Perry, 1970) indicates a developmental trend in the nature of thinking during higher education in which students gradually shift from a belief in dualism (right answers exist) to recognition of relativism (conclusions rest on evidence which learners interpret themselves). In building upon this work, King and Kitchener (1994) devised a model of reflective judgement based on findings from their ten-year longitudinal empirical study. They use the term reflective judgement to denote epistemological cognition, which is underpinned by the assertion that some problems cannot be resolved with certainty. In their study, university students were asked to work with ill-structured problems and discuss their respective experiences of having worked through the process to resolve them. The findings led King and Kitchener to devise a model characterised by seven distinct, yet developmentally related, sets of assumptions. These assumptions are concerned with the process of knowing (view of knowledge) and of how that knowledge is acquired (justification of beliefs). Their model can broadly be summarised in three phases:

- *Pre-reflective reasoning* (stages 1–3) characterised by the *belief* that: 'Knowledge is gained through the word of an authority figure or through first-hand observation,

Reflective task 2.3 **Progressive stages of epistemological development**

In her studies, Baxter Magolda (1999) identifies four progressive stages of epistemological development: *absolute knowing, transitional knowing, independent knowing* and *contextual knowing.*

- Research the work of Baxter Magolda to find out how she distinguishes between progressive stages of epistemological development.
- Compare the criteria used by Baxter Magolda to that used by King and Kitchener in their model of reflective judgement and note the similarities and differences between them.
- Reflect upon where you might situate yourself in relation to Baxter Magolda's stages of epistemological cognition and King and Kitchener's model of reflective judgement.
- Justify how you have reached this conclusion.
- What evidence can you draw upon to support your own judgements?

Discuss the main points of your argument with a colleague/peer or professional tutor.

rather than through the evaluation of evidence ... people who hold these assumptions ... believe that what they know is absolutely correct, and they know with complete certainty. People who hold these assumptions treat all problems as though they were well structured' (King and Kitchener, 1994: 39).

- *Quasi-reflective reasoning* (stages 4 and 5) characterised by the *recognition* that: 'Knowledge – or more accurately, knowledge claims – contain elements of uncertainty, which – people who hold these assumptions ... attribute to missing information or methods of obtaining evidence. Although they use evidence, they do not understand how evidence entails a conclusion (especially in light of the acknowledged uncertainty), and thus tend to view judgements as highly idiosyncratic' (ibid.: 40).
- *Reflective reasoning* (stages 6 and 7) characterised by the *acceptance* that: 'Knowledge claims cannot be made with certainty, but (they) are not immobilised by it: rather, (they) make judgements that are "most reasonable" and about which they are "relatively certain", based upon their evaluation of available data. They believe they must actively construct their decisions and knowledge claims must be evaluated in relation to the context in which they were generated to determine their validity. They are also willing to re-evaluate the adequacy of their judgements as new data or new methodologies become available' (ibid.).

The developmental nature of King and Kitchener's model indicates that each successive set of epistemological assumptions is characterised by a more complex and effective form of justification. The most advanced stage indicates a level of understanding has been reached which enables individuals to work with provisional or uncertain knowledge and information. At this stage, individuals acknowledge there is not necessarily any one correct answer to a given situation but several possible solutions.

Recognition is also given to the notion that expert practitioners may have competing views.

In her review of King and Kitchener's study, Moon (1999) raises an important consideration. She notes that although the focus of their research might have been to measure epistemological cognition, an influence from variables that affect the ability to express or represent those cognitions, whether orally or in written tasks, was inevitable. She raises concern that 'the difficulty of distinguishing the processes of learning from the representation of that learning is common to many studies of reflection and learning' (ibid.: 7).

Critical thinking

Moon (2005: 12) uses Baxter Magolda's model to trace the progressive development of students' ability to think critically and defines *critical thinking* as the capacity 'to work with complex ideas whereby a person can make effective provision of evidence to justify a reasonable judgement. The evidence, and therefore the judgement, will pay appropriate attention to the context of the judgement'. To this she adds that the fully developed capacity to think critically relies upon an understanding of 'knowledge as constructed and related to its context' (relativistic), which is not possible if 'knowledge is viewed only in an absolute manner' (knowledge as a series of facts). This has resonance with King and Kitchener's characterisation of reflective reasoning.

With reference to the development of writing skills, Moon (2005: 34) describes progressive stages of critical thinking in terms of reflective learning as 'a form of cognitive processing of complex issues when the material under consideration is largely already known'. She argues that the 'quality of reflective learning' can be seen as along a continuum from 'descriptive writing' in which ideas are displayed but not subjected to further processing, through three more stages of 'deepening' (ibid.). The deepest level of reflective writing incorporates the consideration of: multiple perspectives, engagement with prior experiences, the broader context surrounding issues, and meta-cognition. Moon (ibid.) defines *metacognition* as 'a form of reflection in which a process of cognitive work, itself, is reviewed. The focus is not on the content of the work, but on the cognitive processes – and, as such, this is an activity that is part of good quality critical thinking'. There is also an awareness of relevant emotional issues and an understanding of how emotions can relate to, and influence, thinking.

Psychological researchers with expertise in learning theory, view reflection as a means to metacognitive awareness, which they explain in terms of: knowing what one knows; having strategies for getting and using that knowledge; and knowing that one has those strategies (e.g. Moshman, 1999). Moon (2005: 34) draws a parallel between deep reflective thinking and critical thinking but notes some shades of difference in connotation: 'there is a sense of critical thinking being more purpose driven toward the reaching of a judgement, and more focused on the identification and evaluation of evidence. In this connection, there is a connotation of precision about critical thinking that is not generally associated with reflection' . She suggests meta-cognition is common to both reflection and critical thinking, and the development of effective reflection and critical thinking are contingent on the learner's progression away from the *dualist* position of absolute knowing toward the *relativist* position of contextual knowing.

Reflective task 2.4 **Critical analysis of critical thinking**

In Chapter 1 of *Learning to Think Things Through: A Guide to Critical Thinking Across the Disciplines*, Nosich (2005) argues the need for critical thinking at the level of:

1   practical decision making
2   meaningfulness
3   concepts.

In *The Miniature Guide to Critical Thinking Concepts and Tools*, Paul and Elder (2006: 4) argue that 'the quality of our thinking reflects the quality of our lives'.

- Research these literary sources and make notes on how critical thinking has been defined and conceptualised within each.
- Compare and contrast ways in which their theories are similar and/or different.
- To what extent do you engage in critical thinking?
- Is this an area you need to further develop?
- Identify at least three ways in which critical thinking may inform your planning, teaching and assessment.

Discuss your ideas with a critical friend and try them out in practice.

Themes common to the work of Baxter Magolda, King and Kitchener, and Moon are the views that reflective and cognitive activity can operate on a range of levels dependent upon how knowledge is generated, developed and processed. Also, the capacity to reflect is developmental and progressive in nature, from working with certain basic, concrete knowledge to working with provisional or uncertain knowledge. There is also an emphasis on the notion that reflective skills can, in part, be learned through a range of strategies and techniques and applied to practice to resolve issues or concerns. An awareness of the components embedded within these common themes is of central importance in coming to understand different patterns of thinking which can be exemplified by teachers at various stages of their professional development.

Reflective and routine practice

Dewey (1933) not only places an emphasis on the need to develop certain skills of thinking and reasoning in order to become a reflective practitioner but also draws a sharp contrast between *reflective* and *routine* action which has shaped the way many researchers and teacher educators distinguish between different types and forms of reflection (McIntyre, 1993; van Manen, 1977; Zeichner and Liston, 1987, 1996).

At the core of Dewey's argument is the notion not only that the chain of linked ideas that focus on resolving a problem involves a stream of consciousness, but also the anticipated outcome determines the process of operations that lead to it. He describes reflective action as the 'willingness to sustain and protract that state of doubt which is the stimulus to thorough inquiry, so as not to accept an idea or make a positive assertion of a belief until justifying reasons have been found' (Dewey, 1933: 16). The need to resolve a problem is what drives the enquiry forward as 'the exercise of thought is, in the literal sense of that word inference; by it, one thing carries us over to the idea of and belief in another thing. It involves a jump, a leap, a going beyond what is surely known to something else accepted on its warrant' (Dewey, 1910: 26). Reflective action considers the assumptions underpinning any form of knowledge or belief and the consequences which might follow from action that incorporates such knowledge or beliefs, which includes 'a conscious and voluntary effort to establish belief upon a firm basis of evidence and rationality' (Dewey, 1933: 9).

Conversely, Dewey argues that routine action is guided by a disposition to accept the most commonly held view of resolving a problem in a given situation in a routine almost thought-less way. No attempt is made to experiment with alternative strategies or viewpoints; rather, attention is directed toward the means to achieve specific ends which are taken for granted, guided by such factors as authority, custom, expectations, institutional definitions and tradition. Dewey (1910: 4–5) describes such thoughts as prejudices or 'prejudgements, not judgements proper that rest upon a survey of evidence'.

From a phenomenological perspective, van Manen (1977: 264) suggests that much of teachers' daily 'practical' thinking about such issues as 'planning, adapting materials, developing courses, arranging subject matter content, teaching and evaluating' can be described as technical and routine as the 'practical' in this sense 'expresses itself in the routines or taken for granted grounds of daily activities'. He does however distinguish between three forms of rationalisation underpinning the *nature* and *focus* of questions teachers may ask about their practice, which can lead to different interpretations of teachers' 'practical' work.

Van Manen's *technical rationality* is characterised by the application of existing knowledge to reach a given end, which is not open to criticism or modification and refers to acting efficiently on an everyday basis. The primary focus of teachers' questions is to resolve concerns about aspects of their own practice, and social contexts are taken for granted. A parallel can be drawn between van Manen's interpretation of technical rationality and the first level of reflective teaching identified by Grimmett, MacKinnon, Erickson and Riechen (1990), which applies research findings to practice and 'essentially represents thoughtfulness about action'.

Van Manen's *practical rationality* is characterised by the process of analysing and clarifying assumptions, experiences, goals, meanings and perceptions, which underpin practical actions. Teachers' questions focus more on the 'educational' aspects of their work to gain 'an interpretive understanding both of the nature and quality of educational experience, and of making practical choices' (van Manen, 1977: 226–227). Teachers come to recognise that meanings are not absolute, rather they are embedded in and negotiated through language (Fosnot, 1996; Hatton and Smith, 1995). A parallel can be drawn between van Manen's interpretation of practical rationality and the second level of reflective teaching identified by Grimmett *et al.* (1990) in that 'reflection is essentially a deliberation among choices of competing versions of good teaching'.

Van Manen's (1977: 227) *critical rationality* is characterised by moral and ethical questions teachers can raise which focus on 'the worth of knowledge and the nature of the social conditions necessary for raising the questions of worthwhile-ness in the first place'. Teachers analyse the wider cultural, social and political contexts, challenge their taken-for-granted assumptions and question their practice in relation to ideological and equity issues: 'universal consensus, free from delusions or distortions, is the ideal of a deliberative rationality that pursues worthwhile educational ends in self-determination, community, and on the basis of justice, equality, and freedom' (ibid.). A parallel can be drawn between van Manen's interpretation of critical rationality and the third level of reflective teaching identified by Grimmett *et al.* (1990) in which 'new understandings of previously taken-for-granted assumptions about practice are developed'.

Zeichner and Liston (1987: 27) draw similar distinctions to van Manen between reflective and routine practice and express these in terms of the teacher as *technician, craftsperson* and *moral craftsperson:*

> The teacher as technician would be concerned primarily with the successful accomplishment of ends decided by others. The craftsperson teacher would consider the educational justification for classroom actions and how well the educational goals are being accomplished. The teacher as moral craftsperson would also be concerned with the moral and ethical implications of particular institutional arrangements.

The nature of particular types of question, which van Manen and Zeichner and Liston use to distinguish between routine and reflective practice, has raised concern. Although moral and ethical questions are important, particularly when the needs and interests of pupils must be addressed, Furlong and Maynard (1995) caution that to prioritise and separate moral and ethical questions from those which might focus on other aspects of teaching, such as the nature of pedagogy and of how pupils learn, could be perceived as inappropriate. Calderhead (1989: 45) also claims that van Manen and Zeichner and Liston provide inadequate 'conceptions of professional learning as it occurs in classrooms or of how it might occur'.

The arguments underpinning the distinction drawn by Dewey between reflective and routine action has also been challenged. Furlong and Maynard (1995: 45) question the interpretation of teaching as routine and argue that this view does not capture the 'multifaceted, unpredictability and sheer complexity of teaching'. Moreover, whether teachers are aware of them or not, 'teaching is never "merely" technical; it always involves educational and moral assumptions' (ibid.). Zeichner and Liston also assert that educational and moral dimensions are always implicit within teaching even when viewed as a technical process. They clarify that the purpose behind the distinctions they have drawn between the teacher as technician, craftsperson and moral craftsperson was to shape their own teacher education programme and they claim that by explicitly placing an emphasis on each of these components, pre-service teachers are better able to recognise them in their own teaching.

Taking this line of argument further, Barnett (1997) suggests that by reflecting on their own situation student teachers gain awareness as to the causes and consequences of their actions and come to understand their true situation sufficiently to create the freedoms they need for themselves and proposes a system, which includes both *action* and *critique*, within a frame of reference that focuses on the student teacher as a developing person. He identifies *action, self-reflection* and *understanding* as three key domains that higher education needs to focus on and considers empowered student teachers are capable of critical self-reflection and critical action. He aligns this

---

Reflective task 2.5 **Engaging in and with critical reflection**

- Review a range of literature on critical reflection and extract the main concepts and themes advanced within each.
- Write a 2,000-word reflective narrative which explores how through critical reflection you can challenge your taken-for-granted assumptions and question your own practice in relation to ideological and equity issues.
- Debate the following claim with a critical friend: the expression 'critical reflection' is a tautology.

---

disposition with the capacity to size up the 'real world' in all its manifestations yet not to kowtow to it. Important attributes of 'critically' empowered student teachers are they have the clarity of thought and emotional strength to justify what they value and demonstrate, in their actions, that there are alternative ways of understanding and teaching in the 'real world'.

Barnett concludes his argument by suggesting critically reflective practitioners view their professional lives in terms of what they can and want to do in order to improve the quality of pupils' educational experiences as opposed to what they are permitted to do. They are risk-takers who strive continuously through their 'desire to think again' (Clandinin and Connelly, 1995) to explore new ways of doing things. Underpinning the goal toward becoming a critically reflective practitioner is the metaphor *liberation*. Zeichner and Liston (1987: 23) describe the liberated person as one 'free from the unwarranted control of unjustified beliefs, unsupportable attitudes and the paucity of abilities which can prevent that person from completely taking charge of his or her own life'.

In light of the preceding discussion, particularly in relation to critical thinking, and reflective and routine practice, it is evident that there are anomalies in the ways in which qualitative distinctions in reflective practice have been interpreted. These anomalies reflect the complex, multifaceted nature of concepts associated with this phenomenon. There are however also a number of commonalities and recurrent themes, which can be synthesised from the eminent scholars, researchers and practitioners. To that end, the following sections capture salient features, which can distinguish between three types of discourse you can engage in and exemplify in your own practice. It is useful to reiterate here that the term discourse is used in a broad sense to denote ways of thinking and speaking about teaching as well as of practising teaching.

Descriptive reflective conversations

This type of discourse is based on concrete experience as you examine and frame aspects of your own classroom practice. It can be characterised as a retrospective personal account of teaching, which involves returning to experience (Boud, Keogh and Walker, 1985) and providing a detailed description of that experience. As individuals experience the world through their own lens, sense of reality and 'form of consciousness' (Stevens, 1996), descriptive reflective conversations enable you to search for patterns and trends that may emerge as you try to make sense of your own teaching. Of significance to the ways in which you see and interpret any teaching situation are theories associated with different patterns of thinking and of how you construct knowledge. You can examine the situational, context-specific nature of your experience by asking yourself such questions as:

- What was taught?
- How was it taught?
- Did pupils achieve the intended learning outcomes?
- What teaching strategies were effective, or ineffective?
- How do I know?
- What does this mean?
- How does this make me feel?
- How might I do things differently next time?

Descriptive reflective conversations have potential for making the implicit explicit and should enable you to construct a pedagogical vocabulary of shared meanings and understandings (Ghaye and Ghaye, 1998). Teachers must account for their actions and provide reasons why they responded to a particular teaching situation in a particular way with a particular group of pupils in a particular context at a particular moment in time, e.g. if the intended learning outcomes were achieved by some pupils, yet not by others, they must question why this was the case. Problems can be identified as you analyse what actions may have given rise to particular outcomes and, importantly, what the implications are for your own future teaching. This provides an important foundation for the generation of 'living educational theory' (Whitehead, 1993) and the development of your own 'epistemology of practice' (Schon, 1987).

Comparative reflective conversations

This type of discourse requires you to reframe the focus of your reflection in light of multiple perspectives, alternative views and possibilities, research findings from literature and your own engagement with prior experiences. Comparative reflective conversations can be evidenced when teachers relate personal assumptions, beliefs, theories, values and conceptions of teaching to that of others. It is a meaning-making process, which moves you from one experience into the next with a deeper understanding 'of its relationships with and connections to other experiences and ideas' (Rodgers, 2002: 845). You can engage in comparative reflective conversations by asking yourself such questions as:

- What alternative strategies might I use in my teaching?
- What are the advantages/disadvantages of using particular strategies for diverse learners?
- How might colleagues and/or pupils explain what is happening in my classroom?
- What research enables me to gain further insights into this matter?
- In what ways can I improve the ineffective aspects of my practice?
- Having established learning objectives, in what ways can these be accomplished?
- How do colleagues accomplish these same goals?
- For each alternative perspective, whose learning needs are addressed and whose are not?

This type of discourse is essentially 'a deliberation among choices of competing versions of good teaching' (Grimmett *et al.*, 1990) and involves moral, ethical and value commitments as well as questions concerning such aspects of teaching as 'how pupils learn' and 'the nature of pedagogy' (Furlong and Maynard, 1995). You should come to recognise that meanings are not absolute but embedded in and negotiated through language (Fosnot, 1996) – a form of contemplative enquiry that involves clarifying the assumptions underpinning teaching. Teachers may, for example, believe that they divide their time equally between each group of pupils within the class or that the resources they have prepared are appropriate for a diverse range of learners. However, engaging in discourse with pupils to seek their opinions, views and perspectives might reveal that personal perceptions are markedly different to those of their pupils. This highlights the need for you to search beyond personal assumptions and theories as a range of possibilities concerning one particular aspect of your teaching might emerge dependent upon whose perspectives you have considered.

Teachers also come to recognise that knowledge, or more accurately knowledge claims, contain elements of uncertainty which those who hold these assumptions might attribute to missing information or methods of obtaining evidence. They can expect to have an opinion, to think through issues and express themselves in a valid manner, and to consider colleagues might also have useful contributions to make. However, the idea of judging some perspectives as better or worse than others tends to be overlooked. For example, although teachers might use evidence, they do not necessarily understand how evidence entails a conclusion, particularly in light of the acknowledged uncertainty, and tend to view judgements as highly idiosyncratic. Comparative reflective conversations thus have resonance with 'transitional knowing' (Baxter Magolda, 1999) and 'quasi-reflective reasoning' (King and Kitchener, 1994).

Critical reflective conversations

Critical thinking is at the core of this type of discourse, which can be characterised by the acceptance that knowledge claims cannot be made with certainty. Teachers make judgements that are 'most reasonable' and about which they are 'relatively certain' based on the evaluation of available data. Expert practitioners also need to be able to use a 'deliberative rationality' to appraise what they do and a 'calculative rationality' to make decisions in novel situations (Dreyfus and Dreyfus, 1986). This type of discourse has resonance with 'contextual knowing' (Baxter Magolda, 1999) and 'reflective reasoning' (King and Kitchener, 1994).

Critical reflective conversations can be evidenced when you ask searching questions about your teaching to consider the implications behind alternative perspectives and demonstrate a willingness to suspend judgement until these avenues have been fully explored, in response to such questions as:

- What are the implications of using particular strategies in my teaching when viewed from alternative perspectives?
- On the basis of these perspectives and their implications, what strategies would be the most effective in helping pupils to achieve the intended learning outcomes?
- Are these particular learning outcomes appropriate for the diverse range of learners within this class? How do I know? Where is the evidence?

Reflective task 2.6 **Designing questions to shape reflective conversations**

- Select one of the nine dimensions of reflective practice presented in Figure 1.1 and, in relation to a specific teaching and learning activity or task, think about questions you can ask to engage in descriptive, comparative and critical reflective conversations.
- Use the template shown in Table 2.2 (p. 28) to record these questions.
- Plan to use some of these questions in a specific lesson.
- After the lesson, reflect upon whether these questions were the right questions to ask – how do you know? What additional questions spring to mind? Share the outcomes of this experience with a critical friend.

- Why select this particular strategy for this particular group of pupils on this particular occasion within this particular context rather than an alternative? What criteria can support my decision-making?
- How does my choice of objectives, learning outcomes, teaching and assessment strategies reflect the cultural, ethical, ideological, moral, political and social purposes of schooling?

The complex issues associated with power and politics as they relate to schools need to be understood if you are to meaningfully engage in critical discourse about your practice (Ghaye and Ghaye, 1998). This can be exemplified when you engage in reflective conversations that address questions concerned with *why* the educational, ideological, political and professional systems of which you are an integral part serve either to constrain or to empower you (Barnett, 1997; Moon, 2005), which can give rise to 'new understandings of previously taken-for-granted assumptions about practice' (Grimmett *et al.,* 1990) and lead to 'a renewed perspective' (Jay and Johnson, 2002).

Summary of key points

This chapter clarifies how qualitative distinctions between descriptive, comparative and critical reflective conversations have been interpreted within the Framework of Reflective Practice and explored how reflective conversations and narrative enquiry incorporate different types of discourse and different patterns of thinking. It has considered how some key theorists distinguish between reflective and routine practice and how concepts advanced by others may signal progressive stages of epistemological cognition, reflective reasoning and critical thinking as individuals move from the dualist to the relativist position.

Although several theorists distinguish between reflective and routine practice by positioning certain types of question with different forms of rationalisation, one must question whether some interpretations are entirely appropriate or justified, particularly given the complex nature of professional environments within which teachers work. Thus, caution needs to be exercised when making judgements about the capacity of individuals to engage in reflective as compared with routine action or practice. The

Table 2.2 Questions to shape descriptive, comparative and critical reflective conversations

Dimension of reflective practice:	
Teaching and learning activity or task:	
Reflective conversation	**Questions**
Descriptive	
Comparative	
Critical	

notion of qualitative distinctions in the types of discourse and reflective conversations teachers can engage in and exemplify, however, is an important indicator of the extent to which they move from *surface* to *deep* to *transformative* learning.

Recommended reading

Ghaye, A. and Ghaye, K. (1998) *Teaching and Learning through Critical Reflective Practice*, London: David Fulton.
The authors present a comprehensive five-part typology to explore different components of reflective practice: descriptive, perceptive, receptive, interactive and critical reflection on practice.

Hatton, N. and Smith, D. (1995) Reflection in Teacher Education: towards definition and implementation, *Teaching and Teacher Education*, 11 (1), 33–49.
Research undertaken at the University of Sydney, Australia sought to investigate the nature of reflection in teaching, and based on the relationship between theory and practice the authors identified and categorised four types of writing: descriptive writing, descriptive reflection, dialogic reflection and critical reflection.

Jay, J. and Johnson, K. (2002) Capturing complexity: a typology of reflective practice for teacher education, *Teaching and Teacher Education*, 18, 73–85.
This article reports findings of work undertaken at the University of Washington's Teacher Education Programme with teacher educators and teaching assistants, to guide their understanding of pedagogy during reflective seminars. It introduces a three-dimensional typology of reflection and questions to guide and scaffold thinking.

Part II

Dimensions of reflective practice

Key features and processes

Chapter 3

Dimension 1

Study your own teaching for personal improvement

Learning objectives

In this chapter you will consider:

- how critically constructive self-reflection and considered response underpin the *art of self-study*;
- the centrality of *reflection* and *evaluation* within the improvement process;
- how Schon (1987) draws links between *knowing in action* and *reflection on action*;
- *experiential learning theory*, preferred *learning styles* and the concept of *learning spaces*.

Introduction

Stenhouse (1975) identifies the art of self-study as one of the key attributes of extended professionals, which can give rise to new possibilities for 'qualitative research to focus on the everyday practices by which individuals constantly construct and reconstruct their sense of individual identity' (Elliott, 2005b: 124). In writing and speaking of personal experiences, teachers engage in discourse which can explore 'vulnerabilities, conflicts, choices and values' and take measure of the 'uncertainties, mixed emotions, and multiple layers' (Ellis and Bochner, 2000: 748) of their experience. Reflective conversations thus become a powerful agent of understanding 'self' as teachers recount not only what they observed in a given context, but also their emotions, feelings, ideas and thoughts as to 'future possibilities' (Pollard, 2002).

Central to your development as a teacher is your capacity to reflect regularly on what is happening in your own lessons to improve the learning experiences you provide for pupils. In so doing, you reflect on the intended learning outcomes, consider the content and pedagogical approaches you used, how individuals and groups of pupils were engaged during the lesson and importantly, what your pupils have learned. Amongst other things, this enables you to refine and tailor your teaching strategies and consider alternative approaches you can try in future lessons. Discussions with a colleague/peer or critical friend to explore reasons that may underpin the outcomes of your lesson can also open your eyes to new possibilities. A genuine commitment to your own development thus arises from critically constructive self-reflection and considered response, which situates *reflection* and *evaluation* at the heart of the improvement process.

Wider aspects of school life, such as peer counselling, after-school clubs and activities, enrichment programmes and the pastoral care system, also play a significant role in pupil learning. The impact of these on your pupils' overall development and wellbeing should be reviewed regularly to ensure they accommodate the diverse needs of a range of learners. Rapid advances in media and new technologies, as well as initiatives and strategies rolled out by education and government departments nationwide, can have an impact on the learning experiences of pupils and thus provide important focal points for reflection and evaluation. These exemplars illuminate that teachers also need to reflect on and evaluate factors associated with the whole-school curriculum and wider aspects of school life to gain a holistic view of their pupils' learning and development.

This chapter explores how you can learn about what you do through analysing the effectiveness of your own actions and how you can develop different ways of working to study and improve your own teaching. The prelude to such improvement is reflection, as this provides the vehicle through which the effectiveness of teaching and learning can be evaluated. Reflection is an integral part of *Experiential Learning Theory,* which Kolb (1984) describes as 'self-perpetuating' in that you shift from actor to observer, from direct involvement to analytical detachment, which creates a new form of experience to reflect on and conceptualise. His theory is built on the notion that experiential learning is a process, which involves re-creating personal lives and social systems rather than the application of a series of techniques to current practice. It is distinguished by attending to the organisation and construction of learning from observations made in some practical situation so that learning can then lead to improved practice.

Reflection

An understanding of *reflection,* how it might be structured and used to guide practice, lies at the heart of self-study and professional development planning for personal improvement. Dewey (1933: 7) identifies reflection as one of the modes of thought: 'active, persistent, and careful consideration of any belief or supposed form of knowledge in light of the grounds that support it and the future conclusions to which it tends'. He associates reflection with the *kind of thinking* that involves turning a subject over in the mind to give it serious consideration and thought and identifies five phases or states of thinking: *problem, suggestions, reasoning, hypothesis* and *testing.*

The *problem* phase relates to seeing 'the big picture' rather than discrete, small entities on their own and identifying the real cause for concern. Through recognising and understanding the perplexity of a situation, a plan of action can be intellectualised and thought through more fully.

Suggestions incorporate the possibilities and ideas that spring to mind when confronted by a puzzling situation. When suggestions are plentiful, each must be considered in an appropriate manner, and thus there is need to suspend judgement as suggestions provide an impetus for further enquiry.

Reasoning involves linking ideas, information and previous experiences in order to extend the knowledge of, and thinking about, the subject. It facilitates the expansion of hypotheses, suggestions and tests since 'even when reasoning out the bearings of a supposition does not lead to its rejection, it develops the idea into a form in which it is more apposite to the problem' (Dewey, 1933: 112).

The *hypothesis* phase reconsiders a suggestion in relation to how it might be used and what can be accomplished with it. Acting upon a working hypothesis involves examining how it stands up to tentative testing, considering more information and undertaking more observations. Thus, 'the sense of the problem becomes more adequate and refined and the suggestion ceases to be a *mere* possibility, becoming a *tested* and, if possible, a measured probability' (ibid.: 110).

Testing refers to the stage at which the hypothesis is tested and the outcome may be used to corroborate or negate the conjectural idea. Although overt testing provides the opportunity to discover how well the problem situation has been thought through, the results need not corroborate the thinking that preceded the action. 'It either brings to light a new problem or helps to define and clarify the problem on which he has been engaged. Nothing shows the trained thinker better than the use he makes of his errors and mistakes' (ibid.: 114). Thus, in reflection failure can be instructive. Covert testing may also occur which involves conducting a 'thought-experiment' to test the hypothesis.

Teachers must place each phase within the context of past and future actions and experiences, and some might be expanded or overlap, dependent upon the nature of the problem. When pieced together, the phases form a process of *reflective thinking,* which involves a state of 'doubt, hesitation, perplexity, mental difficulty, in which thinking originates, and an act of searching, hunting, inquiring, to find material that will resolve the doubt, settle and dispose of the perplexity' (Dewey, 1933: 12). This form of problem solving enables you to resolve 'a situation in which there is experienced obscurity, conflict (and) disturbance of some sort' into one that becomes 'clear, coherent, settled (and) harmonious' (ibid.: 100). The ultimate goal is to find a solution to improve the effectiveness of your teaching to enhance pupil learning. The capacity to effectively engage in this process requires you to develop a range of specific skills, e.g. keen observation, logical reasoning and analysis, as the process of thinking incorporates:

> the suggestion of a conclusion for acceptance and also search or enquiry to test the value of the suggestion before accepting it. This implies (a) a certain fund or store of experiences or facts from which suggestions proceed; (b) promptness, flexibility and fertility of suggestions; and (c) orderliness, consecutiveness and appropriateness in what is suggested.
>
> (Dewey, 1910: 30)

Dewey notes that limitations can be prevalent in any of these three regards. Your thinking might, for example, be irrelevant or narrow as you may not possess enough raw material from which to base conclusions or because raw material and concrete facts, even when extensive, 'fail to evoke suggestions easily and richly' (ibid.). Furthermore, even if these two conditions are fulfilled, when ideas are suggested they may be 'incoherent and fantastic' as opposed to 'pertinent and consistent' (ibid.). In such circumstances, perhaps a more appropriate approach would be to place an emphasis on *suggestions for practice* (McIntyre, 1993) as opposed to a *systematic enquiry into aspects of practice* through

---

Reflective task 3.1 **Reflective thinking**

LaBoskey's (1993: 30) categorisation of cognitive abilities incorporate the higher levels of thinking in Bloom's (1956) taxonomy of educational objectives (analysis, synthesis, evaluation) and exemplify Dewey's stages of reflective thinking. She argues that teachers must be able to:

> describe and analyse the structural features of an educational situation, issue, or problem – problem definition; gather and evaluate information as to the possible sources of the dilemma under consideration and to generate multiple alternative solutions and their potential implications – means/ends analysis; and integrate all of the information into a tempered conclusion about or solution for the problem identified – generalisation.

- Think about a situation or problem you need to resolve, e.g. how to accommodate pupils with specific learning needs or disabilities in your lesson; limited knowledge and understanding of factors that may trigger low-level disruption or inappropriate behaviour; how to use multi-media technologies to accelerate learning and challenge pupils on the gifted and talented register.
- Using the template given in Table 3.1, think through your situation or problem and provide some ideas and suggestions as to how you can try to resolve it.
- Plan to use some of these ideas and suggestions in your next lesson.
- After the lesson, try to identify whether your ideas and suggestions led to the solution you had anticipated by reflecting on:
    - What worked well and/or what did not work well;
    - Whether your pupils learned and/or did not learn;
    - Why they learned and/or did not learn.
- In light of your findings you will then need to reflect on:
    - What you can continue to do in your next lesson;
    - What you might need to do differently in your next lesson to enhance pupil learning.
- Discuss your findings with a peer/colleague or professional tutor and identify areas in which you feel there is need for further improvement.
- Set yourself SMART targets to plan how you can gain support and experience in developing these areas.

Dewey's stages of reflective thinking. This consideration is important, particularly for those with limited knowledge or direct experience of teaching and for those reluctant to challenge deeply ingrained assumptions, beliefs and personal theories about particular aspects of teaching.

Dewey's association of reflection with problem solving has received a measure of agreement in that one central concern of reflection is to find solutions to real problems encountered by practitioners (LaBoskey, 1993; Pollard *et al.*, 2005; Rodgers, 2002; Schon, 1987). However, questions have been raised as to whether solving problems should be viewed as an inherent characteristic of reflection. Hatton and Smith (1995: 3)

Table 3.1 Ideas and suggestions as to how to resolve a problem

Problem definition:	
Means/ends analysis:	
Generalisation:	

argue that if the essential nature of reflection is to think about action, this may involve processing information while a group event is taking place, or debriefing a student teacher after a particular experience to gain insights and understanding of 'relationships between what took place, the purposes intended, and difficulties which arose viewed within broader cultural or professional perspectives'.

Rodgers (2002: 845) examined the theoretical underpinnings of Dewey's reflective thinking framework for its significance within teacher education and suggests it might usefully be broken down into four components; notably, reflective thinking:

- is a meaning-making process that moves a learner from one experience into the next with deeper understanding of its relationships with and connections to other experiences and ideas;
- is a systematic, rigorous, disciplined way of thinking, with its roots in scientific enquiry;
- needs to happen in community, in interaction with others;
- requires attitudes that value the personal and intellectual growth of oneself and of others.

Several of these components find synergy with Schon's (1987) exposition of *reflection in action* and *reflection on action* as well as Kolb's (1984) *Experiential Learning Theory*.

Reflection in action and reflection on action

Within the context of teaching you constantly encounter situations that are unique; no two groups of pupils are the same. Even when you become familiar with a particular teaching group, how you explain and present new material to promote pupil learning and understanding can also be unique. Schon (1987) argues that the repertoire of teaching approaches and strategies teachers gain from experience provide *exemplars, images* and *metaphors* they can draw upon to structure and frame each new teaching situation. *Framing a situation* involves interpreting it one way as opposed to other possible ways and this process must be viewed as experimental since imposing meaning onto the situation by taking action leads to particular consequences, which should then be evaluated. At the heart of Schon's (1987: 22) discourse is the emphasis placed on *professional artistry* described as:

> the kinds of competence practitioners display in unique, uncertain and conflicted situations of practice ... a high powered esoteric variant of the more familiar sorts of competence all of us exhibit everyday in countless acts of recognition, judgement and skilful performance.

What emerges from Schon's discourse is that competence or *intelligent action* can be shown in the ability of practitioners to respond effectively in particular situations. This contrasts sharply with Dewey's interpretation that competence can be demonstrated through an ability to articulate and justify behaviour. Schon (1987: 25) elaborates further and describes intelligent action as *knowing in action*, which he claims can be intuitive as 'we reveal it by our spontaneous, skilful execution of the performance; and we are characteristically unable to make it verbally explicit'. Although this knowledge is inherent, intangible, intuitive, spontaneous and tacit, it 'works' in practice. This intuitive form of *knowing in action* is aligned to *reflection in action* (Schon, 1987: 28), which occurs when practitioners encounter an unknown situation or a surprise occurrence in the learning environment triggers it off:

> reflection-in-action has a critical function, questioning the assumptional structure of knowing-in-action ... (and) ... gives rise to on the spot experiment. We think up and try out new actions intended to explore the newly observed phenomena, test our tentative understandings of them or affirm the moves we have invented to change things for the better.

This involves simultaneous reflecting and doing, which implies the professional has reached a stage of competence where he is able to analyse what is taking place and modify actions virtually instantaneously. The process of interpreting and providing solutions to complex, situational problems happens during an action as events unfold, 'the period of time in which we remain in the same situation' (Schon, 1983: 278). The expressions 'thinking on your feet' and 'keeping your wits about you' aptly portray reflection in action, which Kounin (1970) associates with *contemporaneous reflection* and 'withitness'. McIntyre (1993: 43) suggests reflection in action is likely to be more characteristic of how experienced teachers respond in the teaching context as they have a richer vocabulary of exemplars, images and metaphors from which to frame teaching situations, along with the confidence to shape and try these out in new ways:

> Expert practitioners ... (have) ... extensive repertoires of past experiences on which they can draw in order to illuminate current problems; and, when they use the possibilities of constructing new frames by modifying and combining old ones, they have very rich, even although bounded, capacities for thinking creatively through reflecting in and on their experience.

Reflection in action can often be very rapid as split-second decisions need to be made and as Tickle (2000: 127) cautions, it is not always possible to:

> judge the effects of action and to assess the nature of newly created situations, because of the rapid pace of decision making and volatile nature of circumstances in densely populated classrooms and schools ... the selection of information may be rapid and impressionistic; the likelihood of information being missed is considerable, and the potential for misjudgement enormous.

This highlights the need to reflect on your teaching through rigorous, systematic evaluation procedures. Schon recognises that many professionals find it difficult to reflect on practice as whatever language they use, descriptions of practice will always be *constructions*. Also, by trying to capture 'intelligent action' which originates from being spontaneous and tacit through language, reality is distorted as 'knowing in action is dynamic' whereas 'facts, procedures, rules and theories are static' (Schon, 1987: 25). However, Polkinghorne (1995: 16) suggests the very act of bringing these happenings into language 'imposes a higher level of order on them than they have in the flux of everyday experience'. Similarly, Stringer (1996: 97) notes that when teachers reflect on their situation they can 'conceive solutions to their problems with a degree of clarity that escapes them in the rush and clutter of their day-to-day lives'. This is an important consideration in coming to understand the complex mosaic of factors underpinning the decisions you make in the teaching environment.

Thus, although your verbal (re)constructions of situations and events might seem inadequate, reflection on action is an important process in learning about the professional activity of teaching as it moves you from *knowing in action* toward *reflection on action* (Schon, 1987). The journey serves to make much that was implicit explicit and enhance your level of awareness and consciousness of how you frame teaching situations. This enables you to gain control of your teaching and develop 'artistry' as reflection on action encourages the questioning of principles and theories which underpin what you do, and engaging in the conscious exercise of discernment as you provide reasons to support the judgements you make. Reflection on action provides a frame of reference in coming to recognise how you make sense of, and gain control over, your situated knowledge. It also acknowledges that your personal reflection must be subject to systematic questioning so that your practice can be justified. Schon does not privilege one particular form of questioning over another. Any of the foundation disciplines in education such as philosophy, psychology and sociology may provide the source of questioning to gain an understanding of principles that underpin your teaching.

Reflection on action involves looking back on action some time after the event has taken place. Within teacher education, certain models are based on thinking about skills and competencies with a view to evaluating their effectiveness almost immediately after an attempt at implementation, and then making changes to behaviour. Some models encourage deliberation over a relatively extended period of time about the purposes of action with a view to exploring alternatives that might be implemented in the future, whereas others involve conscious detachment from an activity followed by a distinct period of contemplation.

Reflective task 3.2 **Reflecting on feelings and emotions**

Korthagen and Vasalos (2005: 48) also emphasise feelings and emotions and recommend that when you engage in reflection on action the following questions should be probed:

- What was the context?
- What did I want? What did the pupils want?
- What did I do? What did the pupils do?
- What was I thinking? What were the pupils thinking?
- How did I feel? How did the pupils feel?

Use these questions to guide your reflections and evaluations over a series of lessons:

- How do your responses compare with those of your pupils?
- Has anything surprised you?
- What have you learned about your pupils?
- What have you learned about yourself?
- What have you learned about your approach to teaching?
- How might the responses to these questions shape your future practice?

Feelings and emotions are woven into Boud, Keogh and Walker's (1985: 19) approach to reflection on action as teachers are encouraged to 'recapture their experience, think about it, mull it over and evaluate it' through:

- *association* – relating new data to that which is already known, making links between feelings and ideas we have about teaching;
- *integration* – seeking relationships among the data, making sense of associations in some way;
- *validation* – determining the authenticity of the ideas and feelings which have resulted, trying out new ways of viewing and understanding teaching;
- *appropriation* – making knowledge one's own, taking ownership of new insights and learning to inform future teaching.

This said, Boud (1999: 125) cautions that this framework has been interpreted 'in such a reductionistic manner' as to be unrecognisable as reflection. He reports that some staff within placement schools asked student teachers to reflect by numbers '1 – return to the experience, 2 – attend to feelings, 3 – reevaluate by stages ...' as though it were a simple, linear process of 'working through a series of prompts to reach deeper understanding' (ibid.). He persuasively argues that *recipe following* is wholly inappropriate as it does not take account of the 'uniqueness of learners, their prior experience, the particular context in which they are operating nor the need to address any unhelpful dynamics of power or oppression which may intrude' (ibid.: 128). Also, the emphasis placed on the need for personal disclosure was often found to be beyond the capacity of some student teachers. Boud suggests these shortcomings can

Table 3.2: Propositions that underpin experiential learning theory

I	Learning is best conceived of as a process, not in terms of outcomes. To improve learning ... the primary focus should be on engaging students in a process that best enhances their learning ... one that includes feedback on the effectiveness of their learning efforts.
2	Learning is best facilitated by a process that draws out the students' beliefs and ideas about a topic so that they can be examined, tested and integrated with new, more refined ideas ... thus, all learning is relearning.
3	Learning requires the resolution of conflicts between dialectically opposed modes of adaptation to the world. Conflict, differences and disagreement are what drive the learning process ... thus, in the process of learning one is called upon to move back and forth between opposing modes of reflection and action and between feeling and thinking.
4	Learning involves the integrated functioning of the whole person ... thinking, feeling, perceiving and behaving ... thus, learning is not just the result of cognition but a holistic process of adaptation to the world.
5	In Piaget's terms, learning occurs through equilibration of the dialectic processes of assimilating new experiences into existing concepts and accommodating existing concepts to new experience ... thus, learning results from synergetic transactions between the person and the environment.
6	A constructivist theory of learning is proposed in that social knowledge is created and recreated in the personal knowledge of the learner ... thus, learning is the process of creating knowledge.

Source: adapted from Kolb and Kolb (2005: 194)

be addressed when practitioners build a context for reflection, unique to every learning situation, and create an environment of trust.

Experiential learning theory

Reflection is an integral part of experiential learning, which has at its roots the work of such eminent scholars as Dewey (1958), Lewin (1946) and Piaget (1967) who situated the role of experience at the heart of their theories of human learning and development. As Dewey (ibid.: 25) writes:

> I assume that amid all uncertainties there is one permanent frame of reference: namely, the organic connection between education and personal experience ... all genuine education comes about through experience (but) ... not all experiences are genuinely or equally educative.

Kolb (1984) developed a model of the experiential learning process and a multi-linear model of adult development based on the propositions outlined in Table 3.2.

Experiential learning theory defines learning as 'the process whereby knowledge is created through the transformation of experience. Knowledge results from the combination of *grasping* and *transforming* experience' (Kolb, 1984: 41). The two dialectically related modes concerned with grasping experience are *concrete experience* and *abstract conceptualisation*, and those concerned with transforming experience are *reflective observation* and *active experimentation*. As a process for constructing knowledge, experiential learning involves a creative tension among the four learning modes that is responsive to contextual demands.

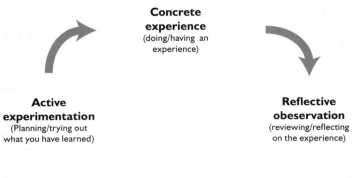

Figure 3.1 Model of experiential learning (adapted from Kolb, 1984)

Table 3.3 Reflecting on experience

Learning mode	Experience 1	Experience 2	Experience 3
Concrete experience			
Reflective observation			
Abstract conceptualisation			
Active experimentation			

Portrayed as a spiral or an idealised learning cycle, the learner must 'touch all the bases' – experiencing, reflecting, thinking and acting – in a recursive process that is both responsive to the learning situation and to what is being learned. Immediate or concrete experience provides the basis for observations and reflections. These reflective observations are distilled and assimilated into abstract concepts from which new possibilities and implications for action can be drawn. These possibilities and implications can be tested through active experimentation, which in turn serve as guides to create new experiences, as illustrated in Figure 3.1.

Kolb associates experiential learning with Piaget's theory of cognitive development in that both consider the processes of *assimilation* and *accommodation* to underpin stages of development. Assimilation incorporates receiving information from the environment, and accommodation incorporates modifying that which is already known by the learner in light of the new learning. Reflection is used to move the learner beyond current thoughts and ideas and to progress in their learning.

Eraut (1994: 107) suggests experiential learning can refer to those situations where experience 'is initially apprehended at the level of impressions, thus requiring a further period of reflective thinking before it is either assimilated into existing schemes of experience or induces those schemes to change in order to accommodate it'. LaBoskey's (1993) research into the cognitive processing ability of student teachers found that *common sense thinkers* and *alert novices* engage with experiential learning in different ways, which has implications for how they assimilate and accommodate information from the environment and learn from their respective experiences.

Reflective task 3.3 **Reflecting on experience**

Think of three concrete experiences you have recently had with pupils, e.g. using guided discovery in your teaching to promote independent learning; a confrontation with a particular group of pupils who refused to engage with a task; accompanying pupils off-site on an educational school trip. Take each experience in turn and use Kolb's four learning modes in a chart as in Table 3.3 to deconstruct and reconstruct these experiences.

In relation to each experience:

- Explore how you grasp experience by examining the connection between concrete experience and abstract conceptualisation.
- Explore how you transform experience by examining the connection between your reflective observations and active experimentation.

In relation to the four learning modes:

- Do you touch 'all the bases' when analysing and evaluating your experiences?
- Do any patterns emerge which might characterise your approach to learning?
- In what ways can experiential learning theory inform and shape your future practice?

Learning style

The concept of learning style is used to describe individual differences based on a learner's preference for using different phases of Kolb's learning cycle. We develop a preferred way of selecting among the four learning modes due to the demands of our immediate environment, our particular life experiences and hereditary make-up. We resolve the tension between being active or reflective and between being concrete or abstract in patterned and characteristic ways. Development can be conceived as multi-linear in terms of an individual's particular learning style and life trajectory, for example, the development of:

- active experimentation increases behavioural complexity
- reflective observation increases perceptual complexity
- concrete experience increases affective complexity
- abstract conceptualisation increases symbolic complexity.

Early research on experiential learning theory, using both the original and revised Learning Style Inventory (Kolb, 1971, 1999) identified four learning styles associated with different approaches to learning and characteristic patterns of behaviour, as summarised in Table 3.4.

Hunt and his associates (Abbey, Hunt and Weiser, 1985; Hunt, 1987) identify four additional learning styles, which they describe as Northerner, Southerner, Westerner and Easterner; and Mainemelis, Boyatzis and Kolb (2002) identify a 'balancing' learning style, which integrates abstract conceptualisation – concrete experience – and active experimentation – reflective observation. This research expands the original four learning styles to illuminate nine distinct styles.

Garner (2000) cautions there is a marked tendency in research and practice to view learning style as a fixed personality trait or as a fixed characteristic, which fails to take into account the dynamic nature of learning style. To clarify the latter point, Kolb (1984: 63–64) writes:

> The way we process the possibilities of each new emerging event determines the range of choices and decisions we see. The choices and decisions we make to some extent determine the events we live through, and these events influence our future choices. Thus, people create themselves through the choice of actual occasions they live through.

Learning space

The experiential learning theory concept of learning space elaborates further on the complex, dynamic nature of learning style and its formation through transactions between a person and his environment. Reflective task 3.4 (p. 46) enables you to explore this concept more fully and relate it to your own practice.

Summary of key points

In gathering evidence of personal strengths and areas in need of further improvement you are developing the art of self-study, which lays the foundation for your professional

Table 3.4 Characteristic patterns of behaviour associated with different learning styles

Learning style	Dominant learning abilities	Characteristic patterns of behaviour
Diverging	Concrete experience and reflective observation	View concrete situations from many different points of view Perform better in situations that call for the generation of ideas, e.g. a 'brainstorming' session Are interested in people and have broad cultural interests Tend to be imaginative and emotional Like to gather information Tend to specialise in the arts In formal learning situations prefer to work in groups, listen with an open mind and receive personalised feedback
Assimilating	Abstract conceptualisation and reflective observation	Are best at understanding a wide range of information and putting it into concise, logical form Less focused on people and more interested in abstract concepts and ideas Generally find it more important that a theory have logical soundness than practical value, which is an important skill for effectiveness in information and science careers In formal learning situations prefer readings, lectures, exploring analytical models and having time to think things through
Converging	Abstract conceptualisation and active experimentation	Are best at finding practical uses for ideas and theories Have the ability to solve problems and make decisions based on finding solutions to questions or problems Prefer to deal with technical tasks and problems rather than with social and interpersonal issues, which are important skills for effectiveness in specialist and technology careers In formal learning situations prefer to experiment with new ideas, simulations, laboratory assignments and practical applications
Accommodating	Concrete experience and active experimentation	Have the ability to learn primarily from 'hands-on' experience Enjoy carrying out plans and involving themselves in new and challenging experiences Rely more heavily on people for information than on their own technical analysis in solving problems, which is important for effectiveness in action-orientated careers such as sales or marketing In formal learning situations prefer to work with others to get assignments done, to set goals, do field work and test out different approaches to completing a project

Adapted from Kolb and Kolb (2005: 196–197).

Reflective task 3.4 **Exploring the concept of learning space**

Research the work of the following theorists and make notes on conceptual frameworks they have advanced:

1   Bronfrenbrenner's (1979) work on the ecology of human development
2   Lave and Wenger's (1991) work on situated learning theory
3   Nonaka and Konno's (1998) work on knowledge creation.

Write a 2,000-word reflective narrative which explores how the learning spaces you inhabit within your role as a teacher can be used constructively to create a positive environment for a diverse range of learners. Discuss the key points of your argument with a critical friend.

---

development planning. This chapter explores how theorists position reflection at the core of the improvement process and explain the multifaceted nature of this concept. It introduces Dewey's framework of reflective thinking and association with problem-solving; Schon's discourse on reflection in action and reflection on action and how professionals frame each unique teaching situation and develop professional artistry; and Boud, Keogh and Walker's framework of reflection, which integrates feelings and emotions.

Kolb's exposition of experiential learning theory, which captures the learning modes of concrete experience, reflective observation, abstract conceptualisation and active experimentation, has been explored within the process of learning, in addition to the concepts of learning styles and learning spaces.

Several strategies have been introduced enabling you to engage in reflection in a number of ways and evaluate how your reflections can inform, guide and shape your own thinking, approach to learning and future practice. At this point you are encouraged to use the template presented in Table 2.2 to devise descriptive, comparative and critical questions related to a task you have undertaken within this dimension of reflective practice.

Recommended reading

Kayes, D. (2002) Experiential learning and its critics: preserving the role of experience in management education, *Academy of Management Learning and Education*, 1 (2): 137–149.
Kayes offers his own critique of some critics of experiential learning theory and proposes an extension based on Lacan's poststructuralist analysis, which elaborates the discord between personal and social knowledge in addition to the role language can play in shaping experience.

Kolb, D. (1999) *Learning Style Inventory, Version 3*, Boston, MA: Training Resources Group Hay/McBer.
To gain insight into your dominant learning style, access the most recent version of Kolb's Learning Style Inventory via the following link: trg_mcber@haygoup.com

Weil, S. and McGill, I. (1989) *Making Sense of Experiential Learning*, Milton Keynes: Open University Press.

These authors developed a 'village' metaphor to categorise four diverse but not mutually exclusive contexts and varieties of experience based learning. Village 4 has particular significance in its focus on personal growth and development to increase group effectiveness and self-awareness.

Zull, J. (2002) *The Art of Changing the Brain: Enriching Teaching by Exploring the Biology of Learning*, Sterling, VA: Stylus.

Zull (ibid.: 18–19) suggests experiential learning is related to the process of brain functioning in that: 'concrete experiences come through the sensory cortex, reflective observation involves the integrative cortex at the back, creating new abstracts occurs in the frontal integrative cortex, and active testing involves the motor brain. In other words, the learning cycle arises from the structure of the brain'.

Chapter 4

Dimension 2

Systematically evaluate your own teaching through classroom research procedures

---

Learning objectives

In this chapter you will consider:

- key characteristics of action research and processes embedded within this paradigm;
- ethical implications behind research involving human participants;
- research instruments and techniques used to gather, collate, analyse and evaluate data;
- criteria appropriate for assessing the validity of action research.

Introduction

As the term evaluation means to empower or strengthen, it should be an integral part of all teachers' professional growth and development irrespective of career stage. Formative evaluation as interpreted within this dimension involves the systematic exploration and judgement of pedagogical experiences, processes and outcomes in relation to specific goals, developmental needs, perceptions, resources and values. To use Eisner's (1998: 63) analogy, teachers need to become *connoisseurs* and *critics* of their own practice to determine whether what is happening as a result of their teaching is ultimately for the better:

> Connoisseurship is the art of appreciation. It can be displayed in any realm in which the character, import, or value of objects, situations, and performances is distributed and variable, including educational practice.

From the Latin word *cognoscere*, which means coming to know, connoisseurship is concerned with developing the capacity to see (rather than merely to look) so that the nuances and complexities inherent within different experiences and situations teachers encounter can be fully recognised and understood. This requires teachers to:

- examine ways in which these experiences and situations are enacted and might relate to one another;

- place them within the wider educational, ideological, political, professional and social contexts;
- consider how they might link to personal, situational and professional values and commitments (e.g. an appreciation of what constitutes effective teaching and learning).

There are a number of research strategies and procedures teachers can draw upon to systematically evaluate their own teaching in order to become more informed critics of their own practice. Action research is commonly used for this purpose, and building on Lewin's (1946) legacy of the action research spiral a number of models have been developed, which provide a highly structured approach to this research paradigm.

Action research for improving practice, thinking and creating more meaningful work environments seeks to take the value-laden, socially constructed nature of practice as its starting point. When teachers identify action for improvement this can usefully be viewed as both a dialogical and reflective process. The commitment to learn from and improve practice are characteristic principles of action research, as is the concern to generate and produce new knowledge. Reflecting on practice is a core component of action research and an important vehicle through which you can gain greater insight, understanding and awareness of your professional growth and development as a teacher, identify possible avenues for alternative practice, gain a greater sense of autonomy over your own work and internalise the processes associated with the art of self-study.

This chapter traces the historical roots of action research, explores its key characteristics and introduces a range of strategies and techniques for gathering information about the impact of your teaching on pupil learning. It also considers the ethical principles involved in practitioner-based research and criteria that can be drawn upon to assess the validity of action research.

Action research

Historical roots

The history of action research can broadly be divided into two stages. The first stage stems from developments in the United States between the 1920s and 1950s when there was growing interest 'in the application of scientific methods to the study of social and educational problems' (Wallace, 1987: 99). This is exemplified in the early work of Lewin (1952: 564) who introduced the metaphor *action research* to describe a form of enquiry that would enable 'the significantly established laws of social life to be tried and tested in practice' and portrayed action research as a spiral of steps, 'each of which is composed of a circle of planning, action and fact finding about the result of the action' (Lewin, 1946: 206). Thus, in its initial formulation, action research was defined as a method that enabled theories produced by the social sciences to be applied in practice and tested on the basis of their practical effectiveness. At that time, action research could only legitimise its claim to be a genuine social science by conforming to the methodological principles prescribed by the epistemology of positivism, which led to its rejection in the 1950s by the American social scientific community.

The second stage in the evolution or revival of interest in action research occurred within the context of curriculum and educational research in the United Kingdom in the early 1970s in response to such factors as:

- a growing conviction of the irrelevance of conventional educational research in relation to the real practical concerns of teachers and schools (Kemmis, 1988);
- the belief that the professionalism of teachers could be significantly enhanced if they adopted the role of teacher as researcher (Stenhouse, 1975);
- a revised version of Lewin's original model that would enable teachers to test out the curriculum proposals and policies enacted in their own classrooms and schools to stimulate innovative curriculum change and improve pedagogical practice (Elliott, 1998).

The version of action research that emerged during this period rejected the positivist approach to research in favour of 'interpretive' methodologies that were 'coming of age', gaining acceptance and being used in the social sciences. Consequently, action research was increasingly viewed as a form of enquiry that could use qualitative as opposed to quantitative research methods, and focused on the perspectives of research participants and social actors. There was also a notable shift in how the object of study was conceptualised, for example, 'the objects of educational action research are educational practices ... practice as it is understood by action researchers is informed committed action' (Kemmis, 1988: 44–45). Practitioners could test educational theories implicit within their own practice by treating them as experimental hypotheses to be systematically assessed in specific educational contexts. Lewin's original cycle was transformed from a method that applied social scientific theories to practice into one that enabled practitioners to assess the practical adequacy of their own tacit theories in action. The purpose behind this cyclical process, writes Elliott (1991: 69), is:

> to feed practical judgement in concrete situations, and the validity of the 'theories' or hypotheses it generates depends not so much on 'scientific' tests of truth, as on their usefulness in helping people to act more intelligently and skillfully. In action research 'theories' are not validated independently and then applied to practice. They are validated through practice.

Characteristic features of action research

Building on the historical origins, Table 4.1 exemplifies some ways in which theorists have defined and described action research.

Action research for improving personal practice

Action research incorporates a number of processes that teachers can use to investigate their own practice and answer questions about the quality of teaching and learning taking place. These processes include analysing and evaluating information about a particular experience, occurrence or situation after the event through critical self-reflection: 'the systematic and deliberate thinking back over one's actions' (Russell and Munby, 2002: 3). The components embedded within these processes have usefully been broken down by Carr and Kemmis (1986: 162) into a 'self-reflective spiral of cycles of planning, acting, observing, reflecting then re-planning, further action, further observation and further reflection'. McKernan's (1996) time process model of action research, shown in Figure 4.1, illustrates these processes and emphasises the

Table 4.1 Theorists' interpretations of action research

Bassey (1998: 93)
An enquiry which is carried out in order to understand, to evaluate and then to change, in order to improve educational practice.

Carr and Kemmis (1986: 162)
A form of self-reflective enquiry undertaken by participants in social situations in order to improve the rationality and justice of their own practices, their understanding of these practices, and the situations in which these practices are carried out.

Cohen and Manion (1994: 192)
Essentially an on-the-spot procedure designed to deal with a concrete problem located in an immediate situation. This means that ideally, the step-by-step process is constantly monitored over varying periods of time and by a variety of mechanisms (e.g. questionnaires, diaries, interviews and case studies) so that the ensuing feedback may be translated into modifications, adjustments, directional changes, redefinitions as necessary, so as to bring about lasting benefit to the ongoing process itself rather than to some future occasion.

Elliott (2005a: 359)
Critical self-reflection is integral to action research when conceived as the systematic organisation of action, which aims to realise educationally worthwhile and socially just learning experiences for pupils ... the power to transform practice is dependent upon an awareness of the habitual patterns of interaction that shaped (student teachers') lives in classrooms and the norms and beliefs embedded in them.

Hopkins (2002: 41)
Combines a substantive act with a research procedure; it is action disciplined by enquiry, a personal attempt at understanding while engaged in a process of improvement and reform.

Kemmis and McTaggart (2005: 5-6)
A form of collective self-reflective enquiry undertaken by participants in social situations in order to improve the rationality and justice of their own social or educational practices, as well as their understanding of those practices and the situations in which the practices are carried out ... the approach is only action research when it is collaborative, though it is important to realise that action research of the group is achieved through the critically examined action of individual group members.

Koshy (2005: 9)
Constructive enquiry, during which the researcher constructs his or her knowledge of specific issues through planning, acting, evaluating, refining and learning from the experience. It is a continuous learning process in which the researcher learns and also shares the newly generated knowledge with those who may benefit from it.

Lomax (2002: 122)
A self-reflective, self-critical and critical enquiry undertaken by professionals to improve the rationality and justice of their own practices, their understanding of these practices and the wider contexts of practice.

Macintyre (2000: 1)
An investigation where, as a result of rigorous self-appraisal of current practice, the researcher focuses on a problem (or topic which needs to be explained), and on the basis of information (about the up-to-date state of the art, about the people who will be involved and about the context) plans, implements, then evaluates an action then draws conclusions on the basis of their findings.

O'Leary (2004: 139)
A strategy that pursues action and knowledge in an integrated fashion through a cyclical and participatory process. In action research, processes, outcome and application are inextricably linked.

Reason and Bradbury (2001: 2)
Is about working towards practical outcomes, and also about creating new forms of understanding, since action without understanding is blind, just as theory without action is meaningless. Since action research starts with everyday experience and is concerned with the development of living knowledge, in many ways the process of inquiry is as important as specific outcomes. Good action research emerges over time in an evolutionary and developmental process, as individuals develop skills of enquiry and as communities of enquiry develop within communities of practice.

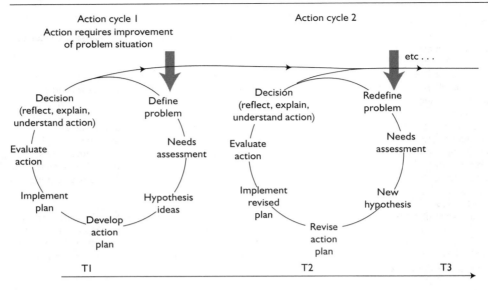

Figure 4.1 McKernan's (1996: 29) time process model of action research

importance of not allowing a particular problem to become too rigidly fixed from the outset, as the purpose behind action research enquiry should be to engage in rational problem solving.

This model reveals an important feature of action research, notably, the cyclical nature of an on-going process to improve the quality and effectiveness of practice. In seeking to improve practice and personal understanding the model shows that an enquiry must be undertaken by the practitioner, first to clarify and define the problem (as shown in the wide vertical arrow of Action Cycle 1). Once the action that requires improvement has been identified the next step is to undertake a literature search into

---

Reflective task 4.1 **Key characteristics of action research**

- From the interpretations presented in Table 4.1, extract the recurrent themes to identify key characteristics of action research.
- Three traditional approaches to action research are embedded within these interpretations – practitioners undertaking research:
  - to change, improve and evaluate their own practice for personal professional growth and development;
  - collectively for the purpose of emancipation in social situations to contribute toward greater democracy and equity in schools and society;
  - to generate new knowledge which can be shared to support and build upon the professional practice of others.

Identify which theorists belong to each tradition and conduct a search to examine how these traditions are distinctive and how they complement one another.

the area. This search should establish the major concepts and theories relevant to the area and any related research studies that have been undertaken. This literature review should give rise to hypotheses and ideas you may have about teaching, which enables you to develop an action plan outlining the different teaching approaches you anticipate you will use, data you will collect and research instruments you will use to gather this data.

In light of the specific class you will be teaching, you plan the first lesson, drawing from the cluster of approaches you have already identified. You implement the plan as you teach the first lesson and you (or an observer) gather data, as you teach and possibly after the lesson, so as to capture the pupils' response to your teaching. You then interrogate the data in much the same way as you analyse a lesson evaluation and reflect upon and decide how you will teach the following lesson. According to the nature of the data analysed, you may stay with your original action plan or decide to modify this in light of your reflections. As Figure 4.1 shows, you then plan and teach the next lesson (Action Cycle 2), collect and reflect on data and so the cycle continues.

Ideally, 'the step-by-step process is constantly monitored over varying periods of time' (Cohen, Manion & Morrison, 2007: 192), which alerts you to the fact that you do not solve a problem or unpack all aspects of an issue in one lesson. Rather in each lesson you try a particular combination of teaching strategies. Successful strategies should be retained and built upon, whereas less successful ones should be modified or discarded in light of your reflection. This relies on your skills of observation, reflection and evaluation.

You should come to recognise that reflection has at least two distinctive roles within action research. First, to form the basis for the planned action: reflection focuses on the meaning of observing an event or situation to devise the plan of action. Second, to evaluate the effect of the action: reflection focuses on the meaning of observing the effects of the action. In both phases of the cycle, reflection is retrospective and provides a link between the considered events of the past with future planning and development. Systematically reflecting on data gathered, lesson by lesson, to consider why particular outcomes were realised in the light of a particular strategy is the hallmark of this particular approach to action research.

The focus of your action research

Action research characteristically begins by selecting a topic for investigation in relation to: an aspect of teaching that needs developing; solving a particular issue or problem to promote pupil learning; achieving a particular goal; enabling pupils to achieve a specific learning objective; exploring an area of personal interest; or, evaluating the impact of a particular strategy or new initiative. The rationale and justification behind selecting a particular research topic needs to be context specific, appropriate and manageable within a given time frame. Some examples of topics student teachers decided to investigate during final school placement include:

- the effectiveness of grouping strategies to promote pupils' self-esteem;
- how strategies to control different aspects of the teaching environment can influence low-level disruption;
- the effects of teacher feedback on the performance of year 7 pupils;

- gifted, Talented and Able pupils' perceptions of teaching styles that enhance their own learning;
- how resource-based teaching can raise the participation levels of 11- and 12-year-old pupils with Attention Deficit Hyperactivity Disorder.

The following excerpts originate from the rationale presented by two of these student teachers.

The effects of teacher feedback on the performance of year 7 pupils

Throughout my teacher training I have been faced with such questions as 'How can you be an effective teacher?' and 'What should the teacher be striving to achieve?'. I have generally been given the answer, 'To be an effective teacher you should strive to achieve pupil learning'.

I am aware that there are many factors that have an effect on pupil learning. However, I am going to single out one variable, feedback, and look at how different types of teacher feedback affect pupil performance. I am aware that one would find it hard to find conclusive results from this due to the mass of alternative variables, however, I am confident that some types of feedback will show a positive effect on pupil performance.

During this piece of research, I will critically reflect on the findings and use this information to improve my teaching as a result. The inspiration for choosing this particular aspect of teaching comes from three main sources. Firstly, it was advised in documented feedback by my mentor as an area of teaching to try to improve on. Secondly, I personally feel this is a weaker area of teaching for me. Looking back at my reflective evaluations of lessons, they show a weak area of not using constructive feedback. Thirdly, as a trainee I also need to look at this focus in relation to achieving the standards for Qualified Teacher Status, which are a pre-requisite to completing my initial teacher training.

This piece of action research aims to show the best type of feedback to give pupils to aid their performance. It does not claim to provide the reader with a conclusive paradigm to follow in using feedback most effectively, the intention is to explore the area of feedback in a specific setting, and discover which types of feedback are beneficial to that particular setting and may be transferable to other classes.

How resource-based teaching can raise the participation levels of 11- and 12-year-old pupils with Attention Deficit Attention Hyperactivity Disorder

This action research investigation aims to improve educational experiences for children with Attention Deficit Hyperactivity Disorder (ADHD). The inspiration for this area has come from working at a school which has a high number of pupils with ADHD, during my year 4 teaching placement. As a result of this I have been made aware of an area of my teaching which needs to be improved to enhance the quality and work rate of pupils with ADHD.

This aim relates to several standards for the award of Qualified Teacher Status, which when achieved could offer inclusion without isolation for ADHD pupils in a good working environment through the use of resources, target setting and teaching styles.

A second reason for this investigation is that I have observed in other schools that pupils with ADHD are rarely challenged, being viewed as just difficult, and the pupils just get sent out of the lesson and are isolated or confronted, which research has shown makes the pupils more determined not to participate.

Holmes (2004: 2) identified that pupils with ADHD do not respond positively to confrontation, rather 'they will respond best to calmness ... so aim not to raise your voice too high when addressing the class generally and them specifically'. As a result of confrontation, pupils suffer from lower participation levels thus hindering their opportunities to learn. Holmes develops this claim further by observing that 'the pupil is fidgety and chatty, distracting himself and others, gathering the tempted into his realm of scattered attention. An observer would say the child's simply disobedient, unable to take instructions and to respect those around him, but on closer inspection, it is clear that this is not so. This is likely to be a child suffering from attention deficit hyperactivity disorder' (ibid.).

In acknowledging the above statements I feel that pupils would gain the chance to develop through understanding and catering for their needs and improving their participation levels and time on task in lessons. Through resource-based teaching, in particular using Information Communication Technology, I aim to improve the participation levels of pupils with ADHD, and to establish which resources keep the pupils engaged and on task. I think this is an important area that needs to be addressed and researched to improve the pupils' opportunities for learning.

Ethical considerations

Ethical issues arise in research undertaken with human participants when the conduct of the researcher involves the interests and rights of others. By its very nature, research in the social sciences involves studying people's activities in one way or another. Research involving interviews or observations, particularly where veridical records are kept, on audio or video tape for example, may impinge on the confidentiality, privacy, convenience, comfort or safety of others. Such threats constitute ethical problems.

Many professions which undertake research with human participants have devised an ethical code of practice or set of principles, such as the *Revised Ethical Guidelines for Educational Research* of the British Educational Research Association (BERA, 2004), which provide important benchmarks and reference sources in coming to recognise the researcher's responsibilities to protect the well-being of research participants. BERA (2004) provides indicative guidance in relation to: voluntary informed consent; deception; right to withdraw; children, vulnerable young people and vulnerable adults; incentives; detriment arising from participation in research; privacy; and disclosure. Also, educational establishments will have ethical principles and procedures in place for undertaking research with human participants in specific contexts. Thus, before undertaking action research you will need to fully understand the ethical implications and rigidly adhere to these throughout your study.

Busher (2002: 75) suggests ethical decisions need to be made in relation to each of the following factors:

1   The nature of the project, e.g. how does the project relate to ethical considerations in today's socio-political climate?
2   The context of the research, e.g. how does the subject area relate to the institutions, its people and wider contexts you are working in?
3   Procedures adopted, e.g. how will you ensure participants are aware of what you are doing? How will you ensure anonymity of participants?
4   Methods of data collection, e.g. who will you choose to collect data from?
5   Nature of participants, e.g. how will you ensure child protection matters are considered if using pupil interviews?
6   Types of data collected, e.g. is the data you propose to collect ethically appropriate in the context of the research?
7   What is done with the data and how it is disseminated, e.g. who is the audience for your research and how will you protect sources of information that might be sensitive if published?

Reviewing the literature

Once you have decided on a topic for action research you need to undertake a review of the relevant literature so that you can situate your study within the wider context of theory and practice. This includes the identification and synthesis of appropriate concepts and frameworks that might be applicable to your own study and other empirical research on the topic. Different types of literature you need to consider encompass those related to policy documents and guidance material, theoretical concepts and constructs advanced by theorists and existing research studies undertaken within your chosen field. As you read through this literature, particularly the latter type, it is important to make notes on the research methodologies employed by other researchers, what data was gathered and how that data was analysed, as this kind of information should guide decisions you make in relation to your own research. Table 4.2 presents a summary template of the type of information you can extract from each source of literature.

Reflective task 4.2 **Planning your action research project**

•   Select an action research topic that aims to bring about improvement in your own practice or some change within your school.
•   Write a 1,500-word rationale for your proposed study and consider what ethical decisions need to be made.
•   Discuss this proposal with your tutor or a professional colleague.
•   Review your proposal in light of the feedback received.

Table 4.2 Summary template for literature review

Author/s	Title	Source
Key words:		
Aims/purpose:		
Research participants:		
Methodology:		
Analysis:		
Key findings:		
Conclusions:		
Recommendations for further studies:		
Quotes:		
Relevance to specific research question/s:		
Evidence base (high, medium or low):		
Date reviewed:		

The review of literature does not simply consist of a list of ideas and quotations gathered from a range of sources and presented as an annotated bibliography. You must reflect upon these ideas, compare and contrast them with ideas from other sources, critically analyse, synthesise, organise and categorise them. Your literature review should therefore make reference to previous research on the topic/concept in relation to established views concerning: the value of the topic; definition of concept/s; and how this relates to research on teaching and learning. You need to discuss this critically and draw out that which is of value for your own research project. The literature review should be used to identify your research question/s and relevant theoretical frameworks. You can use subheadings as a funnelling exercise, working from the general to the specific within the focus of your study.

Reflective task 4.3 **A critical review of literature**

- Select five recently published articles related to your proposed action research study and extract the relevant details from each using the template shown in Table 4.2.
- Compare and contrast their: key findings and recommendations in relation to the original aims and purpose; research participants and methodologies employed; and evidence base drawn upon to support their respective conclusions.
- Consider how the outcomes of this activity might inform your original proposal (see task 4.2) and make any necessary adjustments to refine the focus of your research.

Data collection techniques

An important feature of action research is gathering data, which provides an accurate record of the outcomes of your teaching in relation to pupil learning. Two kinds of data should be collected for this purpose:

1 data that monitors what you, as the teacher, do within each lesson and to evaluate how successful you are at putting your plans into practice;
2 data that demonstrates the effectiveness of your innovation as a whole, e.g. whether pupils' performance improves in response to your modified teaching strategies.

Data collection techniques are of two types:

- *quantitative* techniques – any method which produces data that can be reduced to a numerical form and analysed statistically, e.g. a record of the number of times an event occurs. Quantitative data is normally collected in a structured format using some type of rating scale, e.g. those recording
  - *duration* (when an event starts and when it finishes);
  - *interval* (what event occurs in a set period of time);
  - an *event* (the number of times an event occurs in a lesson).
  'Closed' questions on questionnaires can also be quantitative;

- *qualitative* techniques – any method used to gain insight rather than statistical analysis, e.g. unstructured observations, personal perceptions about what is observed, reflective journals/diaries, some rating scales, documents, interviews, and 'open-ended' questions on questionnaires.

The following sub-sections introduce some data collection techniques commonly used in classroom-based research.

Field notes and diaries

Very often field notes are used as a first step prior to narrowing down the focus of an investigation. They are particularly relevant for observations designed to allow you to describe events in a lesson, either considering the whole range of events that occur (e.g. recording your general impressions of a teaching environment) or describing all events in a broadly defined area of concern (e.g. pupil behaviour). Such observations enable you to identify any issues or problems and determine what you want to look at in more detail. You can then collect information systematically to focus further investigation on the issue or problem. McKernan (1996) distinguishes between three types of field notes and diaries you can maintain when undertaking research:

- intimate journal – a personal diary to record events on a day-to-day basis;
- log book – used regularly to summarise key happenings and events;
- memoir – entries made infrequently which allows time to reflect on events and interpret them more objectively.

Lesson evaluations are an example of a form of diary or log book. Also, many of the reflective tasks introduced throughout this book can be viewed as the forerunner to more focused research-based field notes and diaries. Field notes are particularly useful if you wish to undertake a case study of an individual pupil or group of pupils, e.g. if you are involved in a 'shadowing' exercise. In such instances observations and field notes are made over a period of time and can then be collated in a diary. This can be used to reflect on and analyse patterns and trends over a period of time. It is important to maintain confidentiality and avoid direct reference to individuals and specific schools in field notes.

Questionnaires

These can be a useful means of acquiring information about learning and teaching from the perspectives of both the teacher and pupils, e.g. by asking pupils specific questions about the lesson, you can gather valuable information about the impact of your teaching on their learning. The way your questions are constructed is of considerable importance to the effectiveness of your questionnaire. Questions should be:

- *accessible* – the language needs to be appropriate for the research participants and complicated grammar such as double negatives should be avoided;
- *concise* – to avoid information overload and minimise ambiguity;

- *unbiased* – structured impartially, and leading questions that can bias responses avoided;
- *clear* – constructed simply and combining questions avoided.

Several types of question can be incorporated into questionnaires to provide varying degrees of quantitative and qualitative data. *Closed questions*, for example, can give pupils definitive choices and limit their responses to a 'yes' or 'no' type of format whereas *open-ended* questions can elicit a phrase or comment and may be more illuminating, but rely on the language ability of pupils. If care is taken in their construction, questionnaires can be quick and easy to administer and provide a large amount of pertinent information. One problem is that in a normal teaching situation questionnaires take time to give out, complete and return. Another is they depend upon whether or not pupils have the ability to understand the questions. When constructing a questionnaire or selecting one already developed, ensure the language is at the right level for pupils and jargon free so they understand exactly what you are asking. There is also a danger that pupils may not be truthful as they might try to please you by writing the type of answer they think you wish to hear.

Interviews

There are three main types of interview: structured, semi-structured and unstructured.

- *Structured* interviews allow you to work through an interview schedule and are usually composed of closed questions which direct the response options of those you interview. With such limited flexibility however, your data may lack evidence that is pivotal to your research, as the questions you ask may not offer a sufficient range of responses to gain a fully comprehensive overview of the topic.
- *Semi-structured* interviews offer a more flexible style and can be used to collect information equivalent to that of structured interviews. You begin by identifying a number of key questions that not only elicit specific types of response but also act as prompts. Further probing can be used to ensure that those interviewed understand the question. A technique described by Oppenheim (1992) as 'funnelling' questions helps you to gain more information about an area of interest by pursuing further questions around the same theme.
- *Unstructured* interviews are the most flexible style and can allow you to gather complementary evidence. This approach is generally used to explore an area in preliminary research for people with access to specialised information. However, the success of such interviews relies heavily on the dexterity and expertise of the interviewer, e.g. when the interviewer poses informed questions and adapts to the situation by reacting perceptively to new leads as they arise during the interview.

Although interviews are usually undertaken on a one-to-one basis, you can interview research participants in groups. The main advantage of group interviews is they can elicit rich data as participants listen to one another. Further benefits include: people are often less intimidated, feel more at ease and can freely engage in discussion; they are less time consuming than individual interviews; and subsequent individual interviews

Reflective task 4.4 **Research instruments and techniques**

- To further develop your knowledge and understanding of data collection techniques appropriate for classroom-based research, conduct an in-depth literature search to identify the key features, uses, advantages and disadvantages of:
  - audio tape recording
  - case studies
  - documentary analysis
  - field notes and reflective diaries
  - interviews
  - observation schedules
  - questionnaires
  - video tape recording.

The following authors provide a useful springboard for this search in addition to advice and guidance on how you might design a range of research instruments: Bell (2005); Cohen, Manion and Morrison (2007); Hopkins (2002); Robson (2002); Wilson (2009).

can explore issues that arose from the group interview (Cohen, Manion and Morrison, 2007). However, major disadvantages of group interviews are 'the results cannot be generalised, the emerging group culture may interfere with individual expression … the group may be dominated by one person and "groupthink" is a possible outcome' (Fontana and Frey, 2000: 652).

Using information gathered

An important point to note is that the information you decide to collect is only the starting point for your action research investigation. The data collected from your research instruments should enable you to describe and reflect on each lesson in relation to:

- key events
- teacher, pupil and/or observer behaviour
- problems encountered.

In light of your response to the above areas you should make the necessary adjustments to your plan of action and/or refinements to your data collection techniques. You need to record this process with consistency and clarity throughout your investigation, indicating the basis upon which any changes were made to the strategy and used to modify and develop your teaching and pupil learning, from lesson to lesson through *formative evaluation*. Your results and discussions provide opportunities for reflection and cross-referencing your findings. What is important in this record of on-going research is the clear explanation of a development based on sound evidence and the quality of conclusions you have drawn.

Collation and analysis of data

Having undertaken an action research investigation, you need to present, interpret and analyse your findings. You should collate your raw data and organise your research evidence into appropriate categories. Findings can be presented in the form of data summaries rather than the raw data itself, along with tables, graphs, transcripts of significant conversations and records of illuminating incidents. Having established appropriate categories, you can examine the findings and look for evidence of similarities and differences, groupings, patterns, trends and events or incidents that are of particular significance to your research focus and question/s. You should be able to survey all the data you have collected over the research weeks to interpret, analyse and critically reflect on your overall findings.

The importance of your analysis cannot be overstated as this resides at the heart of your study and is where you demonstrate your capacity to reflect and understand, organise information, explain its significance and justify your conclusions. You should take the opportunity to compare your findings with the concepts and data reviewed in your reading. Your analysis should include the following:

- clear exposition of complex arguments and issues
- elucidating and explaining
- sustaining a logical argument
- comparing and contrasting
- identifying and challenging assumptions.

The emphasis of your action research should be on Why? rather than What? Two things you should try to avoid are a straightforward descriptive narrative and a subjective account, which has little value. Although your opinions are valid, they must derive logically from the evidence base. Your literature review can help you develop a conceptual framework to explain your data in the following ways:

- using the literature to help you classify your data
- interpreting your findings in terms of the theory or conceptual framework
- challenging assumptions
- evaluating your action research by relating outcomes to stated objectives
- establishing causal relationships.

Your approach should be critical, explanatory and explicitly link theory and practice to derive valid conclusions. The usefulness and validity of your findings for teaching should be judged realistically and considered in light of prior reading and relevant research. You need to acknowledge that your findings have arisen from a specific context, one that involves you as the researcher focusing on a particular aspect of teaching or pupil learning, with a particular group of pupils in a particular environment. Therefore, care needs to be exercised to avoid making claims or generalisations based on limited data which has emerged from a small-scale investigation.

Triangulation is often used in action research as one of several techniques designed to measure the trustworthiness or validity of a category or hypothesis. It is characterised by collecting data about a particular teaching situation from three different perspectives:

Table 4.3 Assessing the validity of action research

Process validity
Are appropriate methods used to answer the questions:
a) Does the research focus on a problem that is of practical concern to the teachers involved?
b) Does the research involve gathering data from different points of view, for example the teacher, an observer, and students (triangulation)?
c) Does the research enable the teacher/researcher to call their existing stock of practical knowledge (tacit theories) into question, and test it against evidence gathered in their practical situation?
d) Does the research extend teachers' understanding of their situation in a way that opens up new possibilities for action?

Democratic validity
Are the researchers and researched engaged and included in the inquiry?
Is the research a rigorous conversational process in which the teacher opens up his/her practice to the rational scrutiny of students and peers, 'in-voices' their views of the action situation, and in the process demonstrates a disposition to subordinate his/her own prejudices to the search for an overlapping and un-coerced consensus?

Catalytic validity
Is the research transformative?
a) Is the research a deliberative and self-reflexive process in which the teacher calls into question both his/her teaching strategies (means) and the aims (ends) to which they are directed, and modifies each by reflecting on the other?
b) Is the research a process in which the teacher displays:
  • integrity in the pursuit of his/her educational aims and values?
  • curiosity about other people's interpretations of the action situation?
  • objectivity and honesty about his/her own motives and reasons for action?
  • open-mindedness towards the views of others and respect for their freedom of thought and action?

Outcome validity
Has the process led to a resolution and/or reframing of the problem?
a) Does the research enlarge the teacher's sphere of personal agency in the practical situation through the realisation of his/her educational aims in a sustainable form?
b) Does the research enable a teacher to generate a description of the complexities of the case in sufficient detail to be of universal significance to other teachers?

usually those of the pupils, an observer and the teacher/researcher. In this way different sources of data can be cross-referenced to validate whether something has occurred. The criteria that Elliott (2006) devised explicitly for the purpose of assessing the validity of action research, as shown in Table 4.3, can be drawn upon to guide you here.

In drawing conclusions you might suggest changes that, if you were to undertake your study again, you could make to improve some aspect of the research. Also, you might consider whether your findings have relevance to other teaching and learning situations. Perceived limitations of your study should be identified and you might recommend possible future research and developments.

The value of research into your teaching

Research into your own teaching investigates aspects of educational theory. You come to appreciate the complex ways in which theory and practice are related and realise

---

Reflective task 4.5 **Undertaking your action research project**

In light of the action research processes introduced throughout this chapter:

- Refine the focus of your proposed study (see task 4.2) and justify why the research is important.
- Provide a critical analysis of the theory and published research to produce a conceptual framework as the basis for your study.
- Select appropriate methods of data collection, and design (and pilot) your research instruments.
- Conduct your research, collect and analyse your data.
- Present the analysis of your findings and discuss them in relation to the literature in your review.
- Draw conclusions on the outcomes of your study as a whole and make appropriate recommendations for future action and further research.

---

that while there is much common ground in teaching, every situation creates a specific context for using theory to inform practice. As you work in this way you will come to understand the range of variables that influence good practice, e.g. the school context, the social dynamics in a class and the way pupils perceive the activity or subject you are teaching. You apply the outcomes to your own teaching and pupil learning to address an issue, solve a problem or achieve a particular goal. You may then look at the same issue, problem or goal in more depth or from a different perspective, or move on to another focus.

The following excerpt illuminates, in part, what impact undertaking a small-scale action research investigation during final school placement had on one student teacher introduced earlier in this chapter.

Reflections and conclusions

The aim of my study was to try and improve the participation levels of pupils with ADHD through resource-based teaching. My findings over the unit suggest that pupils with ADHD respond well to independent learning with ICT resources that outline exactly what to do, how to do it, why and when. Examples of the resources I used were reciprocal teaching cards, key words and outlining the teaching points for each lesson. One factor that arose during my data analysis was the observation that the self check style had a negative effect on the pupils' participation, which suggests that ADHD pupils might prefer to work with other pupils rather than alone. During my study I also observed that the pupils liked to work with other ADHD pupils. One research participant was unaware that she has ADHD which suggests that the pupils are drawn to one another for reasons unknown. My findings further suggest that these pupils respond well to being given responsibility and knowing that I trusted them to teach their partners.

I observed these pupils in other lessons and the approach adopted by some teachers with ADHD pupils was to use a command style approach, giving them no responsibility within the lesson. This did not seem to be effective with regard to the participation levels of the pupils. From observing these lessons, the ADHD pupils were often isolated from the rest of the group as a result of their behaviour and that of their peers.

Within the school where I conducted my study, I hope that I highlighted my aims and helped staff to identify different ways to attempt to accommodate ADHD pupils in their classes. The school has a number of pupils with ADHD and although the school accommodates pupils well, I feel that there are many issues which could be improved to include the ADHD pupils further.

Findings made during my study also reveal major differences between ADHD pupils' behaviour. These were very prominent in the interviews. One pupil adopted an aggressive demeanour, another discussed very promiscuous topics throughout the interview, whilst two others were focused, attentive and very positive throughout their interviews. All of these pupils suffer from ADHD yet their reactions to interviews were so very different. I feel this requires further inquiry.

This may be a result of individuality, mood and many other factors, but I feel there is a lot to be considered regarding the effects of ADHD on behaviour. This study was particularly difficult as the personalities of the pupils were so varied.

What I have found is that the pupils do want to learn and the problem is just getting them into that state of mind where they will do what they are supposed to do as there were so many little challenges.

I think I have learned a lot from this research, particularly in relation to the way I approach my teaching by focusing more now on pupils, learning to see what has or has not worked and what I need to do in the next lesson to move their learning forward.

I would not say that I always got it right because to some extent action research is trial and error; however, I endeavoured to use the data and feedback received formatively and to draw some insightful conclusions about my teaching to inform future planning and practice. I do think that many of the modifications I made had a positive effect on the pupils' learning but I do not think that the process ends here. There are many things I could extract from this research and then go back and do more to improve still further. What has become very clear to me is the importance of searching for the reasons behind the outcomes of my teaching and trying to understand why some strategies were effective whereas others were less so.

Reflecting upon my study, I feel that I have uncovered some aspects of ADHD which need more research. I feel the main finding in my investigation is that there is not enough literature and understanding of the disorder which affects so many children across the world and that we, as a profession, know so little about ADHD and its effects on pupils. Research needs to be conducted to investigate the cause of the disorder, the learning behaviours and patterns of pupils with ADHD, factors affecting the social interaction of sufferers, the effects of Ritalin on sufferers, and how sufferers' motivation and participation levels differ across the curriculum in different subject areas within the school.

I feel I have developed professionally as a direct result of this study. Through critically reflecting on my own teaching I believe that I can continue to improve pupil learning through further development of my teaching as I enter the profession. I would like to research the effects of different teaching strategies and the use of different groupings on the participation of pupils with ADHD through more reflective teaching to develop my understanding of ADHD and ways to improve the learning of ADHD pupils even further.

Reflective task 4.6 **Analysis of discourse**

- Read the narrative through several times and use Table 2.2 (p. 28) to identify the descriptive, comparative and critical reflective conversations evident within this discourse.
- In your view, are the conversations used in a considered way, given that this excerpt is indicative of reflections and evaluations following a piece of action research?
- Are some types of reflective conversation more prevalent than others?
- How might your engagement with this task shape the way you draw upon evidence to substantiate your own research conclusions?

Summary of key points

This chapter has introduced a range of classroom strategies and research techniques that can be drawn upon to systematically evaluate your own teaching. The historical roots of action research have been traced and the key characteristics and processes of this paradigm explored. It has considered the ethical principles involved in practitioner-based research and appropriate criteria to use in assessing the validity of your own action research investigation.

Undertaking action research should help you to identify issues and address problems identified through observation, reflection and evaluation. This means thinking critically about what you are doing, finding ways of systematically investigating it and making sense of your investigations. As you gain experience, confidence and learn to challenge, communicate and explore ideas, you will become a more effective teacher and both a connoisseur and a critic of your own practice.

Recommended reading

Bell, J. (2005) *Doing your Research Project: A Guide for First-Time Researchers in Education and Social Science (4th edition)*, Maidenhead: Open University Press.
This book is designed for people undertaking small-scale research projects. Part 2 'Selecting methods of information collection' provides examples of data collecting techniques.

Hopkins, D. (2002) *A Teacher's Guide to Classroom Research (3rd edition)*, Buckingham: Open University Press.
This book is a good starting point for anyone wishing to research aspects of personal practice. It contains practical ideas and examples of a variety of data collection techniques to improve classroom practice and guidance on each aspect of the research process.

Wilson, E. (2009) *School-based Research: A Guide for Education Students*, London: Sage.
An invaluable text and contemporary resource with comprehensive sections that feature: using existing research to understand and plan your classroom-based research; carrying out and reporting on classroom-based research; methodologies and paradigms.

Chapter 5

Dimension 3

Link theory with your own practice

Learning objectives

This chapter enables you to consider:

- the nature of *theory* relevant to teachers;
- how *episteme* and *phronesis* relate to teacher cognition and teacher behaviour within a Gestalt framework;
- sources of the *knowledge base* for teaching and how these may be developed;
- the significance and use of processes inherent within *pedagogical reasoning and action*.

Introduction

Theories associated with learning to teach emerge from at least two perspectives. *Espoused theories* are those seen by a profession to guide action and encompass the formal philosophy of the profession (e.g. propositional or explicit knowledge) whereas *theories-in-use* incorporate those patterns of behaviour, learned and developed in the day-to-day work of the professional (e.g. procedural knowledge and tacit knowing). This distinction originally arose from concern that there was a gap between espoused theories that purport to underpin professional activity and the reality of how a professional behaves in practice. Schon (1987) suggests the latter type more aptly characterises the real behaviour of a professional. Although he recognises the need for professionals to acquire a body of specialised knowledge, he cautions that such knowledge cannot simply be applied in a rule-governed way to guide practice and presents the view that professionals generate their own theories-in-use or personal epistemology of practice, which in turn enables them to ground and validate curriculum theory through their own practice.

A third perspective on theories relevant to teachers, stems from *cultural knowledge,* which is also context specific and embedded within the 'shared assumptions and beliefs that are used to perceive and explain classroom reality and assign value and significance to new information and ideas' (Wilson, 2009: 4). The pursuit of linking theory with practice also implies that teachers must be able to critically analyse the research evidence they read as part of their professional role, and judge its findings and conclusions 'from a well-informed point of view' (Campbell *et al.*, 2003: 2). This builds on Stenhouse's (1983) view that the purpose of educational research is to develop thoughtful reflection so as to strengthen the professional judgement of teachers, which can be realised when teachers subject their own practice to critical scrutiny and rational reflection, informed by literature and research (Humes, 2001). These examples illustrate the breadth and diverse nature of theoretical constructs underpinning this dimension.

To gain an understanding of the relationship between theory and practice, this chapter predominantly draws on work from two key sources. Korthagen and Kessels (1999) present two related theoretical bases to support their discourse on the nature of theory relevant to teachers. The first uses the concepts of *episteme* and *phronesis* derived from Aristotle, to explain different meanings attributed to the word 'theory'; the second explores the relationship between teacher cognition and teacher behaviour, which leads to a model that incorporates three levels in learning about teaching: the *Gestalt* level, the *schema* level and the *theory* level. The focus then turns to Shulman (1987) who presents a view of teaching that seeks to capture sources of the knowledge base for teaching. Against this backdrop he provides a model to highlight processes embedded within *pedagogical reasoning and action,* which enables *praxis* to be interpreted as thought-full-action and action-full-of-thought (Freire, 1972).

Theory relevant to teachers

A significant amount of educational, psychological and sociological research has emerged in past decades, which in principle provides professional practitioners with a useful body of knowledge. Teacher educators for example, have made *a priori* choices about which particular theories (axioms, principles, rules) should be transferred to student teachers during teacher education. Experts working in universities have traditionally taught this knowledge and tried to simulate its transfer to the classroom context. However, as Ben Peretz (1995: 546) cautions:

> The hidden curriculum of teacher education tends to communicate a fragmented view of knowledge, both in coursework and field experience. Moreover, knowledge is 'given' and unproblematic. These views of knowledge are likely to become quite problematic as teachers gain experience.

Studies have shown that placing an emphasis on expert knowledge and the tendency to focus on specific knowledge bases in teacher education often fail to influence the practice of many student teachers. Reporting from a cognitive psychological perspective, Korthagen and Kessels (1999) identify three major factors that can inhibit the transfer of knowledge from teacher education to the school context:

1   The *prior knowledge* of student teachers can exert a powerful influence on their comprehension and learning as many have developed preconceptions about teaching that differ from theories they are taught in teacher education. In part, as a result of the socialisation process of being a pupil in school for many years, they have built preconceptions about the nature of teaching, e.g. how to teach subject matter, plan lessons and create a purposeful active learning environment. Many have also developed a restricted view of their pupils' learning styles. Corporaal

(1988) concludes that the poor transfer of theory to practice often arises when there is a lack of integration of the theories presented in teacher education into the conceptions that student teachers bring to their course.

2   The *feed-forward* problem can arise if student teachers are introduced to theories in teacher education that they are unable to connect to their own actions in concrete practical situations, e.g. the fruitfulness of a given theory might be perceived as untimely or wholly irrelevant to other more pressing concerns they experience, which can influence their motivation and willingness to study it.

3   The type of abstract, systematised, expert knowledge presented in teacher education might lack *relevance* to the authentic school context as student teachers need concrete solutions for situations that may arise, particularly when trying to accomplish complex and often conflicting goals.

Although the traditional *application-of-theory* approach is still evident in many programmes worldwide, these examples illuminate the need to bridge several gaps that can emerge between theory and practice. In promoting the transfer of knowledge from teacher education to school practice, Brouwer (1989) notes that one important factor is the extent to which theory and practice follow an integrative design within the teacher education curriculum. In recent decades, alternative ways of preparing teachers for the profession have been developed, placing a strong emphasis on reflective teaching (Korthagen and Kessels, 1999: 6) and conceptualise teacher development as:

> the on-going process of experiencing practical teaching and learning situations, reflecting on them under the guidance of an expert, and developing one's own insights into teaching through the interaction between personal reflection and theoretical notions offered by the expert.

The nature of theory within such programmes takes on a different shade of meaning when compared with the traditional application-of-theory approach.

Reflective task 5.1 **Teacher education experience**

Consider the ways in which your teacher education programme draws links between theory and practice. Is the curriculum designed in an integrative way or are notable gaps evident between theory and practice?

Episteme and phronesis

Drawing on Aristotle's concepts of *episteme* and *phronesis,* Korthagen and Kessels explain two different meanings associated with the term theory. For example, when a teacher educator offers epistemic knowledge, he uses general conceptions that can apply to a wide variety of situations: this knowledge is based on research and can be characterised as *objective* theory. This type of knowledge plays a central role in the traditional application-of-theory approach to teacher education. Although epistemic knowledge serves an important purpose, teachers also need context-specific knowledge related to the situation in which they meet a problem or develop a particular need. This type of knowledge, termed phronesis, brings a teacher's pre-existing, subjective perception of personally relevant classroom situations one step further. The character of phronesis is more *perceptual* than conceptual and often, subconsciously, focuses the attention of the teacher in the situation on certain characteristics of the situation that assume significance to the question of how to act within the situation.

Expressed succinctly, the principle aim of episteme is in helping us to know more about many situations whereas that of phronesis is in helping us to perceive more in a particular situation and finding an appropriate course of action on the basis of heightened awareness. The heightened awareness of concrete characteristics within specific situations is also the fundamental distinction between phronesis and procedural knowledge, e.g. knowing 'how to' apply theory to the concrete situations of practice. The danger in emphasising procedural knowledge is that teachers may learn numerous strategies and techniques for different types of situation yet do not necessarily learn how to discover, in specific situations occurring in everyday teaching, which strategies and techniques to use.

Teacher cognition and teacher behaviour

During the 1970s, some research into *teacher thinking* portrayed teachers as *conscious decision makers* based on the assumption that teachers possess theoretical structures they apply to practical situations. The common line of thinking about the relationship between teacher cognition and teacher behaviour mirrored the *process-product* approach to research on teaching prevalent at that time. The general view was that once inside school and involved in making practical decisions, teachers would simply apply and use the research-based knowledge available to them. Questions concerning how teacher cognition might actually influence teacher behaviour were seldom raised.

Two decades later developments in cognitive psychology, linguistics, neurophysiology and social psychology pointed toward the central role of *analogue* and *figurative* mental structures in terms of constructing meaning and directing behaviour. For example, during an *immediate teaching situation* (Dolk, 1997) perception, interpretation and reaction happen within a split second and together form a *unity* shaped by and rooted in many former life experiences. This unity may not be rational or reach the teacher's level of consciousness, which raises the question: What factors guide teacher behaviour?

Gestalt formation

Korthagen (1993) uses the term *Gestalt* to capture the dynamic and holistic unity of feelings, meanings, needs, values and behavioural inclinations that are triggered by an immediate teaching situation. A central tenet in Gestalt psychology is that the most fundamental way in which individuals acquire a grasp of their environment is through the formation of Gestalts. These often enable us to see objects or situations as an entity and respond to them as such. This means that during an immediate teaching situation the conditions and events embedded within that situation are combined into one holistic perceptual identity, which implies a complex interplay between cultural, physical, psychological and sociological factors. For example, the knowledge embedded within Gestalts is first and foremost linked to concrete situations that have previously

Reflective task 5.2 **Observing teacher behaviour**

- Observe three different teachers as they work with pupils and record the behavioural characteristics each exhibits. This may include such behaviours as: actively listening to pupils; using praise, reinforcement and encouragement; organising and managing the environment; using pupils' names; interacting with individual pupils, small groups and the whole class; using humour, gestures and eye contact; and idiosyncratic mannerisms.
- As you record each characteristic, make a note of the corresponding pupil behaviour.
- Compare and contrast these teachers to identify ways in which their behaviour is both similar and distinctive.

Reflective task 5.3 **Personal teacher behaviour**

- Think of an event or occurrence that has recently happened in your own teaching and make notes on: what preceded the event, what triggered the event, what actually happened, who was involved, the context, how you behaved, how your pupils behaved.
- Consider how your *feelings, former similar experiences, values, role conception, needs or concerns* and *routines* may have guided your behaviour.
- Consider how your own behaviour may have influenced the behaviour of your pupils.
- What have you learned about your own behaviour?
- Has anything surprised you?
- Are there any elements of your teaching behaviour that need developing? If so, plan how you can go about accomplishing this goal.
- Discuss your thoughts and ideas with your mentor or professional tutor.

been encountered by the person and shaped by the value-laden and subjective experiences of such situations. This has resonance with van Manen's (1990) discourse on the interplay between a situation and the person experiencing that situation as well as the role of context in that experience.

To describe the direct and holistic relationship between behaviour, context, person and situation, Korthagen and Kessels (1999: 9) draw on the notion of *closure* from Gestalt psychology: 'the tendency of an organism to complete incomplete information'. Teachers may, for example, close situations with responses located in their existing repertoires and which exemplify well-known ways of behaving in similar situations. This means Gestalts can often reflect and reproduce socio-cultural norms and patterns. The split-second ways of reacting in situations during a lesson, rooted in Gestalts triggered by characteristics of the situation, may however not always be wholly appropriate.

Korthagen and Lagerwerf (1996) explored how Gestalts relate to the epistemic knowledge teachers must acquire as the basis of their professional thinking, along with

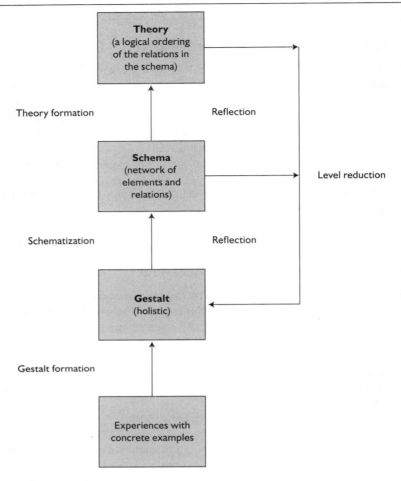

Figure 5.1 Levels in the process of learning with regard to a certain domain
Adapted from Korthagen and Kessels (1999: 10)

how reflection on action (Schon, 1987) can develop epistemic knowledge by using levels in the process of learning a certain domain, as illustrated in Figure 5.1.

Gestalts form at the base of this model. When teachers are encouraged to take time, stand back and look closely at their own teaching or come across unexpected situations, reflection on their own Gestalts is promoted. By analysing what factors guide their own behaviour, teachers may become more aware of the elements that constitute these Gestalts and explore relationships between them. The processes of perception → interpretation → analysis → decision → action can be analysed when the teacher is operating at a conscious level, particularly when engaged in reflection-on-action after the lesson. This involves analysing and clarifying 'individual and cultural experiences, meanings, perceptions, assumptions, prejudgements, and presuppositions, for the purpose of orienting practical actions' (van Manen, 1977: 226). This process enables teachers to develop a consciously available *schema*, which on the one hand is tied to concrete experiences and on the other, becomes more detached from these experiences.

Therefore a schema can be described as a conscious mental framework of concepts and relationships. The kind of knowledge embedded within a schema shows characteristics of phronesis as it builds on Gestalts connected to specific situations and personal perception. However, the knowledge in schemata is often more generalised over different situations and makes use of concepts, which means that schemata can also show characteristics of episteme.

When the focus for reflection is at the schema level this can lead to the development of *theory* as the teacher can make logical connections between the relationships in his schema. For example, some relationships within the schema might appear to be logical consequences of others or appear to be if–then relationships, which apply to a whole range of situations.

The formulation of axioms (basic relationships), definitions and logically derived propositions occurs at the theory level, which has the clearest characteristics of episteme. After a period of time, knowledge in the schema or theory level can become self-evident to the teacher and be used in a less conscious, more intuitive way, as though the whole schema or theory has been reduced to one Gestalt. Van Hiele (1986: 46) refers to this as *level reduction:* the relevant schemata and theories need less attention and enable teachers to focus their thinking on other aspects of their practice.

An understanding of this model should help you to recognise that any episteme not connected to already existing phronesis is unlikely to influence or change practice. Even if a teacher develops Gestalts into his schemata and then into sound theories, level reduction should take place before any level of theory attained can influence split-second behaviour. This means the theory in the teacher's mind 'should itself become a Gestalt, that is, a dynamic unity intertwined with behaviour in a certain type of situation' (Korthagen and Kessels, 1999: 13), which no longer requires much conscious reflection.

Reflective task 5.4 **Linking theory with your own practice**

- Review the section in Chapter 3 on Schon's (1987) exposition of reflection in action and reflection on action.
- What connections can you make between the arguments advanced by Schon and those by Korthagen and Kessels on Gestalt formation?
- Write a 2,000-word reflective narrative (which draws on a range of personal experiences) to critically analyse how your teacher behaviour is guided by your understanding of theory.

Discuss the main points of your argument with a critical friend.

The knowledge base for teaching

There are several frameworks in the literature that seek to capture the knowledge base for teaching (e.g. Banks, Leach and Moon, 1999; Grossman, 1990). To exemplify the extensive range of knowledge required by teachers, Shulman (1986) identifies seven categories, as shown in Figure 5.2, which are explored briefly below.

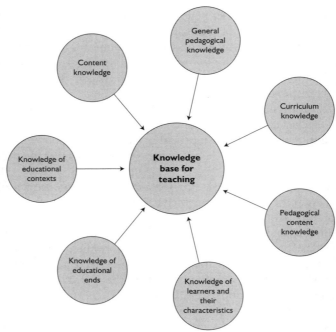

Figure 5.2 Knowledge base for teaching

- *Content knowledge* goes beyond knowledge of the facts or concepts *per se* within a given subject area and requires an understanding of the *substantive* and *syntactic* (Schwab, 1978) structures of the subject matter.
  i   The substantive structures are ways in which the basic concepts and principles of the discipline are organised to incorporate its facts and focus on the *nature of enquiry* within a discipline.
  ii The syntactic structures are ways in which truth or falsehood, validity or invalidity within the discipline are established. Teachers must be able to define the accepted truths within a subject area and explain why a particular proposition is justified, why it is worth knowing and how it relates to other propositions, within the discipline and beyond (in theory and practice), and focus on the *methods of enquiry* within a discipline.
  Teachers must also understand why a particular topic is central to a subject or discipline whereas another may be more peripheral.
- *General pedagogical knowledge* requires an understanding of the broader principles and strategies that transcend subject matter, which are designed to guide classroom teaching, classroom organisation and classroom management to ensure the content knowledge can be transformed into meaningful learning activities for pupils. Teachers must be responsive to the immediate demands of teaching and exercise flexibility in adapting content knowledge for a range of learners, e.g. developing strategies to motivate disaffected pupils and support those with specific learning needs.
- *Curriculum knowledge* requires an understanding of the full range of programmes designed for teaching particular subjects and topics at a given level, the variety of

guidance material available related to those programmes, and characteristics that serve as the indications and contraindications for the use of particular curriculum or programme materials in particular circumstances, e.g. knowledge of alternative curriculum materials available for a given subject or topic within a specific age range such as alternative texts, multimedia technologies and visual materials. This type of knowledge serves as the 'tools of the trade' for teachers. This category also includes *lateral* curriculum knowledge, e.g. the ability to relate the content of a series of lessons to topics being taught simultaneously in other curriculum areas, and *vertical* curriculum knowledge, e.g. familiarity with topics and issues that have been and will be taught in the same subject area during the preceding and subsequent years in school, along with materials that embody them.

- *Pedagogical content knowledge* goes beyond knowledge of subject matter *per se* and requires an understanding of the subject matter knowledge for teaching, which encompasses the most useful and powerful ways of representing and formulating the subject so that it can be understood by others, e.g. through analogies, demonstrations, exemplars, explanations, illustrations, images and the use of metaphor. This category includes an understanding of what makes learning particular topics within the subject area easy or difficult, e.g. the conceptions, misconceptions and preconceptions learners bring to the learning of these topics.

- *Knowledge of learners and their characteristics* requires an understanding of the cognitive development of learners which incorporates knowledge of how child development informs practice and how knowledge of working with a particular group of learners over time enables teachers to personalise learning as they gain insight into what their learners can know, do or understand and what they might struggle to know, do and understand. This category incorporates knowledge of the emotional, physical, psychological and social development of learners and how numerous factors might influence their behaviour, self-esteem, communication skills and interpersonal relationships.

- *Knowledge of educational ends* requires an understanding of the aims and purposes of education based on historical and philosophical grounds, which shape the values and priorities of the type of education pupils receive. Teaching is both effective and normative: it is concerned with means and ends, e.g. teaching is a purposeful activity, which can be evidenced in the short-term goals and objectives teachers identify for a particular lesson or series of lessons. Some teachers might argue that education should be viewed as intrinsically worthwhile, in and of itself, whereas others might see education in relation to long-term goals, such as preparing young people to become socially responsible citizens and ready for the world of work.

- *Knowledge of educational contexts* requires an understanding of all settings where learning may take place within school and beyond and which can affect development and classroom performance. These range from the workings of the group or classroom, school governance and financing, to the character of cultures and social communities and include: the size of classes, how learners are grouped and supported within class, size and type of school, the catchment area, parent-teacher-governor organisations, school council and pupil voice, school rules, policies and procedures, school leadership and management, curriculum development, processes for monitoring, assessing and reporting, staff appraisal, priorities and expectations, and the overall ethos and vision of the school.

Reflective task 5.5 **Knowledge base for teaching**

Using Shulman's knowledge base for teaching, consider which categories:

1   you are confident about and have a firm grounding in and those which need further development;
2   interrelate when teaching a topic in a particular curriculum or subject area.

Identify three SMART targets to enhance your knowledge base for teaching and monitor your on-going progress in these areas.

Reflective task 5.6 **Content knowledge**

•   Analyse the syllabus in your school to identify the subject matter included within a particular curriculum or subject area.
•   Research the *Range and Content* proposed by the National Curriculum in this curriculum or subject area across two Key Stages.
•   Audit your personal subject knowledge in relation to these sources and seek ways to enhance your knowledge in areas that need developing.

Banks, Leach and Moon (1999) suggest every teacher develops a *personal subject construct* which is a set of educational and philosophical views about the nature of a subject, how to teach it and what they hope to achieve through teaching it. Shulman's categories of knowledge are thus brought together in the personal subject construct you develop about a particular subject area, which in turn reflects your own particular view about the value of that subject.

Reflective task 5.7 **Pedagogical content knowledge**

•   Select a topic you plan on teaching to a particular group of pupils and identify:
    –   the conceptions, preconceptions and misconceptions pupils might bring to learning this topic;
    –   ways of representing and formulating the topic so that pupils can learn about and understand the topic.
•   Consider how you might apply your knowledge of these components to develop pupils' *personal, learning* and *thinking skills* and help them become more *independent learners.*
•   Try your ideas out in practice and reflect on the outcomes in relation to your development of pedagogical content knowledge.
•   Critically evaluate whether your personal subject construct has been transformed.

Pedagogical reasoning and action

Teachers must draw on their knowledge base for teaching to provide sound reasons for the decisions they make and actions they take. Sound reasoning involves the process of thinking about what you are doing and requires an adequate base of experiences, facts and principles from which to reason. In response to Shulman's (1986: 4) aphorism 'those who can, do – those who understand, teach', Petrie (1986) argues that such understanding must necessarily also incorporate judgement and action, as comprehension alone is insufficient.

Shulman's (1987) discourse on pedagogical reasoning and action places an emphasis on teaching that incorporates: comprehension and reasoning – transformation and reflection. He begins from the premise that most teaching is initiated by some form of text, e.g. a syllabus, textbook or piece of material that the teacher wants to make comprehensible. The challenge presented to the teacher is in how to prepare something she already understands for effective instruction. Pedagogical reasoning and action involve a cycle through the processes of comprehension, transformation, instruction, evaluation, reflection and new comprehension, as summarised below.

Comprehension

Shulman asserts that to teach is first to understand: teachers must understand what they teach and, where possible, understand it in several ways. They must also comprehend how a given idea relates to other ideas within the same subject area and ideas in other subjects. An understanding of purpose is also important as we engage in teaching to achieve educational purposes and accomplish ends that have to do with such aims as developing pupil literacy, independence, responsibility, respect and in developing the skills, understandings and values needed to function effectively within a globalised society. We also strive to balance the goals of nurturing individual potential and excellence with those involving equality of opportunity among pupils from different backgrounds and cultures. Thus, although most teaching begins with some sort of text, and learning that text can be a worthy end itself, the text can also be a vehicle for achieving other educational purposes.

Transformation

Shulman argues that the key to distinguishing the knowledge base for teaching lies at the intersection of content and pedagogy, e.g. the capacity to transform the content knowledge a teacher possesses into forms that are pedagogically powerful and adaptive to variations in the ability and background presented by pupils. To reason through an act of teaching, from the subject matter as understood by the teacher into the minds and motivations for learners, requires some ordering or combination of the following processes:

1   Preparation (of the given text materials) including the process of critical interpretation, which involves examining and critically interpreting the materials to be taught in relation to the teacher's own understanding of the subject matter. This usually includes: detecting and correcting errors in the text and segmenting

and structuring the material into forms adapted to the teacher's understanding and suitable for teaching. Educational goals or purposes are also scrutinised.

2   Representation of ideas in the form of new analogies, exemplars, images and metaphors, which involves thinking through key ideas in the text or lesson and identifying alternative or multiple ways of representing them to pupils, e.g. thinking about what particular analogies, demonstrations, examples and simulations can help to bridge the teacher's comprehension and that desired for the pupils.

3   Selection of teaching strategies drawn from a repertoire of approaches and models of teaching, which can range from conventional demonstrations, lectures, modelling or seatwork to active learning, guided discovery, settings outside of the classroom, project-based work, reciprocal teaching and Socratic dialogue.

4   Adaptation of representations to the general characteristics of pupils to be taught, and tailoring adaptations to specific pupils in the classroom, e.g. what aspects of pupil ability, culture, gender, motivation or prior knowledge and skills might affect their responses to different forms of presentation and representation? What pupil conceptions, difficulties, expectations, misconceptions, motives or strategies might influence ways in which they approach, interpret, understand or misunderstand the material? Tailoring teaching not only entails fitting representations to particular pupils, but also to a group with a particular disposition, interpersonal relationships and group dynamics, receptivity and size.

These processes result in a plan of action or set of strategies designed to present a specific lesson, unit of work or course. Reasoning does not end when the teaching begins, as comprehension, transformation, evaluation and reflection also occur during active teaching. Teaching is therefore a stimulus for thoughtfulness as well as action.

Instruction

Instruction incorporates the observable performance of varied teaching acts, which includes such aspects of pedagogy as: organising and managing the classroom; presenting clear explanations and vivid descriptions; assigning and monitoring work; interacting with pupils through question and answer, constructive criticism, specific focused feedback and praise. It thus includes discussion, explanation, management, and all the observable features of organisation along with heuristic instruction that is well documented in the research literature on effective teaching.

Evaluation

Evaluation involves regularly checking for understanding and misunderstanding a teacher must employ while teaching interactively, in addition to more formal assessment and evaluation that teachers do to provide feedback and grades. To comprehend what a pupil understands requires a deep grasp of the material to be taught and the processes embedded within learning. This understanding must be specific to particular school subjects and individual topics within the subject. Evaluation is also directed toward the enactment of teaching as well as the lessons and materials used in those activities.

Reflection

Reflection is what a teacher does when she looks back at the teaching and learning that has occurred, and reconstructs, re-enacts, and/or recaptures the events, emotions and accomplishments. It incorporates processes through which a teacher learns from experience and uses particular kinds of analytical knowledge to reflect on her work. Central to this process should be a review of the teaching in comparison with the ends that were sought.

New comprehension

Through acts of teaching, which are both reasoned and reasonable, the teacher achieves new comprehension of the purposes and subjects to be taught, the pupils and the processes of pedagogy. New comprehension does not occur automatically however, even after evaluation and reflection. Specific strategies are required for analysis, discussion and documentation.

The processes embedded within Schulman's model of pedagogical reasoning and action do not represent a set of fixed phases, stages or steps. Many processes can occur in a different order, or may not occur at all during some acts of teaching, and others may be elaborated or truncated.

Shulman also recognises that pupils can initiate the process of pedagogical reasoning and action when they discover, invent or engage in enquiry to prepare their own representations and transformations. He argues that the flexibility to respond, judge, nurture and promote such acts of creativity within pupils depends upon the teacher's capacity for sympathetic transformation and interpretation.

Reflective task 5.8 **Pedagogical reasoning and action**

- Using Shulman's model of pedagogical reasoning and action, critically analyse the development of your knowledge base for teaching in relation to a particular topic you have recently taught to a particular group of pupils.
- What processes within this model do you perceive as:
  - personal strengths?
  - areas in need of development?
- Set yourself three SMART targets to improve aspects of your knowledge base for teaching and review your progress in relation to the processes embedded within the model of pedagogical reasoning and action.

Summary of key points

This chapter has explored the nature of theory relevant to teachers and considered the origins and meanings associated with espoused theories and theories-in-use. The Aristotelian concepts of episteme and phronesis have been introduced and the relationship between teacher cognition and teacher behaviour discussed in relation to Korthagen and Kessels' model of Gestalt formation.

The extensive range of knowledge required by teachers has been captured and presented within Shulman's categorisation of the knowledge base for teaching. From this springboard his model of pedagogical reasoning and action has been explored through the cyclical processes of comprehension, transformation, instruction, evaluation, reflection and new comprehension.

This enables you to consider the relationship between theory and practice as you engage in praxis: that is, thought-full-action and action-full-of-thought (Freire, 1972).

Recommended reading

Argyris, C. and Schon, D. (1974) *Theory into Practice: Increasing Professional Effectiveness,* San Francisco, CA: Jossey Bass.
To support the claim that people hold maps in their mind about how to plan, implement and review their actions, yet few are aware that the maps they use to take action may be incongruent with theories they espouse, Argyris and Schon distinguish between espoused theory and theory-in-use. Governing variables, action strategies and consequences (intended and unintended) are drawn upon to explain processes that develop and maintain theories-in-use, which are considered in relation to single-loop and double-loop learning.

Korthagen, F. (in cooperation with) Kessels, J., Koster, B., Lagerwerf, B. and Wubbels, T. (2001) *Linking Practice and Theory: The Pedagogy of Realistic Teacher Education,* London: Routledge.
This text, based on 15 years' experience in teacher education and research, presents Korthagen's concept of 'realistic teacher education' along with guidance material, practical solutions and research-based theoretical foundations for analysing and linking the relationship between practice and theory.

Whitehead, J. (2009) Generating living theory and understanding in action research studies, *Action Research,* 7 (1): 85–99. Available: http://arj.sagepub.com/cgi/content/abstract/7/1/85
The author builds upon his educational living theory research programme and enquiries of the kind 'How do I improve what I am doing?' from the perspectives of inclusionality and multi-media explanations, which focus on the embodied knowledges of action researchers through live URLs.

Chapter 6

Dimension 4

Question your personal theories and beliefs

Learning objectives

In this chapter you will consider:
*   how personal theories and beliefs have been defined and the multiple sources from which they originate;
*   how findings from research inform our understanding of ways in which personal theories and beliefs may influence teaching and learning;
*   the relationship between social cognitive theory and self-efficacy beliefs.

Introduction

An exploration of this dimension begins with the following task for reasons that will become apparent as the chapter unfolds.

Reflective task 6.1 **Personal biography**

Imagine you are meeting a new group of people for the very first time and, as an icebreaker, you are asked to introduce yourself. What would you say or rather not say about yourself and where might you begin? Whilst it goes without saying that much of what you choose to share about yourself with others will depend upon the nature of the group and the underlying reasons why the group has been formed in the first place, use the following headings to guide your thinking and write a brief biography to introduce yourself:

*   Family background – origins and composition.
*   Community – where you grew up and social groups you once and still belong to.
*   Education – all formal learning experiences since pre- or primary school.
*   Religious affiliations.
*   Personal – (i) interests, (ii) likes and dislikes, (iii) strengths and weaknesses, (iv) goals and aspirations.

This chapter seeks to explore the nature of personal theories and beliefs by examining how they have been defined, sources from which they emanate and what impact they may have on the professional practice of teachers, and opportunities they provide to enhance pupil learning and development. It draws on findings from a wealth of research undertaken in the area of teacher cognition within recent decades, which has focused on the knowledge, beliefs and conceptions of teachers underpinning their teaching practice. Teacher cognition as a concept has, however, been very broadly used within educational research to capture the knowledge, beliefs and thinking of teachers (Calderhead, 1996), which Kagan (1990: 420) cautions can be somewhat ambiguous as:

> researchers invoke the term to refer to different products, including teachers' interactive thoughts during instruction; thoughts during lesson planning; implicit beliefs about students, classrooms and learning; reflections about their own teaching performance; automatised routines and activities that form their instructional repertoire; and self-awareness of procedures they use to solve classroom problems.

This highlights one major problem associated with much of the available literature on teachers' personal theories and beliefs: notably, that of researchers failing to agree on a definition of precisely what comprises teachers' personal theories and beliefs.

Social cognitive theory is drawn upon to explain that the decisions teachers make and the ways in which they exercise control and personal agency are strongly influenced by efficacy beliefs. An understanding of this complex relationship is particularly important, as researchers have found links between pupil achievement and three kinds of efficacy beliefs: the self-efficacy judgements of pupils (Pajares, 1996); the self-efficacy judgements of teachers (Tschannen-Moran, Woolfolk Hoy and Hoy, 1998); and teachers' beliefs about the collective efficacy of their own school (Goddard, Hoy and Woolfolk Hoy, 2004). Bandura (1997) identifies four sources of information that can shape efficacy beliefs: *mastery experience, vicarious experience, social persuasion* and *affective state*.

The role of reflection is important in helping individuals to identify their personal theories and beliefs. Bandura argues that self-reflection mediates between *knowledge* and *action* as teachers can evaluate both their own thought processes and their own experiences. In so doing, they shift from that which is 'subjectively reasonable' for them to believe to that which is 'objectively reasonable' for them to believe (Fenstermacher, 1986).

This backdrop provides fertile ground in arguing the need for you to challenge and confront your personal theories and beliefs and study the origins and sources of efficacy beliefs, particularly as they have been found to underpin the choices and decisions teachers make within their roles and are considered to be a strong predictor of teacher behaviour.

Personal theories and beliefs

The study of personal theories and beliefs is essential in coming to understand both the complexity of teachers' knowledge and what constitutes effective teaching. However, terms such as 'teacher cognition, self-reflection, knowledge and belief', as Kagan (1990: 456) highlights, have each been used to refer to different phenomena ranging from the 'superficial and idiosyncratic to the profound and theoretical', which makes this area of cognitive research difficult to investigate. For example, Pajares (1992: 309) argues that:

Reflective task 6.2 **Thinking about your role as a teacher**

Answer each of the following questions and provide examples to support your responses:

1 What difference do you make to the lives of your pupils?
2 How do you know when your pupils are learning?
3 What are your greatest achievements as a teacher?
4 Which aspects of teaching do you find most challenging?
5 What would your colleagues/peers and pupils say about you as a teacher?
6 Why did you decide to become a teacher?

- Discuss your response to each question with a critical friend who knows you well and identify ways in which your perspectives are complementary and/or contradictory.
- Consider how this discussion might have reinforced and/or challenged your thinking about your role as a teacher.
- Return to your response to task 6.1 and identify aspects of your personal biography which may have shaped your answers to questions 1 through 6 above.
- To what extent are the perceptions you have about your role as a teacher influenced by your personal theories and beliefs?

... defining beliefs is at best a game of player's choice. They travel in disguise and often under alias – attitudes, values, judgements, axioms, opinions, ideology, perceptions, conceptions, conceptual systems, preconceptions, dispositions, implicit theories, explicit theories, personal theories, internal mental processes, action strategies, rules of practice, practical principles, perspectives, repertoires of understanding and social strategy, to name but a few that can be found in the literature.

Several decades ago, Rokeach (1972: 113) defined a belief as 'any simple proposition, conscious or unconscious, inferred from what a person says or does, capable of being preceded by the phrase 'I believe that ...', and he described an attitude as an 'organisation of beliefs' (ibid.: 112). Fishbein and Ajzen (1975: 131) defined a personal theory or belief as a 'representation of the information someone holds about an object', or a 'person's understanding of himself and his environment'. This object can be 'a person, a group of people, an institution, a behaviour, a policy, an event ... and the associated attribute that may be any object, trait, property, quality, characteristic, outcome, or event' (ibid.: 12). They defined a belief system in terms of a hierarchy of beliefs according to the strength held about a particular object.

More recent researchers have used a number of definitions to study teachers' personal theories and beliefs at the primary and secondary levels of schooling. Kagan (1990: 423) defines these as 'the highly personal ways in which a teacher understands classrooms, students, the nature of learning, the teacher's role in the classroom, and the goals of education'. Calderhead (1996: 715) refers to them as 'suppositions, commitments and ideologies' and Richardson (1996: 103) as the 'psychologically held understandings, premises or propositions about the world that are felt to be true'.

In reviewing the beliefs and conceptions of mathematics teachers, Thompson (1992: 149) notes that 'thoughtful analyses of the nature of the relationship between beliefs and practice suggest that belief systems are dynamic, permeable mental structures, susceptible to change in light of experience'. Conversely, Block and Hazelip (1995: 27) found 'teacher beliefs and belief systems are grounded in their personal experiences and, hence, are highly resistant to change', which supports the argument that the capacity to change personal theories and beliefs is directly related both to the strength and kind of theories and beliefs teachers hold (Kagan, 1992; Pajares, 1992).

Although findings from research into teachers' personal theories and beliefs appear to yield discordant messages, some consensus has been reached over several issues:

- Student teachers enter teacher education programmes with pre-existing theories and beliefs based on their own experiences as pupils in schools (e.g. Bullough, 1997; Richardson, 1996). Lortie (1975) attributes this phenomenon to their 'apprenticeship of observation', which Pajares (1992) argues has both personal and universal facets as all children grow up with a well-painted portrait of 'teacher' and play 'school' in various ways. Individual experiences and interpretations colour these portraits in ways that form well-developed and hardy beliefs.
- Personal theories and beliefs are often robust and resistant to change (e.g. Block and Hazelip, 1995; Clark, 1988; Kagan, 1992; Richardson, 1996). Pajares (1992) argues that accommodating new information and adjusting existing beliefs under familiar circumstances can be nearly impossible as student teachers have often made commitments to prior beliefs and see little reason to adjust them. As a result 'folkways of teaching' are often reinforced.
- Personal theories and beliefs can act as filters, which *allow in* or *filter out* new knowledge that is either deemed compatible or incompatible with current theories and beliefs (e.g. Nespor, 1987; Pajares, 1992; Weinstein, 1990). When left unattended, new ideas are simply incorporated into old frameworks. This means that the 'intuitive screens' through which new information is filtered must be made transparent if they are to be recognised and fully understood, e.g. the taken-for-granted assumptions that can influence thinking and teacher behaviour.
- Personal theories and beliefs are implicit and tacit, which makes them difficult to articulate (e.g. Clark, 1988; Nespor, 1987; Trumbull, 1990). They are however embedded within craft knowledge, which Leinhardt (1990: 18) defines as 'the wealth of teaching information that very skilled practitioners have about their own practice'. On the one hand, this includes 'deep, sensitive, location-specific knowledge of teaching' whereas on the other, it may include 'fragmentary, superstitious and often inaccurate opinions' (ibid.).

These findings indicate that teachers are unable to change personal theories and beliefs they are unaware of, and are often unwilling to confront those they are aware of unless they see good reason to do so. Goodman (1988: 15) recognised implications behind these assertions in case studies with his own teachers:

the 'need' for external rewards and punishments to 'make kids learn' was taken for granted; the educational and ethical implications were not addressed ... definitions of good kids as 'quiet kids', workbook work as 'reading', on task time as 'learning' and getting through the material as 'good teaching' – all went unchallenged.

This highlights the need for personal theories and beliefs to be subjected to a form of interrogation and questioning, which can establish their origins and legitimacy so that the views we hold about teaching are not merely idiosyncratic preferences or the product of deeply entrenched cultural norms and values of which we may not be aware. Untangling and re-evaluating taken-for-granted practice requires breaking into well entrenched and constructed mythologies that may not always be easily dislodged. Personal theories and beliefs should be explored so the roads they have travelled and directions they are taking can be fully realised.

Reflective task 6.3 **Questioning personal theories and beliefs**

Smyth (1992: 299) argues that the development of informed scholarship requires all personal theories and beliefs to undergo challenge and all must survive careful scrutiny and analysis so that any filters can be exposed and pathways to more informed scholarship can be cleared. To this end, critically reflect upon the following guiding questions:

*   What do your practices say about your assumptions, values and beliefs about teaching?
*   Where did these ideas come from?
*   What social practices are expressed in these ideas?
*   What causes you to maintain your theories?
*   What views of power do they embody?
*   Whose interests seem to be served by your practices?
*   What acts to constrain your views of what is possible in teaching?

Reflective task 6.4 **Critical analysis of subjective theories and beliefs**

Denzin and Lincoln (1998: 28) state:

> There is no clear window into the inner life of an individual. Any gaze is always filtered through the lenses of language, gender, social class, race and ethnicity. There are no objective observations, only observations socially situated in the worlds of the observer and the observed.

*   Write a 2,000-word reflective narrative, which explores the implications behind this statement in terms of the need to subject the personal theories and beliefs you hold about teaching to careful scrutiny and critical analysis.
*   Discuss the main points of your argument with a critical friend.

Reflective task 6.5 **The impact of personal theories and beliefs**

- Select at least five studies from Table 6.1 (p. 88–9) and extract data from each primary source using the literature review summary template provided in Table 4.2 (p. 57).
- Compare and contrast these studies in relation to their:
  i)   aims and purposes
  ii) conceptual frameworks and definitions used
  iii) research participants drawn upon
  iv) research methodologies employed and types of data gathered
  v)   key findings and recommendations in terms of their original aims and purposes.
- What key messages can you take from these studies to inform your own future practice?

In recent decades, numerous studies have investigated personal theories and beliefs, particularly in relation to those held by student and early career teachers, a sample of which are presented in Table 6.1.

These studies illustrate the complexity and range of personal theories and beliefs held by students and early career teachers. They also highlight the difficulty of interpreting research within this particular dimension as finding commonalities across the studies is challenging, particularly when the approaches and contexts used by researchers are many and varied. Some findings from these studies, however, do send encouraging messages in that personal theories and beliefs may not be as stable and fixed as some earlier research suggests. Also, a measure of diversity appears to exist in the personal theories and beliefs of those entering the teaching profession. A common recommendation that emerged from these studies was the need to examine deeply held personal theories and beliefs as an essential first step for your own professional development and teaching practice.

Efficacy belief theory

The seminal work of Albert Bandura (1986) is drawn upon in this section to illustrate how his social cognitive theory informs our understanding of efficacy belief constructs. Bandura argues that individuals possess a self-system, which enables them to exercise a measure of control over their thoughts, feelings and actions. Located within this self-system are cognitive and affective structures that incorporate one's ability to: symbolise; learn from others; plan alternative strategies; regulate personal behaviour; and engage in self-reflection. This self-system also provides reference mechanisms for perceiving, regulating and evaluating behaviour in response to external environmental sources of influence. The self-system thus serves a self-regulatory function by providing individuals with the capability to both alter their environments and influence their own actions.

Bandura (1997) considers self-reflection to be the most uniquely human capability, as through this kind of self-referent thought people can evaluate and alter their own thinking and behaviour. Self-evaluations include perceptions of self-efficacy, which he defines as 'beliefs in one's capabilities to organise and execute the courses of action required to manage prospective situations' (ibid.: 2). Bandura (2006) distinguishes between *efficacy beliefs* and *outcome expectancies:* the former involves judgements about capabilities to perform various types of activities whereas the latter measures outcomes one expects to result from these performances. Beliefs about outcomes are however dependent upon people's beliefs in their own capabilities to perform specific tasks in given settings.

Perceptions of self-efficacy play a key role in human functioning as they affect behaviour not only directly but also by their impact on other determinants such as goals and aspirations, outcome expectations, affective proclivities, and perception of obstacles and opportunities in the social environment (Bandura, 1997). Efficacy beliefs, for example, play a significant role in personal development, particularly in relation to adaptation and change as they can influence:

- whether people think strategically or erratically, optimistically or pessimistically;
- the challenges and goals people set for themselves, their commitment to them and courses of action they choose to pursue;
- how much effort people put into specific endeavours;
- the outcomes people expect their efforts to produce;
- how long people persevere in the face of obstacles and their resilience to adversity;
- how much stress and tension people experience in coping with challenging environmental demands and the quality of their emotional life;
- the life choices people make and accomplishments they realise.

As efficacy judgements are perceptions or beliefs about one's personal capabilities, this does not mean they are necessarily an accurate assessment of those capabilities. This distinction is important as people frequently overestimate or underestimate their actual capabilities, which can influence the courses of action they decide to pursue, the effort they exert in those pursuits and how well they use the skills they possess.

How people interpret the outcomes of their performance will inform and alter their environment and self-beliefs, which in turn can inform and alter their subsequent performances. This principle underpins Bandura's concept of reciprocal determinism, which presents the view that *personal* factors (in terms of cognition, affect and biological events), *behaviour* and influences from the *environment* create interactions, which result in triadic reciprocality, as illustrated in Figure 6.1.

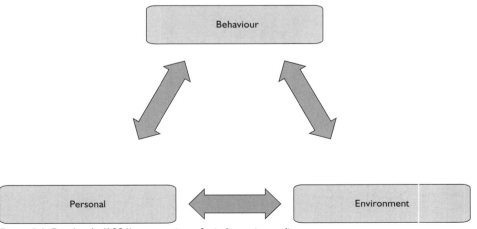

Figure 6.1 Bandura's (1986) conception of triadic reciprocality

Table 6.1 Research studies to investigate personal theories and beliefs

Researcher/s	Focus of study	Research participants	Key findings
Aaronson, Carter and Howel (1995)	Beliefs about inner city pupils	6 pre-service teachers	Personal biographies were influential
Allard and Cooper (1997)	Changing views about gender issues	Pre-service teachers: 7 female and 1 male	Most students altered views about gender relations and no longer took stereotypical roles of men and women for granted; however, female students expressed anxiety about the possibility of offending males and feared retribution
Beynon and Toohey (1995)	Prior aspirations	12 Punjabi Sikh and 22 Chinese university students	Lack of language skills and parental views influenced their decision not to join the teaching profession
Bird, Anderson, Sullivan and Swidler (1993)	Changing students' views during a course	9 White, middle class females	Students failed to consider alternative theories and beliefs
Borko and Mayfield (1995)	Influence of guided teaching relationships	4 pre-service teachers with university tutors and cooperating teachers	Limited change in existing beliefs or practice – cooperative teacher most influential – routine rather than reflective action evident
Calderhead and Robson (1991)	How beginning teachers captured knowledge for use in teaching	12 pre-service teachers	Prior beliefs and existence of varied images often found to be rigid – suggestion made to build on beliefs that already exist
Fosnot (1996)	Promote conceptual change	30 pre-service teachers	Changed views of teaching
Gomez (1994)	Prior beliefs	Empirical studies of pre-service teachers	Attitudes created barriers
Graber (1996)	Perceived impact of a teacher education programme	6 beginning teachers and 10 members of faculty	Combination of factors contributed toward success of the programme
Hollingsworth (1989)	Pre-programme beliefs	14 pre-service teachers	Beliefs filtered coursework and teaching practice
Holt-Reynolds (1992)	How beliefs filter	14 pre-service teachers	Lay theories prevailed
Levin and Ye He (2008)	Develop model to categorise beliefs and describe relationships between the context and sources of beliefs expressed as personal practical theories (PPTs)	94 pre-service teachers	Teacher education programmes can and do influence beliefs about how to teach the curriculum, classroom context, roles and responsibilities of teachers, planning and organisation, the qualities of a good teacher and pupils as learners

Author	Focus	Sample	Findings
McCall (1995)	Developing views of teaching in multicultural classrooms	2 pre-service teachers	Personal backgrounds were significant in the development of views
Mertz and McNeely (1992)	Prior beliefs	52 pre-service teachers (88% female)	Beliefs well formed, influential and varied among pre-service teachers
Rust (1994)	Changes in espoused beliefs over 2 years	2 beginning teachers	Idealistic and child-focused beliefs changed to managing the pupils and methods of classroom discipline
Shapiro (1991)	Change in student thinking	23 pre-service teachers	Limited change in prior theories and beliefs
Stoddart, Stofflett and Gomez (1992)	Belief change in contrasting programmes	27 pre-service teachers across several institutions	Conceptual change occurred as a result of some courses but new perspectives not typically developed as pre-service teachers became more skilful in defending perspectives they already possessed
Sugrue (1996)	Exposure to cultural archetypes of teaching to examine the influence of lay theories and prior beliefs	9 young and 6 mature students	Cultural stereotypes and biographies were influential – teaching personality considered more important than cognitive skills or pedagogical and subject matter knowledge
Tatto (1996)	Beliefs and practice with diverse pupils	552 beginning teachers in 9 programmes	Programmes had little impact on personal theories and beliefs
Valli (1995)	Teaching practice in predominantly Black city schools	9 pre-service teachers (7 White middle class)	Growth shown by working through race-based stereotypes – two opposing cultural myths about race and schooling need to be deconstructed before teachers can learn to teach in a diverse, pluralistic setting
Weber and Mitchell (1996)	Images of teachers	64 pre-service teachers	Predominant image of teachers was of White, nurturing females
Zulich, Bean and Herrick (1992)	How beliefs filter	6 pre-service teachers	Personal biographies were influential and prior beliefs fairly robust and act as filters through which teacher education programmes are viewed

Efficacy-shaping information

Bandura (1997) identifies four sources of efficacy-shaping information of relevance to teachers: *mastery experience, vicarious experience, social persuasion* and *affective state*.

Mastery experience is a powerful source of efficacy-shaping information. For example, the perception that one's performance has been successful tends to raise efficacy-beliefs and contributes toward the expectation that future performances will also be proficient. Conversely, the perception that one's performance has been unsuccessful tends to lower efficacy-beliefs and contributes toward the expectation that future performances will not be proficient. Attributions play a significant role here. For example, if success is attributed to such controllable or internal causes as effort or ability, self-efficacy beliefs are enhanced, whereas if the success is attributed to an intervention by others or luck, self-efficacy beliefs will not necessarily be strengthened (Pintrich and Schunk, 2002).

A vicarious experience involves observing the performance of a particular skill or activity modelled by someone else. When the model with whom an observer identifies performs successfully the efficacy-beliefs of the observer are likely to be enhanced, whereas when the model performs unsuccessfully the efficacy-beliefs of the observer are likely to decrease (Schunk and Zimmerman, 1997).

Social persuasion might entail encouragement, specific feedback about performance or informal discussions about the ability of a teacher to influence his pupils from a peer, colleague or a supervisor. The power of social persuasion will depend on the credibility, expertise and trustworthiness of the persuader (Bandura, 1986) in addition to the open-minded nature of the teacher who receives the advice and feedback.

The affective state or level of arousal, of excitement or anxiety, adds another layer to a person's perception of their capability or competence to perform a given task within a particular context. Affective states can influence how a person interprets and reacts to the numerous challenges he faces within the classroom and wider context of the school on a day-to-day basis.

Ultimately, the exercise of *personal agency* depends upon how people interpret efficacy-shaping information and experiences. The impact of a mastery experience on shaping efficacy-beliefs for example, does not entirely depend upon the actual events of one's performance as efficacy-beliefs are shaped when an individual weighs and interprets his performance in relation to other information. According to Bandura (1997: 81) 'changes in perceived efficacy result from cognitive processing of the diagnostic information that performances convey about capability rather than the performances *per se*'. The same can be said for each source of efficacy-shaping information. In other words, perceptions of self-efficacy arise from cognitive and metacognitive processing of each source of the efficacy-shaping information, for various individual pursuits.

The most fundamental assumption underpinning social cognitive theory is that the choices people make, when they exercise agency, are influenced by the strength of their personal efficacy-beliefs. Individuals are more likely to pursue goals purposefully that seem attainable, challenging and rewarding. When applied to teaching, the higher a teacher's sense of efficacy, the more likely he is to persist in the face of failure and overcome obstacles. In turn, such resilience tends to foster pupil learning through innovative teaching.

Reflective task 6.6 **Teacher self-efficacy beliefs**

Table 6.2 presents an adaptation of Bandura's (2006) Teacher Self-Efficacy questionnaire, which broadly focuses on teachers' beliefs about their control over pupil outcomes.

- Complete the questionnaire.
- In which categories do you rate your degree of confidence highly?
- In which categories do you rate your degree of confidence rather low?
- Select at least three areas in which you would like to increase your level of confidence.
- Discuss with a peer/colleague or professional tutor how you might gain relevant experience in these areas and devise a plan of action to ensure opportunities to gain this experience are realised.

According to Bandura (1997: 469):

> people working independently within a group structure do not function as social isolates totally immune to the influence of those around them ... the resources, impediments, and opportunities provided by a given system partly determine how efficacious individuals can be, even though their work may be only loosely coupled.

He defines collective efficacy as 'a group's shared belief in its conjoint capabilities to organise and execute the courses of action required to produce given levels of attainment' (ibid.: 477). Therefore, teachers' collective efficacy refers to the beliefs teachers possess in their collective capabilities to influence the lives of their pupils. For example, a school in which most teachers are confident about their own capabilities is also likely to be one in which the collective efficacy perceptions are strong and expectations for success high. This *reciprocal causality* is found when teachers think highly of the collective capability of staff within their school, they sense an expectation for successful teaching and thus are very likely to expend the required effort to help pupils learn and achieve. Conversely, when perceived collective efficacy is low, teachers are less likely to feel persuaded by colleagues to persist in the face of failure or change aspects of their own teaching, even when their pupils do not appear to be learning.

Research has shown teachers' self-efficacy beliefs play an important role in influencing several professional and academic outcomes such as pupil achievement and motivation, and they can positively affect teachers' beliefs about teaching and teaching behaviours. For example, Woolfolk and Hoy (1990) discovered that pre-service teachers' self-efficacy beliefs were related to beliefs about student control, and Betoret (2006) found teachers with low self-efficacy beliefs tend to experience low levels of job satisfaction, difficulties in teaching and high levels of job-related stress. Adams and Forsyth (2006) noted that such contextual factors as pupil socio-economic status, age and stage of schooling along with school structure influenced teachers' perceptions about the collective efficacy of their own school. Milner and Woolfolk Hoy (2003) reported the influence of contextual factors on the self-efficacy of a high school teacher of African American origin working in a predominantly European American school. Successful mastery experiences were found to exert a strong influence on self-efficacy beliefs as

Table 6.2 Teacher self-efficacy scale

These questions focus on the types of things that create challenges for teachers in their school activities.

Rate how confident you are that you can do these things by recording a number from 0 to 100 using the scale:

0	10	20	30	40	50	60	70	80	90	100
Cannot do at all					Moderately can do					Highly certain can do

	Confidence (0–100)
Efficacy to influence decision making	
Influence decisions that are made in the school	
Express my views freely on important school matters	
Acquire the teaching materials and equipment I need	
Teaching self-efficacy	
Get through to the most challenging pupils	
Get pupils to learn when there is a lack of support from the home	
Keep pupils on task on difficult assignments	
Increase pupils' memory of what they have been taught in previous lessons	
Motivate pupils who show low interest in schoolwork	
Get pupils to work well together	
Overcome the influence of adverse community conditions on pupils' learning	
Get children to do their homework	
Disciplinary self-efficacy	
Get children to follow classroom rules	
Control disruptive behaviour in the classroom	
Prevent problem behaviour on the school grounds	
Efficacy to enlist parental involvement	
Get parents to become involved in school activities	
Assist parents in helping their children do well in school	
Make parents feel comfortable coming to school	
Efficacy to enlist community involvement	
Get community groups involved in working with the school	
Get businesses involved in working with the school	
Get local colleges and universities involved in working with the school	
Efficacy to create a positive school climate	
Make the school a safe place	
Make pupils enjoy coming to school	
Get pupils to trust teachers	
Help other teachers with their teaching skills	
Increase collaboration between teachers and the administration to make the school run effectively	
Reduce school dropout	
Reduce school absenteeism	
Get pupils to believe they can do well in school work	

Adapted from Bandura (2006: 328).

Reflective task 6.7 **The impact of efficacy beliefs**

- Search the literature to find out what research has been undertaken in your curriculum/subject area (e.g. English, Science ...) to examine the impact efficacy-beliefs may have on teachers' practice and their pupils' academic achievement and sense of self-esteem.
- Write a 2,000-word reflective narrative in response to the following question: Why is it important for teachers to regularly examine their own and their pupils' efficacy-beliefs when preparing to teach (e.g. English, Science ...) to a range of diverse learners?

---

well as the emotional and physiological states that arose from challenges encountered within the teaching situation. Bruce and Ross (2008) investigated the influence of mastery experiences, vicarious experiences, verbal persuasion and affective states on teachers' self-efficacy beliefs and concluded that sources of efficacy-shaping information reinforced one another and resulted in the on-going implementation of new and challenging teaching strategies. Gabriele and Joram (2007) found differences in how experienced and early career teachers used criteria for judging efficacy information; particularly notable was the salience of past experience.

Summary of key points

This chapter has explored the nature of personal theories and beliefs by examining how they have been defined, their origins and the impact they may have on teaching and learning. The research presented indicates that teachers' personal theories and beliefs can influence the development, academic achievement, behaviour and motivation levels of their pupils. This highlights the need for teachers to subject personal theories and beliefs to careful scrutiny and critical analysis to make explicit the taken-for-granted assumptions, ideologies and intuitive screens we may have about teaching and which can unwittingly underpin much of our work. As Palmer (1998: 2) writes:

> When I do not know myself, I cannot know who my students are. I will see them through a glass darkly, in the shadows of my unexamined life – and when I cannot see them clearly, I cannot teach them well.

Social cognitive theory has been introduced and drawn upon to explain, in part, how the decisions we make and the ways in which we exercise control and personal agency are strongly influenced by our self-efficacy beliefs.

Recommended reading

Goddard, R., Hoy, W. and Woolfolk Hoy, A. (2004) Collective efficacy beliefs: theoretical developments, empirical evidence, and future directions, *Educational Researcher*, 33 (3): 3–13.

This article draws on social cognitive theory and research to analyse how teachers' practice and pupil learning are affected by perceptions of collective efficacy, and introduces a model to explain the formation and influence of perceived collective efficacy in schools. It examines the relevance of efficacy beliefs to teachers' professional work and outlines possibilities for future research.

Kennedy, M. (2004) Reform ideals and teachers' practical intentions, *Education Policy Analysis Archives*, 12 (13), (retrieved 20th April 2011) from http://epaa.asu.edu/epaa/v12n13/
This paper describes a study of teachers' interpretations of classroom situations and their intentions for specific things they did in those situations. The author identifies the primary areas of concern that dominated teachers' thinking as they constructed their practices, and introduces a framework which incorporates (i) standing beliefs and values, (ii) accumulated principles of practice, (iii) interpretation of the situation, and (iv) intentions so as to map their lines of reasoning and thinking.

Stooksberry, L., Schussler, D. and Bercaw, L. (2009) Conceptualising dispositions: intellectual, cultural and moral domains of teaching, *Teachers and Teaching: Theory and Practice*, 15 (6): 719–736.
The authors provide a heuristic that organises dispositions around three domains of teaching: intellectual, cultural and moral. They equate dispositions with the teacher's internal filter, shaped by prior experience, beliefs, culture, values and cognitive abilities and which affect ideas about the nature of pupils, teaching and learning.

Chapter 7

Dimension 5

Consider alternative perspectives and possibilities

Learning objectives

In this chapter you will consider:

*   epistemological assumptions consistent with the constructivist approach to learning;
*   interpretation as a meaning-making process;
*   a range of strategies and sources to capture multiple perspectives;
*   the importance of reflecting upon alternative perspectives and possibilities in teaching.

Introduction

Although questions of significance to teaching and learning may involve private, inner *conversations with self,* Freire (1972) argues the need for teachers to adopt a *reflective posture,* one that enters the public arena and examines personal experience through *conversations with others.* Implicit within such discourse is recognition that several possible meanings can be associated with any course of action in relation to a particular teaching group within a particular context. From a social constructivist perspective interpretation is a meaning-making process, which Parker (1997: 40) notes, requires teachers to recognise that:

> problems do not exist 'out there', ready made, well defined and waiting to be solved ... a problem is seen as a human construct which arises out of a particular perception or interpretation formed about a unique educational context with its values and ends; the values, interests and actions of its inhabitants; and crucially, the particular relation of these features to a theoretical perspective which describes and explains them and their interrelations.

This chapter begins with an exploration of epistemological assumptions consistent with the constructivist approach to learning: notably, situating learning in real-world contexts, teaching through cognitive apprenticeship and constructing multiple perspectives. A range of strategies and sources that can be used in authentic learning environments are introduced, which enables you to consider the importance of reflecting upon alternative perspectives and possibilities in teaching.

Constructivist approach to learning

According to Bruner (1996), we construct ourselves through narrative (language) and by telling stories of our lives we can make sense of our lives. The knower is inextricably linked to the known and knowledge making is recognised as an active, creative, interpretive process, in which the telling and retelling of stories provide a framework for the construction of professional knowledge in teaching (Beattie, 2000; Clandinin and Connelly, 1995). The learner builds an internal representation of knowledge or personal interpretation of experience. This representation is open to change as its structure and interconnections form the foundation upon which other knowledge structures can be scaffolded. Successive modes of representation are developed as a person's expertise increases, and the building block for this development is the accumulation of individual cases (Boshuizen, 2003). Early career professional learning is generally characterised by the accumulation of a large amount of experience, and the aggregation of individual cases into increasingly large chunks of recognition and more informed representations of the construction of professional knowledge in teaching, as learning develops.

This view of knowledge does not refute the existence of the real world but argues that all we know of the world are the human interpretations we construct of our experiences of the world. Conceptual growth comes from sharing multiple perspectives and simultaneously changing our internal representations in response to those perspectives as well as through cumulative experience. At the core of such learning is the teacher's propensity to recognise the importance of working with experience as the context that shapes the experience also shapes the kind of learning from experience that is possible (Boud and Miller, 1996).

The constructivist theory of learning does not accept the premise that different types of learning can be identified independent of the context and content of learning. The constructivist perspective argues that it is neither possible to isolate units of information nor to make *a priori* assumptions of how that information will be used. Facts are not simply facts to be remembered in isolation and units of information cannot be remembered as independent, abstract entities. Learning always takes place in a context and the context forms an inexorable link with the knowledge embedded within it. The constructivist approach to learning considers what real people in a particular knowledge domain and real-life context typically do. Cognitive apprenticeship, which reflects the collaboration between real-world problem solving and using appropriate strategies in problem-solving situations, is the key to constructivist learning (Brown, Collins and Duguid, 1989; Resnick, 1987).

From the constructivist perspective, every field has its unique ways of knowing and the overarching goal is to move the learner into thinking within the knowledge domain as an expert user of that domain might think. In geography, for example, the goal would not be to teach geography facts or principles but to teach learners to use the domain of geographic information as a cartographer, geographer or navigator might do. Just as the cartographer or geographer must bring new perspectives to bear and construct a particular understanding or interpretation of a situation, so too must the learner. And just as different geographers identify different relevant information and come to different conclusions, we must also leave the identification of relevant information and 'correct' solutions open in the teaching situation. The process of constructing a perspective or understanding and developing reflexive awareness of that process are essential to the constructive view of learning.

The constructivist view emphasises that learners should be able to construct multiple perspectives on an issue. They must attempt to see an issue from different vantage points. It is essential that learners can make the best case possible from each perspective to demonstrate they truly understand alternative views. One strategy for achieving multiple perspectives is to belong to, and engage with, a professional learning community, which places an emphasis on working collaboratively to develop and share alternative views. It is from the views of others within the community that alternative perspectives are most often realised. Different sorts of argument and different kinds of evidence should support the differing views. It is the rigorous process of developing and evaluating the arguments that is the goal. A second strategy for developing a rich understanding and achieving multiple perspectives is to use examples which reflect real 'slices of life' in authentic contexts. For example, observing video excerpts of different teachers delivering lessons in a particular knowledge domain to a class of learners provides rich contextual knowledge for developing perspectives on teaching. As student teachers are exposed to the perspectives of experts and peers, they can select particular instances and bring to bear whatever perspective they consider most useful, meaningful, or relevant to them in a particular context. The goal is to enable them to see alternative views of how a particular concept can be perceived within authentic examples of teaching. Importantly, student teachers must learn to develop and evaluate the evidence which supports each perspective, and identify any shortcomings as well as the strengths. Valli's (1992) *deliberative reflection*, which involves consolidating several sources of information from a range of perceived experts to weigh up competing claims and give sound reasons for the decisions made, is relevant here, as well as Brookfield's (1995) notion of *hunting assumptions* through a wide range of perspectives and lenses.

Constructing multiple perspectives has two fundamentally important elements: (i) the perspectives that learners develop in the content area must work effectively within that area, and (ii) the learners must be able to defend their judgements. The first element might be referred to as *instrumentality* or the degree to which the learners' constructed knowledge of the field enables them to function effectively within the discipline. An obvious application of instrumentality can be recognised in problem solving. For example, can learners arrive at reasoned solutions to problems within the field? This concept applies equally well to knowledge structures that are not traditionally associated with problem-solving fields, such as in literature when analysing the works of a prominent author; in art when critiquing a particular painting or genre; and in citizenship education when learning how different cultures throughout the world might share universal concerns yet construct very differing perspectives. The second element, which is concerned with the capacity to explain and defend decisions, is related to the development of metacognitive skills: thinking about thinking so as to gain self-conscious awareness of how it is we come to know what we know; an awareness of the assumptions, evidence, justifications and reasoning that underlie different interpretations of experience. Reflexive awareness of one's own thinking can be gained through monitoring both the development of the structure of knowledge being studied and the process of constructing that knowledge representation in relation to a specific context.

Reflective task 7.1   Constructing professional knowledge in teaching

No two individuals would be expected to make the same interpretations of learning experiences or to apply their learning in exactly the same way to real-world problems that do not have one best solution. There is no one 'right' way to:

- approach a topic
- organise a class
- meet children's needs
- teach a lesson
- select and use resources
- support children's learning.

- Write a 2,000-word reflective narrative, which considers how the above claim can be supported by epistemological assumptions consistent with the constructive approach to learning.
- Discuss the key points of your argument with a critical friend and make notes of any issues where your perspectives differ. Pursue this line of enquiry further by scrutinising the arguments drawn upon and the evidence presented to defend each perspective.

The constructivist theory of learning has wide-ranging implications for virtually all aspects of teaching, from selecting appropriate learning goals, objectives and intended learning outcomes to methodologies you decide to employ for analysis, synthesis and evaluation. It has resonance with Dewey's reflective attitude of *open-mindedness*, which Chetcuti (2002: 154–155) describes as the reflective teacher's desire to:

> listen to more sides than one, to give full attention to alternate possibilities … about the content, methods and procedures used in your classroom. You constantly re-evaluate your worth in relation to the students currently enrolled and to the circumstances. You not only ask why things are the way they are, but also how they can be made better.

Professional learning conversations

A learning conversation can be a planned, systematic approach to professional dialogue, which is designed to support you to reflect on your own practice so as to gain new knowledge, insights and understanding to guide the development of your future teaching. A learning conversation can take place with a peer, a professional colleague, an advanced skills or expert teacher, an inspiring manager, a pupil or a group of pupils. They most frequently occur when teachers observe other teachers teach or during coaching and mentoring sessions.

Pendlebury (1995) uses the metaphor *dialogical other* to describe how a learning conversation between a student teacher and a significant other can be structured in a supportive way. Within her three-stage approach, the dialogical other first guides the student teacher to reflect on the aims and means to devise a course of action for a particular situation and teaching group. Second, he challenges and critiques this course of action to invite the student teacher to formulate sound justifications for decisions and judgements made and respond to any perceived developmental needs. Third, he facilitates the construction of an improved course of action as considered necessary. In this way, the dialogical other simultaneously affirms and encourages the interrogation of the student teacher's own voice and assumes the role of a *critical friend*. An important aspect of this process concerns the endeavour to explore their internal representations of knowledge or personal interpretations of experience and add meaning to what the student teacher claims to know. This incorporates the second component of Freire's (1972) *reflective posture* in that learning conversations not only explore previous experience but also focus on the possibilities of future practice.

Schon (1987) presents three models of *coaching reflective practice* designed to show student teachers how a particular setting appears through the eyes of experienced practitioners and how they might frame problems of practice:

- *Hall of mirrors* – the experienced practitioners' practice exemplifies that which student teachers seek to develop and understand in their own practice. As such, student teachers need to experience being a learner in a particular situation to gain greater awareness of the position of their learners when they assume the role of teacher.
- *Joint experimentation* – student teachers are encouraged to lead the reflective enquiry while experienced practitioners offer advice, alternatives and constructive feedback as the need arises. This enables student teachers to question problems concerning practice in a particular setting.
- *Follow me* – experienced practitioners describe and demonstrate their pedagogical knowledge and student teachers endeavour to develop and imitate the appropriate use of that pedagogical knowledge. Discussions about their respective actions, from both experienced practitioners' and student teachers' perspectives, promote learning about the practice setting.

These models juxtapose two perspectives on learning: notably, the student teachers' learning about learning and their learning about teaching. They also highlight the significance of the experienced teachers' role, which incorporates far more than a display of the skills associated with an *expert pedagogue,* as MacKinnon (1989: 23) notes:

> experimenting about the inevitable 'mistakes' and confusions that follow are encouraged and discussed, and viewed as departure points for growth ... a climate of trust, as well as the disposition to take learning seriously ... begins with the supervisor's own capacity for reflection on teaching, together with his or her ability to make this evident to the student teacher.

This consideration is important, as shown in the research undertaken by Eraut (2007) with mid-career teachers, which found explicit routines at the early stages of their careers often become tacit routines after several years of experience. Although this might make it difficult for experienced teachers to explain their knowledge, skills and understanding to student teachers, opportunities to engage in learning conversations

---

Reflective task 7.2 **Professional learning conversations**

- Think back over recent months and identify opportunities in which you engaged in professional learning conversations with others, formally and informally.
- Describe the nature, purpose and outcome of those conversations which supported your professional development most effectively.

---

can help more experienced teachers to make their routines explicit, particularly when required for the purposes of coaching, mentoring and self-evaluation.

Mentoring relationships

Mentors have a significant role to play in the development of future reflective teachers. Moran and Dallart (1995) note that mentors in the teaching practice classroom facilitate the development of reflective skills by modelling reflection on their own practice and directly challenging and affirming the critical thinking process in the student teacher. One principal benefit of a mentoring relationship is the development of 'more self-reflective, metacognitively aware and self-directed learners' (Hine, 2000: 1); by talking, sharing discussion and problem solving, and 'jointly constructing knowledge and meaning' (ibid.: 3) both the mentor and the mentee learn to reflect in ways that will ultimately transform their teaching.

Mentoring has much in common with specialist coaching and is a structured, sustained process designed to support professional learners through significant career transitions. Although ways in which mentors and coaches operate are context specific, ten principles of effective mentoring and coaching, derived from research evidence and through consultation, have been identified (CUREE, 2005):

1 *A learning conversation*: structured professional dialogue, rooted in evidence from the professional learner's practice, which articulates existing beliefs and practices to enable reflection on them;
2 *A thoughtful relationship*: developing trust, attending respectfully and with sensitivity to the powerful emotions involved in deep professional learning;
3 *A learning agreement*: establishing confidence about the boundaries of the relationship by agreeing and upholding ground rules that address imbalances in power and accountability;
4 *Combining support from fellow professional learners and specialists*: collaborating with colleagues to sustain commitment to learning and relate new approaches to everyday practice; seeking out specialist expertise to extend skills and knowledge and model good practice;
5 *Growing self direction*: an evolving process in which the learner takes increasing responsibility for their professional development as skills, knowledge and self-awareness increase;
6 *Setting challenging and personal goals*: identifying goals that build on what learners know and can do already, but could not yet achieve alone, whilst attending to both school and individual priorities;

7 *Understanding why different approaches work*: developing understanding of the theory that underpins new practice so it can be interpreted and adapted for different contexts;

8 *Acknowledging the benefits to the mentors and coaches*: recognising and making use of the professional learning that mentors and coaches gain from the opportunity to mentor or coach;

9 *Experimenting and observing*: creating a learning environment that supports risk-taking and innovation and encourages professional learners to seek out direct evidence from practice;

10 *Using resources effectively*: making and using time and other resources creatively to protect and sustain learning, action and reflection on a day-to-day basis.

Reflective task 7.3 **Support from mentor or specialist coach**

- Think about your past and recent experiences with mentors/specialist coaches and consider how, when and where opportunities were made available for you to:
  - respond proactively to modelled expertise to acquire and adapt new knowledge;
  - discuss practice and core concepts professionally;
  - respond positively to questions and suggestions;
  - understand your own learning needs and goals and develop strategies that respond to these through dialogue;
  - take an increasingly active role to construct your own learning programme;
  - observe, analyse and reflect upon your own and others' practice and make this explicit;
  - think and act honestly on your developing skills and understanding.
- For each professional development opportunity identified, consider the degree to which your experience enabled you to contemplate alternative perspectives and possibilities.
- To what extent have these professional development opportunities influenced your interpretation of experience or internal representation of knowledge?

Peer observation

Peer observation can be a highly effective strategy for gaining access to the alternative perspectives and viewpoints of others, whether you assume the role of the observer or the observed. As professional knowledge in teaching develops cumulatively, opportunities to engage in peer observation should be sustained over time if it is to have a real impact on your development and pupil learning. Based on the findings of several surveys in which teachers perceived the opportunity to observe colleagues teaching was crucial to the development of their own practice, the General Teaching Council for England (GTCE, 2006b) identified the main opportunities provided through peer observation, as shown in Table 7.1.

When observing other teachers, it is important to have a clearly defined focus so you can gather and map evidence directly related to that focus. For example, you may focus your attention on specific aspects of assessment for learning; verbal or non-

Table 7.1 Opportunities provided through peer observation

As the observer	As the observed
Watch and understand the development of complex classroom interactions	Unpack the complexity of what you do in the classroom so that you can develop and pass it on
Observe in a structured way how, when and with what effect a teacher uses different strategies	Look closely into one particular aspect of your teaching, e.g. questioning techniques
Investigate the different effects of a range of teaching styles and strategies on how pupils respond and learn	Experiment with new teaching strategies
	Focus on what is happening to the learning of a particular group of pupils
Internalise new approaches you may see in others' practice so that they become part of your repertoire	Discuss your teaching style/s in a non-judgemental environment
Connect knowledge and practice	Connect knowledge and practice

Source: adapted from GTCE (2006b: 2–3).

verbal communication; classroom management techniques; or personal, learning and thinking skills. When observing you can look for two kinds of information: first, the direct evidence you can observe and second, your personal comment/s as to whether the aspect observed was effective. In preparing to observe other teachers it is useful to record the teacher's learning objectives and intended learning outcomes for the lesson, the pupils' characteristics (e.g. age, gender, stage of development) and the subject/curriculum area being observed. The simplified observation schedule shown in Table 7.2 enables you to gather and map evidence about the same aspect of pedagogy (e.g. assessment for learning strategies) from three different teachers.

Reflective task 7.4 should reveal that different teachers often use very different strategies to achieve the same or similar purposes. A reflective teacher is one who will consider several ways of doing the same thing to ensure they accommodate the different needs of a range of learners and provide a varied approach to engage all pupils.

When your own teaching becomes the focus of lesson observation, you can take a number of steps to ensure you derive maximum benefit from the experience, as detailed in Table 7.3.

A good way to begin the debrief session following an observation is for you to identify your own impressions about the lesson, aspects that went well and aspects that did not go so well. Then ask your observer to comment on various aspects. This needs to be concrete and specific, focusing on observable behaviour and actions. You and your observer may then discuss the extent to which your intended learning outcomes were accomplished. During the debrief session pay particular attention to alternative strategies and possibilities suggested by your observer and take the necessary steps to find out more about these alternatives. You might then select two or three areas where suggestions for improvement have been made.

Peer observation is a collaborative enterprise, and for partners to work effectively and learn from one another a number of common factors should contribute to this success including mutual respect between partners; trust; a supportive environment; and stretching, challenging and pushing each other's thinking and capabilities. One commonly valued attribute to surface from research undertaken by Franz (2005) was

Table 7.2 Observing three different teachers

Focal area	Teacher A	Teacher B	Teacher C
Types/frequency of questions used			
Personal comment/s			
Types/frequency of feedback provided			
Personal comment/s			
Peer assessment strategies			
Personal comment/s			
Self-assessment strategies			
Personal comment/s			

providing personal support that resulted in increased or affirmed self-esteem: partners indicated that this support was key both to personal and partnership success. Other personal attributes found to promote success were captured within the profile of a collaborative personality, as Table 7.4 (p. 106) illustrates.

Reflective task 7.4 **Observations of three teachers**

- Select a specific aspect of teaching you wish to learn more about; design an observation schedule for this purpose and arrange to observe three different teachers.
- Record the teachers' learning objectives, intended learning outcomes, pupils' characteristics and subject/curriculum area to contextualise your observations.
- Conduct each observation and gather the two kinds of information noted above.
- Prepare summary statements about particular strategies each teacher used effectively and reflect upon whether you observed any broad differences between them.
- Does this analysis reveal any assumptions the teachers may have made about (i) the needs and capabilities of their pupils, (ii) their preferred way or style of teaching?
- Select a variety of pedagogical examples used by each teacher and for each describe an alternative or contrasting strategy that may have achieved a similar outcome. For example, 'Another way of promoting X would have been to ask open-ended challenging questions such as …'.
- What implications do your alternatives have for planning pupil learning?
- Discuss with each teacher the reasons why they used particular strategies to achieve specific learning objectives and whether they considered them to be effective.
- Identify learning objectives you thought were achieved particularly well and evaluate why you think the strategies used by teachers to achieve them worked.
- How might you develop this aspect of teaching in your own practice?

Reflective task 7.5 **How collaborative is your profile?**

- Examine the characteristics detailed in Table 7.4 (p. 106) and on a rating scale of 1 (low) to 5 (high) estimate how well you demonstrate each – where possible, provide examples to support your judgements.
- Ask a peer, colleague, mentor or specialist coach who knows you well to rate you using the same scale.
- Compare your perceptions and discuss any differences that may have emerged.
- Select three characteristics which you both agree are at the lower end of the scale and for each, discuss what strategies you might put in place to raise your profile in these areas.
- Review your response to task 1.4 (p. 9) and consider what parallels can be drawn between the two constructs, e.g. emotional intelligence and collaborative personality.
- To what extent does your rating within these constructs reflect your readiness and willingness to learn from others in an open-minded and receptive manner?

Table 7.3 Ways to make peer observation count

1	Prepare well	You need to agree in advance with the other teacher a clear and manageable focus for what is to be observed, e.g. a particular process such as how the lesson begins, or questioning techniques. This helps both of you to explore the detail, and the assumptions, under the surface of the lesson
2	Set ground rules for the style of observation	This is as important as agreeing the focus. Will the observer take part in the lesson, or be a silent 'fly on the wall'? Will they stay in one place, if so where, or observe from different parts of the classroom?
3	Decide in advance how the observation will be recorded	Feedback is a crucial part of the process, so the observer needs to be able to make notes relevant to the teacher's particular concerns and the focus of the observation. Audio and visual technologies can play their part, but might be intrusive and of great intrigue to pupils. Written methods need to be practical, and easy to interpret after the observation, e.g. checklist, rating form, open-ended comments. A school might develop a form for this purpose or use a modified initial teacher trainee observation schedule
4	Ensure an appropriate time and context for observation	Observation for teacher development need not last long. Short observations can lessen cover needs. Some teachers organise team teaching of classes and create the opportunity to observe each other in this way
5	Ensure an appropriate time and context for feedback	Feedback should be given as soon as possible after the session. This could be a summary, with a longer discussion or debrief session a few days later. Feedback should always be given in confidence. It should be explicit, focus on the areas agreed beforehand, and aim to give and provoke reflection. It is more like holding up a mirror to the person's teaching, and posing some questions, than making definitive pronouncements. The observed teacher may then want to move into a more evaluative mode, and identify what went well in the session and where there may be room for improvement
6	Resolve the issue of developmental versus judgemental feedback	Developmental observation should build upon points identified in previous observations and look at progress since the last observation. It would be separated off from performance management and divorced from any kind of capability or competency issues. The emphasis on self-evaluation puts pressure on feedback to become judgemental. If feedback is judgemental – some schools adopt the Ofsted scale – then teachers should mutually agree the judgement so the observed teacher feels involved in the reflection and the observer can point to clear evidence
7	Keep an open-minded teacher-to-teacher dialogue going about what you have observed	Formal feedback can be followed by, or merge into, a broader mutual discussion to explore the many possible interpretations of, and concepts supporting, classroom interactions
8	Look to provide expertise or examples of excellence in what you have observed	Peer observation is least effective in a vacuum, that is without appropriate professional, practical and theoretical follow-up. In particular, teachers developing their practice need clarity about what to aim for and knowledge about possible stepping-stones in between
9	Work with someone in the school who keeps an overview of all peer observation	This need not be another coordinator – it could, for example, be part of the role of an existing CPD coordinator, or within the remit of an assistant or deputy head, depending on the size of the school. Whoever it is, they will keep track of the peer observation taking place, be aware of good practice, and offer support to peer pairs
10	Recognise that peer observation works best within a coaching model	Keep asking the Who, Where, What, When, Why questions. Extend them to: How could you have done better? Why did it happen? What will you do next time? What have you learnt? What will you do better next time? What went well? What went not so well?

Adapted from GTCE (2006b: 4–6)

Table 7.4 Profile of a collaborative personality

Characteristic	Description
Collaborator	Team player, cooperative, easy to work with
Committed	Determined, driven, passionate, focused, diligent, strives to do better
Communicates	Listens, articulate, decisive, shares, takes and gives feedback, writes well, builds rapport, observant, frank, sounding-board
Concrete	Real issue orientation, centred on local needs, well grounded, steady and sure
Connected	Networker, sees connections, systems view
Credible	Stakeholder and peer support, adds value, media savvy, good image, political savvy
Dependable	Responsive, on time, involved, contributes, responsible
Enthusiastic	Energetic, tireless
Ethical	Integrity, confidentiality, trustworthy, fair, honest, shares credit, heart in the right place
Facilitator	Keeps people engaged, stretches people to reflect, coach, advocate, clarifier, career guidance, works well with tough people
Flexible	Good under pressure, willing to learn, creates a permeable organisation, mellow, quick thinker, no preconceived notions
Knowledgeable	Experienced, intelligent, expert, up to date, understands and applies theory, has technology
Likeable	Optimistic, positive, infectious personality
Nontraditional	Big thinker, entrepreneurial, risk taker, creative, out-of-the-box thinker, devil's advocate, challenges
Open	Inclusive, values opinions, respectful, sensitive, equality, objective, selfless, accommodating, honours the grass roots, collegial, win-win approach
Organised	Attention to detail, prepared, systematic
Productive	Effective, strategic, exceeds expectations, role model, hard worker
Supportive	Caring, consoler, comfort focused, compassion, encouraging, legitimiser, counsellor, good advice, boosts self-esteem

Adapted from Franz (2005: 260)

Pupil voice

Pupils appreciate knowing their views and perspectives are important and considered carefully. Using strategies to place these in the foreground often clarifies any confusion or misunderstanding that may arise between your goals and their expectations. Also, to examine how well pupils understand the material, recognise which teaching strategies contribute most effectively to their understanding, and identify any weaknesses in classroom organisation, management, pacing, presentation, resources or workload, you must give them voice if you are to understand such pedagogical issues from their perspective.

Feedback can be gathered from pupils in several ways during your lesson, as the following strategies exemplify:

- During the last five minutes of a lesson, distribute blank index cards and ask pupils to respond to two questions anonymously. General questions might ask: What is going well? What can be improved? How can this be improved? Any problems? What would you like more of? What would you like less of? Specific questions might ask: Are the problems too challenging? Do the resources help you to learn? Does the pace of the lesson cause difficulties?

• During the last few minutes of a lesson, ask pupils to complete a short, simple questionnaire containing four or six multiple-choice or short-answer questions.

• During the last ten minutes of a lesson, arrange pupils in small cluster groups of three to five. Ask each group to nominate a spokesperson and scribe and to identify something they found particularly worthwhile that helped their learning and something that may have hindered their learning and that they would like to change. Each spokesperson reports the views of the group and records these on a board or flip chart. You can then summarise key points of consensus and clarify those of disagreement.

• During the last few minutes of a lesson, ask pupils to write on such questions as: What have you learned today? At the end of today's lesson, what question is uppermost in your mind? This enables you to evaluate how well you conveyed specific material and can signal how you might structure topics in the next lesson.

• Following a series of lessons on a particular topic, ask pupils to list the key concepts and ideas and to write brief summaries on three to five main ideas about the topic. This enables you to gauge whether pupils have grasped the important ideas. You might also organise a class discussion, asking pupils to define and apply the concepts or to compare and contrast their responses.

Ideally you should respond to pupil feedback as soon as possible and consider carefully what their comments reveal. Although some teachers can effectively interpret pupil responses and design appropriate strategies to improve practice, others may find it helpful to review these with a professional colleague to identify possible options for making changes. Important discoveries are often made in response to critical questions

---

Reflective task 7.6 **The importance of pupil voice**

• Plan to gather feedback from pupils in your next lesson by using one of the above strategies.

• Before analysing their feedback, reflect upon the same questions and respond to them from your own perspective.

• Analyse the pupil comments and consider how you might respond to their suggestions for improvement.

• Discuss your ideas with a professional colleague and explore what alternative strategies and possibilities could be pursued.

• In what ways are your perceptions similar to or different from those of your pupils and professional colleague?

• Conduct a literature search to explore the power of pupil voice and write a 2,000-word reflective narrative on how pupil voice can shape your thinking and inform your own professional practice.

that encourage teachers to compare and contrast theory and practice and consider a range of alternative possibilities.

Once decisions have been made in response to pupil feedback, you can share with pupils which suggestions you plan to act upon, how and when, and those you cannot act upon and why (e.g. assessment requirement of a course).

Summary of key points

The epistemological assumptions underpinning the constructive approach to learning have been introduced and their implications for the construction of professional knowledge in teaching have been explored in several ways. These include an analysis of how professional learning conversations, the mentoring relationship, peer observation and pupil voice enable you to reflect upon pedagogical issues from multiple perspectives. The key message is that interpretation is a meaning-making process, contextually driven and situationally bound, and several possible meanings can be associated with any course of action, dependent upon whose perspectives and interpretations of experience are sought.

An open-minded attitude and receptive, collaborative disposition to enquiry enables you to engage with alternative perspectives and possibilities from a wide range of lenses that, in turn, can change your internal representations of knowledge in response to these perspectives as well as through cumulative experience.

Recommended reading

Eraut, M. (2007) Learning from other people in the workplace, *Oxford Review of Education*, 33 (4): 403–422.
Eraut presents an epistemology of practice that treats socio-cultural and individual theories of learning as complementary rather than competing. He explores a range of ways through which people can learn in the workplace (e.g. asking questions, listening and observing, giving and receiving feedback) and provides a useful typology of early career learning.

Korthagen, F. and Vasalos, A. (2005) Levels in reflection: core reflection as a means to enhance professional growth, *Teachers and Teaching: Theory and Practice*, 11 (1): 47–71.
Getting in touch with the core levels of identity and mission should enable you to understand how your personal frame of interpretation has been shaped and build upon your internal representation of knowledge, as you adapt to new learning experiences, e.g. critical incidents and perspectives derived from significant others.

Whitehead, J. and Fitzgerald, B. (2006) Professional learning through a generative approach to mentoring: lessons from a training school partnership and their wider implications, *Journal of Education for Teaching*, 32 (1): 37–52.
This study explores key characteristics of a generative approach to mentoring. One distinctive feature that surfaced was the inclusion of pupil voice within the training school's community of practice. Although a mentor and trainee can analyse video footage, when pupils gave feedback they noticed completely different things and their input was considered vital for changing practice.

Zwozdiak-Myers, P., Cameron, K., Mustard, C., Leask, M. and Green, A. (2010) *Literature review: analysis of current research, theory and practice in partnership working to identify constituent components of effective ITT partnerships,* Report for the TDA, London: Brunel University.
This report presents a model of the constituent components of effective ITT partnerships and concludes that at the core of successful collaborative partnership working was the desire to build an atmosphere of collegiality in which professional learning enhanced the career trajectory of all practitioners, and contributed not only toward the professional development of ITT trainees, but also to the development of plurilingual professionals.

Chapter 8

Dimension 6

Try out new strategies and ideas

> *Learning objectives*
>
> In this chapter you will consider:
>
> • how the achievement of educational goals, objectives and learning outcomes is dependent upon selecting and using the appropriate teaching strategy;
> • why teachers draw on a wide repertoire of strategies to accommodate the needs of diverse learners;
> • trying out active engagement techniques and modelling, questioning, explaining and small group work strategies to extend your current teaching repertoire.

Introduction

The goals of education are many and varied and the relationship between teaching and learning is a crucial aspect of education for all individuals. Freire (1972) views learners as 'critical co-investigators' who engage in dialogue with their teachers; and Rogers (1983) champions the goal of giving pupils the 'freedom to learn'. How then might we support pupils in achieving educational goals such as these? Meaningful and powerful learning does not happen in a vacuum or by some happy accident. It is associated with the creation of an effective learning situation by a skilful teacher and incorporates a combination of knowledge, skills, understanding and attitudes that develop over time through training, experience and focused reflection.

Teachers need to be flexible and responsive in drawing upon a wide repertoire of teaching practices which enables them to match a particular aspect of curriculum content and intended educational outcome to the needs of a particular group of pupils. To this end, teachers themselves must become 'flexible learners' and give serious consideration to the teaching strategies they use to differentiate the curriculum and make it accessible to all learners.

Teaching is a highly complex activity and the dynamics operating in any given classroom will be influenced by a range of contextual and situational factors, the unique blend of qualities, characteristics and experiences that shape each and every pupil in addition to those which shape the teachers themselves. Also, the professional landscape of teaching is in a constant state of flux as it responds to changes within the wider society. Teachers working in twenty-first-century schools are very likely to encounter pupils who are computer literate and expect knowledge and information to be instantly accessible at the touch of a button; alongside those from a range of cultural and ethnic backgrounds who have not been immersed into western culture and for whom English is an additional language; alongside those who have been issued with an antisocial behaviour order; alongside those with a range of special learning and educational needs who are supported in the classroom by adults other than teachers; alongside those recognised as gifted and talented in a range of different ways. Therefore, no two classes will respond to the same teacher or lesson design in exactly the same way and, arguably, this phenomenon is what sows the seed for developing the creativity and professional artistry associated with becoming effective in the classroom.

This chapter invites you to try out a range of active engagement techniques to widen the repertoire of teaching strategies and ideas you currently use. These include an analysis of the purposes and potential uses of modelling, questioning, explaining and small group work to promote pupil learning, which are informed by evidence-based research of effective teaching.

Active engagement techniques

Teachers must acquire a repertoire of teaching strategies to promote learning and develop understanding. They also need a wide variety of techniques to actively engage pupils. When we speak of pupil engagement we usually mean they appear interested, behave well, are on task and work hard. There is however a danger that pupils will simply be encouraged to behave well and work hard yet miss important processes that generate understanding. Teachers must meet two complementary conditions if they are to actively engage pupils:

- an appropriate climate that allows pupils to take full advantage of the knowledge, skills, understanding and experiences presented to them;
- a variety of strategies and techniques which enable pupils to construct their own learning.

Research (DfES, 2004c: 4–6) has identified a number of principles for creating active engagement, which are explored briefly below:

Activating prior knowledge – learning is an active process of constructing knowledge and developing understanding. To aid this process, pupils make meaning by connecting new knowledge and concepts to knowledge and ideas they already possess. It is important that teachers help pupils use what they already know to make sense of new knowledge. This can be accomplished by looking at or handling objects, drawing concept maps, referring to pupils' experiences, telling stories or getting pupils to imagine particular scenes.

Challenge – is about setting high expectations and then teaching *to* them so pupils surpass previous levels of achievement. Where learning is insufficiently challenging, pupils might lack interest and stimulation so their level of involvement quickly declines. One way teachers can create the appropriate level of challenge is to provide learning opportunities pitched on the one hand to avoid repetitive work, and on the other, tasks currently beyond the pupils' capability. Striving to solve challenging problems and thinking through issues can lead to cognitive development and higher achievement for all pupils.

Cooperative group work – when pupils work together on a common task they ask questions for clarification, interpret given information, speculate and give reasons. They share their ideas, knowledge and perspectives and arrive at a fuller understanding than they may have by working alone. When pupils work in this way, Vygotsky's (1986) *zone of proximal (potential) development* is exemplified in that the assistance of peers helps the development of thought in the individual.

Metacognition – simply expressed is thinking about thinking. The ability to stand back from a difficult task to: consider how it should be done; monitor one's progress and priorities; and reflect on successes and weaknesses, is critical in becoming a successful learner. Teachers need to give pupils opportunities to plan, monitor and reflect on their work so they can engage with learning as a process. This is typically done by asking pupils to consider how they will tackle a task or problem or by getting them to reflect on how they accomplished a task.

Modes of representing information – the brain is forced to work hard when it needs to convert information from one mode to another. This could be from text to diagrammatic form or from visual representation, such as film, to music (as in writing a score to accompany silent film footage). Such work is demanding because the individual must think about and make sense of the original information. The same degree of mental work can also be required when transforming information within the same medium (as in summarising a text).

Scaffolds – are structures to guide and support thinking. Complex tasks such as extended writing and problem solving place great demands on the learner, as there are so many things to think about at once. Scaffolds help by focusing attention on one thing at a time and providing a prompt, which reduces the demands placed on the pupil's working memory. The pupil can then move on to the next stage of the complex task. The support is temporary, as the pupil will progress to working independently over time.

Deep and surface learning – some pupils become very motivated learners whereas others do not and many behave differently in different subject areas and with different teachers. These differences partly arise from what the learner brings *to* the classroom (attitudes, background, intelligence, skills, prior knowledge, interests). They are however also the result of what the learner experiences *in* the classroom. When pupils reproduce or memorise given facts and information; accept ideas and information passively; are not required to look for patterns or principles or to reflect on goals and progress, they are engaged in surface learning. When teachers use strategies and techniques underpinned by the principles of active engagement, pupils experience deep learning as they try to understand and make sense of material; relate ideas and information to previous knowledge and experience; do not accept new information uncritically; use organising principles to integrate ideas; relate evidence to conclusions; and examine the logic of arguments.

Some pupils learn more easily by working with diagrams, some by listening and others by physically reorganising information or making models. When there is a mismatch between the way a pupil is being taught and the way a pupil prefers to learn he may lose motivation, underachieve or misbehave. Pupils who have weaknesses in literacy often

Table 8.1 Distinctions between learning orientation and performance orientation

Learning orientation	Performance orientation
A belief that effort leads to success	A belief that ability leads to success
A belief in one's ability to improve and learn	A concern to be judged as able and a concern to perform
A preference for challenging tasks	Satisfaction in doing better than others or in succeeding with little effort
Derives satisfaction from personal success at difficult tasks	Emphasis on interpersonal competition, normative public evaluation
Applies problem solving and self-instruction when engaged in task	Helplessness: evaluates self negatively when task is difficult

choose not to read or write, have poor skills or might lack confidence in their skills. To meet the varied learning styles and needs of different pupils it is important to provide variety in the types of tasks you set.

Motivation and the disposition to learn are important aspects of learning; two major orientations identified by Dweck (2000) are shown in Table 8.1.

Performance-orientated learners are more likely to give up when a task is difficult or when they receive low grades. However, learning-orientated learners are more likely to show resilience and persevere, be less influenced by grades and tend to display such characteristics as creativity, critical curiosity, positive learning relationships and attitudes.

Modelling

Also referred to as 'teacher demonstration' and 'assisted performance', modelling is an effective strategy when used by teachers with pupils who are attempting to learn new and challenging tasks. It is an active process, which calls upon the 'expert' teacher to demonstrate how to do something and throughout the process makes the thinking behind accomplishing the task very explicit. Through modelling a teacher can:

- 'think aloud', making apparent and explicit those skills, decisions, processes and procedures that would otherwise be hidden or unclear;
- expose pupils to the possible pitfalls of the task in hand, showing how to avoid them;
- demonstrate to pupils that they can make alterations and corrections as part of the process;
- warn pupils about possible hazards involved in practical activities, how to avoid them or minimise the effects if they occur.

In effective modelling, the teacher:

- is specific about the task and what pupils will learn;
- does not expect pupils to listen or watch for extended periods of time;
- offers challenge but mediates through providing pupils with the criteria for success;

- explains underlying principles so that pupils understand what is involved;
- shares the thinking so mental processes are explicit;
- involves pupils increasingly in the process by encouraging them to think about the task, ask questions, offer contributions and ideas;
- provides opportunities for pupils to practise the new skill while it is fresh in their memory;
- supports first attempts with prompts, scaffolds and praise;
- enables pupils to see how they can learn from others;
- enables pupils to become independent.

(adapted from DfES, 2004d: 3–4)

Modelling resembles the technique often referred to as 'scaffolding', which teachers can use to structure pupils' learning. This approach has been described as one in which 'learners are supported in carrying out a task by the use of language to guide their action. The next stage in scaffolding is for the learners to talk themselves through the task. Then that talk can, in turn, become an internalised guide to the action and thought of the learner' (Dillon and Maguire, 2001: 145–146). Modelling spans a number of topics and subject areas as it encompasses different approaches ranging from physical demonstration to unpacking complex mental procedures, often regarded as the cornerstone of understanding.

Modelling encourages pupils to develop a 'mental model' of a concept, task or phenomenon and to use metacognitive thinking, which involves planning, monitoring and regulating actions in complex tasks. This is particularly evident when teachers 'think aloud', slow down to examine difficult parts of a process and encourage pupils to do the same. Research suggests that one of the central tenets of reciprocal teaching is the use of metacognition (Palincsar and Brown, 1984). Pupils working in groups, for example, can be taught four strategies (summarising, questioning, clarifying and predicting) characteristically associated with good problem solvers and use them for such tasks as understanding demanding texts and tackling complex mathematical and science problems. Pupils take it in turn to lead the group through very explicit modelling, enabling them to internalise a process to the point where it becomes automatic.

Visual demonstration is a particularly important modelling technique for pupils unable to visualise concepts without prompts or follow a set of instructions simply by listening to them. It also supports pupils with special educational needs and those with sensory impairment who might miss certain steps and experiences through lack of hearing or sight and would benefit from having the skills and processes demonstrated in a concrete, clear way. It is also an effective technique for pupils learning English as an additional language, for pupils whose preferred learning styles are auditory and visual, and extending the experience of pupils who are gifted and talented.

Questioning

One important technique in the scaffolding process for actively engaging pupils in their learning is questioning. However, if not handled effectively, pupils can misunderstand and become confused. To use questioning effectively in your lesson requires planning; you need to carefully consider:

Reflective task 8.1 **Modelling talk**

All subject specialists develop a vocabulary and ways of expressing themselves appropriate to and important within their subject. Through modelling talk you will be able to demonstrate particular features of the language of your subject for pupils. Identify a lesson in which you could model subject-specific talk and plan a talk for that lesson by using the following question sequence as a guide:

- What are the objectives for the lesson?
- What are the subject-specific key words, phrases and concepts you want pupils to learn?
- How can you provide an example or model of these subject-specific language conventions to explain their meanings?
- How will you organise or group pupils for the teacher demonstration?
- What activity or oral task will enable pupils to rehearse and explore these language conventions in a supported context?
- What resources will you need for this lesson to support modelling?
- Who will help you during the lesson?

In preparing to use this modelling strategy you might find it useful to audio record your talk before delivering the lesson and also during the lesson or to have another teacher observe your lesson. After you have taught the lesson, use the following questions to focus your evaluation:

- Were your modelling strategies effective? What worked well?
- Was the talk long enough to provide pupils with the knowledge they needed to undertake the task?
- How did you help pupils to apply the strategies you modelled?
- What examples of subject-specific vocabulary and language that you modelled did pupils use?
- To what extent did the pupils' work match the learning objectives?
- If you ask pupils how modelling talk helped them, what might they say?
- Were there any problems? If so, what might you do next time to overcome them?

- why you are asking the question/s;
- what type of question/s you are going to ask;
- when you are going to ask question/s;
- how you are going to ask question/s;
- who you are going to ask, how you expect the question answered, how you are going to respond if a pupil does not understand the question or gives an inappropriate answer, and how long you are going to wait for a response.

This said, you must not rigidly plan your questioning as you must be flexible and adapt your plan during the lesson to take account of how the lesson unfolds.

Asking questions is not a simple straightforward process. Questions are asked for numerous reasons including: to gain pupils' attention or check they are paying attention; to check understanding of an explanation or instruction; to revise or reinforce a topic; to deepen understanding; to encourage problem solving and critical thinking; or to develop a discussion. Wragg and Brown (2001a: 16–17) classified the content of questions related to learning a particular subject, rather than procedural issues, as one of three types: *empirical questions* requiring answers based on facts or experimental findings; *conceptual questions* concerned with eliciting ideas, definitions and reasoning in the subject being studied; and *value questions* investigating relative worth and merit, moral and environmental issues. These broad categories often overlap and some questions may involve elements of all three types of questions.

Another classification that can support you in planning questions with specific purposes in mind is Bloom's (1956) 'taxonomy of educational objectives' through which questions can be arranged into six levels of complexity and abstraction. Lower-level questions usually demand factual, descriptive answers whereas higher-level questions are more complex and require more sophisticated thinking from pupils. Research suggests that pupils' cognitive abilities and levels of achievement can be increased when they are challenged and have regular access to higher-order thinking (Black and Wiliam, 2002; Good and Brophy, 2000; Muijs and Reynolds, 2011; Wragg and Brown, 2001a). Table 8.2 links the hierarchical levels in Bloom's taxonomy with what pupils might be expected to do and the types of question that could help them to realise those tasks. Examples of possible question stems are provided for each cognitive objective, which you can draw upon when planning questions to ask pupils in your lessons.

Questioning is effective when it enables pupils to engage with the learning process by actively composing and constructing responses. Research (Black and Wiliam, 2002; Good and Brophy, 2000; Muijs and Reynolds, 2011; Wragg and Brown, 2001a) suggests lessons in which questions are used effectively are likely to share the following characteristics:

- Questions are planned and closely linked to the learning objectives of the lesson.
- Frequent use of questioning to follow the exposition of new content, which has been broken down into small steps, enhances pupils' learning of basic skills.
- Closed questions are used to check factual understanding and recall.
- Open questions are a predominant feature of the lesson.
- Sequences of questions are planned so that the cognitive level increases as the questions proceed. This is to ensure pupils are guided to answer questions that demand increasingly higher-order thinking skills and are supported through this journey by questions which require less sophisticated thinking skills.
- Opportunities are planned for pupils to both ask their own questions and seek their own solutions. They are also encouraged to provide feedback to each other.
- Wait time is provided before an answer is required. Three seconds is appropriate for most questions whereas fifteen seconds or much longer might be needed for complex open questions.
- The classroom climate is one in which pupils feel safe and secure enough to take risks, be tentative and make mistakes, and have confidence they will not be ridiculed or criticised if they give a wrong answer.

Reflective task 8.2 **Planning a questioning sequence to promote thinking**

Use the links to Bloom's taxonomy in Table 8.2 to plan a sequence of questions you could use in a lesson you will soon teach. Within your sequence, gradually increase the cognitive demands placed on pupils by moving from concrete questions to more abstract ones. Once you have taught this lesson, use the following guide to focus your evaluation:

- Clarity about why you asked specific questions.
- Balance between open and closed questions.
- Number of questions you asked and how they were paced.
- How you built up toward complex difficult questions.
- Who you asked and why.
- How you responded to wrong answers or misconceptions.
- Wait time you built in for pupils' responses.
- Whether you created a climate where pupils felt safe to make mistakes.
- How you probed pupils' responses to extend understanding.

In light of your findings, review and modify your sequence of questions for future use and consider how you might improve your questioning technique to promote pupil thinking.

  You can undertake this task with a colleague, peer or someone else in your school where both of you plan the sequence of questions and try them out. This enables you to compare and contrast whether the same questions delivered by two different teachers with two different classes were effective and whether any notable differences emerged between you in relation to your respective experiences. Video recording these lessons will also enable you to engage in peer discussion and collaborative evaluation.

This research places an emphasis on the importance of using open, higher-level questions to develop pupils' higher-order thinking skills. However, it also reveals that many questions used both by effective and less effective teachers tend to be lower-level questions, which develop pupils' lower-order thinking skills. It was estimated that 70–80 per cent of all learning-focused questions require a simple factual or closed response, whereas 20–30 per cent guide pupils toward providing an explanation, clarification, expansion, generalisation or making an inference. Teachers must therefore strive to find an appropriate balance between the open and closed questions they use in relation to the topic under investigation and learning objectives for pupils in the lesson.

Muijs and Reynolds (2011) identify three kinds of prompts to help pupils answer questions: *verbal prompts* (cues, reminders, tips, references to previous lessons or giving part of a sentence for pupils to complete); *gestural prompts* (pointing to an object or modelling a behaviour); and *physical prompts* (guiding pupils through motor skills).

Table 8.2 Linking Bloom's taxonomy to what pupils need to do, thinking processes and possible question stems

Cognitive objective	What pupils need to do	Questioning to develop higher-order thinking skills	Links to thinking	Possible question stems
Knowledge	Define Recall Describe Label Identify Match	To help pupils link aspects of existing knowledge or relevant information to the task ahead	Pupils are more likely to retain information if it is needed for a specific task and linked to other relevant information. Do your questions in this area allow pupils to link aspects of knowledge necessary for the task?	Describe what you see … What is the name for … ? What is the best one … ? Where in the book would you find … ? What are the types of graph … ? What are we looking for? Where is this set?
Comprehension	Explain Translate Illustrate Summarise Extend	To help pupils to process their existing knowledge	Comprehension questions require the pupils to process the knowledge they already have in order to answer the question. They demand a higher level of thinking and information processing than do knowledge questions	How do you think … ? Why do you think … ? What might this mean … ? Explain what a spreadsheet does … What are the key features … ? Explain your model … What is shown about … ? What happens when … ? What word represents … ?
Application	Apply to a new context Demonstrate Predict Employ Solve Use	To help pupils use their knowledge to solve a new problem or apply it to a new situation	Questions in this area require pupils to use their existing knowledge and understanding to solve a new problem or to make sense of a new context. They demand more complex thinking. Pupils are more likely to be able to apply knowledge to a new context if it is not too far from the context with which they are familiar	What shape of graph are you expecting? What do you think will happen? Why? Where else might this be useful? How can you use a spreadsheet to … ? Can you apply what you now know to solve … ? What does this suggest to you? How does the writer do this? What would the next line of my modeled answer be?

Analysis	Analyse Infer Relate Support Break down Differentiate Explore	To help pupils use the process of enquiry to break down what they know and reassemble it	Analysis questions require pupils to break down what they know and reassemble it to help them solve a problem. These questions are linked to more abstract, conceptual thought which is central to the process of enquiry	Separate … (e.g. fact from opinion) What is the function of …? What assumptions are being made …? What is the evidence …? State the point of view … Make a distinction … What is this really saying? What does this symbolise? So, what is the poet saying to us?
Synthesis	Design Create Compose Reorganise Combine	To help pupils combine and select from available knowledge in order to respond to unfamiliar situations	Synthesis questions demand that pupils combine and select from available knowledge to respond to unfamiliar situations or solve new problems. There is likely to be a great diversity of responses	Propose an alternative … What conclusion can you draw …? How else would you …? State a rule … How do the writers differ in their response to …? What happens at the beginning of the poem and how does it change?
Evaluation	Assess Evaluate Appraise Defend Justify	To help pupils compare and contrast knowledge gained from different perspectives as they construct and reflect upon their own viewpoints	Evaluation questions expect pupils to use their knowledge to form judgements and defend the positions they take up. They demand very complex thinking and reasoning	Which is more important, moral, logical …? What inconsistencies are there …? What errors are there …? Why is … valid …? How can you defend …? Why is the order important? Why does it change?

Adapted from DfES (2004b: 13–14)

Explaining

The main purpose behind an explanation is to help another person understand something. There are many things which can be difficult or impossible for pupils to understand without an appropriate explanation, including abstract concepts, important ideas, principles, rules, past events and those outside their own direct experiences. Teachers spend a lot of time explaining and this strategy is a common feature of lessons in all curriculum and subject areas, which means that all teachers must acquire and develop the capacity to deliver effective explanations.

Research (DfES, 2004e; Wragg and Brown, 2001b) suggests that explanations teachers use can be categorised in the following ways:

- *Purposes and objectives of the lesson* – it is important to explain why things are done and what pupils are expected to achieve, therefore explanations should clearly distinguish between lesson objectives and intended learning outcomes.
- *Processes, procedures and skills (explaining how)* – performing a skill requires following a set procedure, and explaining the process or procedure will help pupils understand how things happen and work. It is important to emphasise the sequence of events by using such connectives *as first, next, then* and *finally*.
- *Cause and effect (explaining why)* – this type of explanation is characterised by one thing leading to another in a causal sequence and the connective *because* is important. It often begins with something observable and finding ways to explain this in relation to a number of possible causes, which rely on evidence to support one possible cause over another. It is more difficult to explain events that arise from a combination of factors such as: the cause of global warming, the origins of jazz or Impressionism, or the outbreak of World War II. Analogies, concept maps, diagrams and models can support this type of explanation, as can interspersing the explanation with questions.
- *Relationships (how one factor affects another over time)* – when explaining relationships between factors, it is important to consider how one factor affects another and how these might relate to one another over time. Introducing timelines for each event with diagrams and using the connectives, *as the* ... , *so the* ... , can help pupils understand relationships.
- *Concepts (often abstract)* – when defined as ideas or notions, concepts have common features that are recognisable. They can either be *concrete*: (i) familiar terms in everyday usage and observable (amphibian, bridge, essay, ocean) and (ii) unfamiliar terms used by specialists that are observable (ellipsis in writing, gradient, thermosetting plastic) or *abstract*: (i) familiar terms used by specialists that are not easily observable (design, democracy, erosion, health) and (ii) unfamiliar terms used by specialists that are not observable (atom, choreography, irony, urbanisation). Analogy, diagrams and models can help pupils to visualise and construct a mental map or representation of concepts.
- *Attitudes and values (involving some personal judgement)* – the use of judgement comes into play when explaining attitudes and values and it is important to clearly distinguish between an opinion and a fact. This type of explanation should seek to justify an opinion based on some form of evidence.

Good explanations share a number of common characteristics, as highlighted in Table 8.3, which teachers can draw upon in any order or combination according to the

Table 8.3 Characteristics of explanations

Key features	What key points or essential elements will help pupils to understand?
Clear structure	Is the explanation structured in a logical way showing how each part links together using words, images and analogies which pupils understand, and well chosen examples to illustrate key features?
Key features identified	Have you identified the key points or essential ingredients that would 'unlock' pupils' understanding?
Dynamic opening	What is the 'tease' or 'hook' that is used at the start to capture the pupils' interest and attention?
Clarity – using voice and body	Can voice intonation or body language be used in any way to emphasise or embellish certain points to maintain pupils' interest?
Signposts	Are there clear linguistic signposts to help pupils follow the sequence and to recognise which are the key points?
Examples and non-examples	Are there sufficient examples and non-examples to aid pupils' understanding of a concept and to establish the boundary of an idea or concept?
Models and analogies	What models and analogies might help pupils to grasp an idea and visualise it? Will pupils understand the model and analogy? How might you help pupils identify the strengths or weaknesses of the model and analogy?
Props	What pictures, images, concrete objects or visual aids (e.g. practical modelling or demonstration) can be used to help pupils understand more, capture their attention and focus their minds?
Questions	Are there opportunities to check for pupils' understanding at various points, and to note and act upon any misconceptions or misunderstandings? Are there opportunities for pupils to be interactive, involved and to rehearse their understanding?
Connections to pupils' experience	Are there opportunities to activate pupils' prior knowledge so that links between the new and old can be made and the new ideas assimilated?
Repetition	Are there a number of distinct moments in the explanation when the key points, ideas or terminology that should be learned are emphasised and repeated?
Humour	When and how might it be appropriate to use humour to keep attention and help to make some things easier to remember and more memorable?

Adapted from DfES (2004e: 11)

purpose behind an explanation, nature of the topic and learning needs of the pupils. They usually begin with a hook or tease to engage pupils from the outset and end with a summary of key learning points.

Effective explanations support pupils in a number of important ways. Pupils can gain an understanding and a good visualisation of the new concept or idea and know how it fits into their existing knowledge and understanding. They understand and internalise key features of the concept or idea so they can restate it in their own words. They are able to use appropriate analogies and models to restate their own ideas and explain them to others, know how to proceed with their own learning and what next steps they should take.

Reflective task 8.3 **Planning for and structuring explanations**

- Identify a future lesson that will require an explanation. Use the key features and guiding questions identified in Table 8.3 to plan and structure your explanation, design and gather resources and then try it out. Video record this lesson or have a colleague/peer or professional tutor observe the lesson and provide you with specific focused feedback. Discuss which aspects of your explanation worked well and those that did not work particularly well. Review your explanation and make notes on how this could be improved next time.
- Identify another future lesson that will require an explanation, but one you will be teaching to two different groups of pupils. Use the procedure above to plan and structure your explanation but this time vary the inclusion or combination of your ingredients, e.g. include a particular model or concrete object in one class but not the other; change the sequence of when to use repetition. Once you have taught both classes, analyse whether your variations made a difference and evaluate what impact each explanation had on pupils' understanding. Consider how the outcomes of this task might inform your future planning and structuring of explanations.

Small group work

Small group work has a number of distinct advantages over individual practice. The main benefit lies in the cooperative aspects it can help foster as in the development of social skills. Working with others can help develop pupils' empathetic abilities, by allowing them to see others' viewpoints and helping them to recognise that everyone has strengths and weaknesses. Trying to find a group solution to a problem also develops the need to accommodate others' views. Pupils may provide one another with scaffolding in the same way the teacher can during questioning. The total knowledge available in a group is likely to be larger than that available to individual pupils, which enables more powerful problem solving and allows the teacher to pose more difficult problems than she could perhaps pose to individual pupils.

Johnson and Johnson (1999) identified five defining elements of cooperative groups:

- *positive independence* – pupils need to feel their success depends upon whether they work together or not (they sink or swim together);
- *face-to-face supportive interaction* – pupils need to be active in helping one another learn and provide positive feedback;
- *individual and group accountability* – everyone has to feel they contribute toward achieving the group goals;
- *interpersonal and small group skills* – communication, conflict resolution, decision making, leadership and trust;
- *group processing* – the group reflects on its performance, how it has functioned and how to improve.

The organisation of small group work requires teachers to take a number of factors into account when structuring the task. The goals need to be stated clearly and the task explained in such a way that no ambiguity exists about the desired outcomes. Slavin (1996) suggests that to facilitate cooperation the goals need to be group goals accompanied by individual accountability for work done to avoid the effect of free riders. Giving individual and group grades can help accomplish this, as can the use of shared resources and tools. Also, the task can be structured in such a way that each group member is assigned a particular task. One way of doing this is to make the completion of one part dependent upon completion of the previous stage. Another is to assign specific roles to each pupil such as those identified by Johnson and Johnson (1994):

- the *summariser* prepares the group's presentation to the class and summarises the conclusions reached to see if the rest of the group agrees;
- the *researcher* collects background information and looks up additional information that might be needed to complete the task;
- the *checker* verifies the facts the group will use to ensure they are correct and will stand up to scrutiny from the teacher or other groups;
- the *runner* tries to find the resources needed to complete the task, such as dictionaries and equipment;
- the *observer/troubleshooter* takes notes and records group processes, which may be used during the debriefing following group work;
- the *recorder* writes down the major output of the group, and synthesises the work of other group members.

After finishing the group task, results need to be presented to the whole class or other groups and a debriefing session held that focuses on the process of the group work, e.g. the effectiveness of the collaborative effort.

Research suggests cooperative groups should be somewhat heterogeneous with respect to pupil ability. Groups composed of high–medium ability pupils or medium–low ability pupils both gave and received more explanations than groups comprised of high–medium–low ability pupils. Less heterogeneous groups were particularly advantageous for medium-ability pupils. When pupils of the same ability were grouped together it was found that high-ability pupils thought it unnecessary to help one another whereas low-ability pupils were less able to do so (Askew and Wiliam, 1995; Webb, 1991).

Decisions about how to compose groups may be influenced by any class setting that has already taken place. However, the way you choose to group pupils can be based on a range of criteria dependent upon the desired outcomes of a particular activity in which the groups are engaged. At different times and for different reasons you might consider such factors as ability, behaviour, communication skills, English as an additional language, gender, special educational needs and disabilities, or social mix. You also need to consider whether pairs, small groups or large groups are more appropriate for the task at hand. Table 8.4 highlights some benefits and limitations associated with different types of group composition and group size and when it might be appropriate to use them.

Once the principles of group work are firmly established within the classroom, you can introduce several group-work strategies to engage pupils with more challenging subject content to extend their learning styles and skills. The National Curriculum Council and the National Oracy Project (1997) identified some alternative ways of structuring pupils for group discussion:

Table 8.4 Group composition and group size

Grouping	Benefits	Limitations	When to use
Friendship	Secure and unthreatening	Prone to consensus	When sharing and confidence building are priorities
Ability	Work can more easily be pitched at the optimum level of challenge	Visible in-class setting	When differentiation can only be achieved by task
Structured mix	Ensures a wide range of views	Reproduces the power relations in society	When diversity is required
Random selection	Builds up pupils' experiences of different partners and views Accepted by pupils as democratic	Can get awkward mixes and 'bad group chemistry'	When pupils complain about who is allowed to sit with whom When groups have become stale
Single sex	Socially more comfortable for some	Increases the gender divide	In contexts where one sex habitually loses out, e.g. competing to control the computer keyboard
Individual	Has to think for self	Isolated within own experience and knowledge	When you want to be sure it is all their own work
Pair	Obliged to talk Secure Unthreatening No need to move desks Quick	Prone to quick consensus Little challenge from different viewpoints Allocation of loners can be difficult	When the topic is personal or sensitive When you need only a brief discussion
Small group (3–4)	Diversity of opinion without the size of group being too threatening Turning a pair round can create a table of four without moving desks	Social pressures begin to set in: 'We always work together'; 'Do we have to work with girls?'; 'I have no one to work with' Possible for individuals to stay quiet once there are more than two	To build confidence To increase social interaction in the class As an interim stage before whole-class discussion
Large group (5–7)	Diversity of ideas, experience, opinion Bridges the gap between small group experience and contributing to whole-class discussion	Have to move desks Requires chairing and social skills Can easily be dominated More pupils remain silent	For discussion requiring a range of views and ideas For developing teamwork
Whole class	Everyone gets the same experience Teacher can monitor and support the talk	Several pupils remain silent More difficult to contribute and there can be frustration in having to wait, discussion moving on, etc. Risk of domination by the bright, confident and talkative Risk of teacher doing most of the talking	When it is essential that all pupils hear the same message

(adapted from DfES, 2004f: 10-12)

Reflective task 8.4 **Criteria for selecting group composition and group size**

- Think about a class you currently teach. Annotate the cells within Table 8.4 to indicate which benefits and limitations apply to this class and add further points from your own experience. How might you address any limitations identified if you wanted to use the same group composition or group size in a lesson?
- Ask another teacher who works with the same class how they approach group work with them. Discuss in which lessons or circumstances you would each use different group compositions or group sizes. How might this inform your future practice?

- *Listening triads:* pupils work in groups of three and one takes on the role of talker, one the questioner and another the recorder. The talker explains something, or comments on an issue, or expresses concerns. The questioner prompts and seeks clarification. The recorder makes notes and gives a report at the end of the conversation. Next time, pupils change roles.
- *Envoys:* once groups have carried out a task, one person from each group is selected as an envoy. The envoy moves to a new group to explain and summarise the group's work and find out what the new group thought, decided or achieved. The envoy returns to the original group and feeds back. This encourages the envoy to think about his use of language and creates groups of active listeners.
- *Rainbow groups:* once groups have completed a task, each pupil in the group is given a colour or number. Pupils with the same colour or number join up to form new groups comprising representatives of each original group. In their new groups, pupils take turns to report on their original group's work and might begin to work on a new, combined task.
- *Jigsaw:* a topic is divided into sections. In 'home' groups of four or five, pupils take a section each and then regroup into 'expert' groups. The experts work together on their chosen areas, then return to their home groups to report on their area of expertise. The home group is then set a task that requires pupils to use the different areas of expertise for a joint outcome. This strategy requires advanced planning, but is an effective speaking and listening strategy and ensures the participation of all pupils.

Reflective task 8.5 **Group discussion strategies**

Look at a unit of work you are about to teach and identify opportunities to use the group discussion strategies of: listening triads, envoys, rainbow groups and jigsaws. Select one, plan to use it over a series of lessons and test it out. How effective was it? How might you improve further? Repeat this process until you have tried each of the group discussion strategies. Which particular strategy/strategies work/s best with your pupils and why?

Summary of key points

When teachers ask searching questions of educational practice that arise from their own circumstances and interests, they exemplify an active approach to professional learning by seeking new strategies and ideas, evaluating and reflecting on their impact and trying out new practices and ways of working to improve their teaching. As teachers actively critique and challenge what they claim to know, the insights gained are expressed in terms of new possibilities for teaching and they reconstruct and reframe personal theories and assumptions about their own practice. Through integrating new strategies and ideas into their own practice, teachers take ownership of their teaching as they *appropriate* new knowledge, which gives them the degree of autonomy needed to make professional judgements in response to each unique situation.

This chapter has presented a range of active engagement techniques, which research has shown underpins effective teaching to promote pupil learning. These include an analysis of the purpose and potential uses of modelling, questioning, explaining and small group work. As you try out these strategies and ideas and evaluate their impact on your own teaching and pupil learning you will build upon and extend your existing repertoire to provide pupils with powerful and meaningful learning opportunities to achieve a wide range of educational goals.

Recommended reading

Joyce, B., Weil, M. and Calhoun, E. (2009) *Models of Teaching,* 8th edition, Boston, MA: Allyn and Bacon.
Four families or models of teaching are presented; each feature highly structured distinct stages or episodes, underpinned by theoretical constructs of how humans learn. The information processing family, for example, includes the teaching approaches inductive thinking, concept attainment, scientific enquiry and cognitive growth, whereas the social family includes role-play, group investigation and social enquiry.

Mosston, M. and Ashworth, S. (2002) *Teaching Physical Education,* 5th edition, San Francisco: Benjamin Cummings.
Eleven teaching strategies (termed 'styles') are presented along a continuum moving from command, practice, reciprocal, self-check, inclusion, guided discovery, convergent discovery, divergent discovery, learner designed individual programme, learner-initiated toward self-teaching. The O-T-L-O principle (objectives, teacher behaviour, learning behaviour, outcomes) is introduced, based on the philosophy that decision-making is the pivotal element 'in the chain of events that form the teaching–learning relationship' (ibid.: xx). The authors suggest this spectrum can be applied to all subject areas and help guide the selection of an appropriate teaching strategy to achieve a particular outcome.

Muijs, D. and Reynolds, D. (2011) *Effective Teaching: Evidence and Practice,* 3rd edition, London: Paul Chapman/Sage.
Underpinned by research into effective teaching, this text is divided into four parts. Parts 1 and 2 discuss learning and generic teaching skills, Part 3 considers teaching for specific purposes and Part 4 discusses teaching specific subjects and the issue of the

assessment and observation of teaching in classrooms. Chapters 2, 3, 4 and 5 explore the direct instruction method, interactive teaching, collaborative small group work and constructivist teaching, respectively.

Rogers, B. (2011) *Classroom Behaviour: A Practical Guide to Effective Teaching, Behaviour Management and Colleague Support,* 3rd edition, London: Sage.
Written by a former teacher who currently works as an Education Consultant lecturing widely on behaviour management, discipline, effective teaching, stress management and teacher welfare, this book grapples with some important issues facing teachers working in classrooms today such as dealing with bullying, teaching pupils on the autistic spectrum in mainstream classrooms and working with very challenging pupils.

Chapter 9

Dimension 7

Maximise the learning potential of all your pupils

> *Learning objectives*
>
> In this chapter you will consider:
>
> - children and young people's right to education and equal opportunity to learn;
> - the social, historical and political contexts of inclusive education;
> - guiding principles that underpin assessment for learning;
> - how personalised learning aims to narrow the attainment gap and raise achievement for all pupils.

Introduction

The principles of entitlement and inclusion require teachers to recognise that all pupils have an equal opportunity to learn and gain access to education, largely through the convergence of three practices: 'diversity in group, interactive instruction that appeals to a wide variety of learning styles, and an inclusive curriculum' (ETUCE, 2008: 58). This can be challenging within the context of twenty-first-century schools as teachers are increasingly called upon to teach pupils from multicultural backgrounds with a diverse range of social, emotional, intellectual, physical, special educational needs and/ or disabilities as well as different aspirations and preferred learning styles.

Recent emphasis in Europe on developing transversal competencies amongst pupils across traditional curriculum subjects and themes, and in England on personalised learning, illustrate the requirement to tailor provision and accommodate individual aptitudes, interests and needs, so that all pupils realise their potential, irrespective of background and personal circumstances. Considerable emphasis is placed on the development of *personal, learning and thinking skills* (QCA, 2008) and processes involved in the enactment of learning itself, which aim to give pupils greater autonomy over their learning and prepare them for a rapidly changing complex society in which they need to become 'self-directed learners, able and motivated to keep learning over a lifetime' (OECD, 2005: 2).

Key drivers behind the infrastructure of contemporary schools and classrooms lie in stark contrast to those of past decades. This chapter begins with an overview of

Reflective task 9.1 **Educational experiences of inclusion**

- Think about your own experiences as a pupil, particularly as one in a class of between 25–30 others. Provide examples of occasions when you were included:
  - in specific lessons and subject areas
  - by particular teachers
  - in classroom-based tasks
  - by your peers.
- Provide examples of occasions when you may have been excluded.
- Try to capture the *emotions* and *feelings* associated with your experiences and record these in two columns as exemplified in Table 9.1.
- Reflect upon how well you achieved in different subject areas of the curriculum. Think about areas you most enjoyed and spent a great deal of time and effort on and those you least enjoyed or tried to avoid.
- Write a 1,500-word reflective narrative on: 'How educational experiences can positively and negatively impact on pupils' social, emotional and intellectual development'.
- Discuss the key points of your argument with a critical friend.

Table 9.1 Feelings and emotions associated with inclusion and exclusion

Feelings and emotions	
Inclusion	Exclusion
At ease	Uncomfortable
Confident	Threatened
Happy	Marginalised
Important	Rejected
Valued	Low self-esteem
…	…
…	…

the origins of inclusive education to highlight how the path once travelled by some of our most vulnerable children and young people has been transformed in response to the fundamental right not to be discriminated against on the grounds of difference and diversity. Government policy and legislation are chronologically juxtaposed with important milestones in educational reform for this purpose. The focus then turns toward guiding principles that underpin assessment for learning, one of the most powerful ways to maximise pupil learning by emphasising progress and achievement as opposed to failure. The chapter concludes by examining how personalised learning aims to narrow the gaps in attainment and raise achievement for all pupils.

Origins of inclusive education

A number of major stepping stones spanning more than 50 years have led us to where we are today in relation to categorising, educating and identifying pupils with special educational needs and/or disabilities. Prior to the 1944 Education Act, such labels as feeble minded, idiot, imbecile and fool were in common usage and such individuals were, more often than not, *segregated* from society, not given an opportunity to enter mainstream education and placed in workhouses, asylum institutions or sent to prison. In steering this Act through parliament, Butler (1944) proposed:

> ... (clause 31) children with slight disabilities may be taught by special methods adapted to their individual needs in ordinary primary and secondary schools, but for the more seriously disabled we look for an extension of the present inadequate provision of special schools both through local education authorities and voluntary endeavour, and I hope that we shall make our provision of these schools adequate for the purpose ...

> ... (clause 32) to abolish certification under the Mental Deficiency Acts for education purposes. No child who can be dealt with within the education system shall in future be described or treated as mentally defective ... our object is to provide the necessary flexibility, so as to enable advantage to be taken of new developments in medical education or psychological diagnosis and practice as they come along.

This Act introduced the term and educational provision for children with special educational needs, but it was not until the Warnock Report that special educational needs (SEN) was considered in non-medical terms and a major shift toward *integration* in placing these children in mainstream schools was realised. Baroness Warnock (1978: 42) recommended that the term 'children with learning difficulties should be used in future to describe both those children who are currently categorised as educationally sub-normal and those with educational difficulties who are often at present the concern of remedial services'. She argued for each child to be looked at as an individual case and for the introduction of a detailed system or profile to record the child's special needs. Special units were to be set up and attached to mainstream schools as well as 'special boarding schools for pupils who were delicate, neglected or lived too far from the nearest day school to be able to attend it without difficulty' (ibid.: 25).

The 1981 Education Act introduced many of Warnock's recommendations including the introduction of 'statements', specific duties on school governors and local education authorities to make provision for SEN, define responsibilities and procedures for SEN, and establish parental involvement in the child's assessment along with a right of appeal. These placed considerable demands on physical, financial and human resources within already stretched Education and National Health systems, which resulted in a deterioration of services provided for these children (MacFarlane, 1985).

The 1988 Education Act introduced the National Curriculum (DES/WO, 1988) into maintained primary and secondary schools in England and Wales and set out a minimum entitlement to education for all pupils which:

- was broad and balanced;
- promoted spiritual, moral, cultural, mental and physical development;
- prepared pupils for the opportunities, responsibilities and experiences of adult life;
- included religious education and sex education for secondary pupils.

This led to a restructuring of the subject-based curriculum, the creation of national 'league tables' and the availability of the assessment data on individual pupils' level of attainment. General teaching requirements reinforced the duty of teachers to consider special educational needs through three main principles of inclusion:

- setting suitable learning challenges;
- responding to pupils' diverse needs;
- overcoming potential barriers to learning and assessment for individual pupils and groups of pupils.

The Inclusion Charter (CSIE, 1989) was drawn up to clarify what inclusive education meant, based on the fundamental principle that inclusion is a matter of human rights and all pupils should be treated equally. The *Code of Practice on the Identification and Assessment of SEN* (DfE, 1994) became statutory in 1994, introduced the Individual Education Plan (IEP) and emphasised the importance of identifying SEN in the early stages. In the same year, the Salamanca Statement (UNESCO, 1994: ix) proclaimed:

- every child has a fundamental right to education, and must be given the opportunity to achieve and maintain an acceptable level of learning;
- every child has unique characteristics, interests, abilities and learning needs;
- education systems should be designed and education programmes implemented to take into account the wide diversity of these characteristics and needs;
- those with special educational needs must have access to regular schools which should accommodate them within a child-centred pedagogy capable of meeting these needs;
- regular schools with this inclusive orientation are the most effective means of combating discriminatory attitudes, creating welcoming communities, building an inclusive society and achieving education for all; moreover, they provide an effective education to the majority of children and improve the efficiency and ultimately the cost effectiveness of the entire education system.

With the advent and governance of New Labour, the green paper *Excellence for All* (DfEE, 1997) highlighted a significant correlation between school exclusion figures and children and young people with special educational needs. It sought to clarify that 'good provision for SEN does not mean a sympathetic acceptance of low achievement. It means a tough-minded determination to show that children with SEN are capable of excellence. Where schools respond in this way, teachers sharpen their ability to set high standards for all pupils'. Several areas in need of attention included: early identification and intervention, effective behaviour policies, improving achievement, strengthening staff skills and improving specialist support, which provided the impetus to review and reconfigure the way in which public services were working in the interests of all children and young people. Three full terms (12 years) in office resulted in a prolific, almost unprecedented amount of reforms to raise educational achievement and improve the provision for all pupils, each attracting vast amounts of human capital and financial investment.

A revised National Curriculum for England became statutory in 2000 (DfEE/QCA, 1999) and the *Index for Inclusion* (CSIE, 2000) sent to every school defined inclusion as:

> ... the processes of increasing the participation of students in, and reducing their exclusion from, the cultures, curricula and communities of local schools. Inclusion is concerned with the learning participation of all students vulnerable to exclusionary pressures, not only those with impairments or categorised as having special educational needs. Inclusion is concerned with improving schools for staff as well as for students.

In 2001 a revised (Ofsted, 2000) framework incorporated the inspection of inclusive provision within all schools. The *Special Educational Needs Code of Practice* (DfES, 2001) revised the 1995 Disability Discrimination Act and placed a duty on schools and other educational institutions to make 'reasonable adjustments' and ensure that disabled pupils were not disadvantaged. It also stated:

> (6.18) Effective management, school ethos and the learning environment, curricular, disciplinary and pastoral arrangements can help prevent some special educational needs arising, and minimise others ... Schools should not assume that pupils' learning difficulties always result solely, or even mainly, from problems within the young person.

> (6.20) Subject teacher planning should be flexible so as to recognise the needs of all pupils as individuals and to ensure progression, relevance and differentiation ...

Following the tragic death of Victoria Climbié on 25 February 2000 who had *slipped through the net*, Blair (DfES, 2003: 1–2) cautioned: 'her case was a shocking example from a list of children terribly abused and mistreated. The names of the children involved, echoing down the years, are a standing shame to us all ... we all desperately want to see people, practices and policies in place to make sure that the risk is as small as is humanly possible'. *Every Child Matters* (DfES, 2004g) became the key driver to reforms within all public services used by children, and the government's vision was a systemic change to:

- integrate universal and targeted services for children from birth to 19;
- build wrap-around care and services for children, young people and their families;
- promote prevention, early identification and intervention of children at risk and those in need of protection;
- support parents and carers.

Five priority outcomes were identified to realise this vision:

- Be healthy
  - Physically healthy
  - Mentally and emotionally healthy

- – Sexually healthy
- – Healthy lifestyle
- – Choose not to take illegal drugs
- – *Parents, carers and families promote healthy choices.*
- Stay safe
  - – From maltreatment, neglect, violence and sexual exploitation
  - – From accidental injury and death
  - – From bullying and discrimination
  - – From crime and anti-social behaviour in and out of school
  - – Have security, stability and be cared for
  - – *Parents, carers and families provide safe homes and stability.*
- Enjoy and achieve
  - – Ready for school
  - – Attend and enjoy school
  - – Achieve stretching national educational standards at primary school
  - – Achieve personal and social development and enjoy recreation
  - – Achieve stretching national educational standards at secondary school
  - – *Parents, carers and families support learning.*
- Make a positive contribution
  - – Engage in decision-making and support the community and environment
  - – Engage in law-abiding and positive behaviour in and out of school
  - – Develop positive relationships and choose not to bully and discriminate
  - – Develop self-confidence and successfully deal with significant life changes and challenges
  - – Develop enterprising behaviour
  - – *Parents, carers and families promote positive behaviour.*
- Achieve economic wellbeing
  - – Engage in further education, employment or training on leaving school
  - – Ready for employment
  - – Live in decent homes and sustainable communities
  - – Access to transport and material goods
  - – Live in households free from low income
  - – *Parents, carers and families are supported to be economically active.*

The Children Act 2004 (DfES, 2004h) set the legislative spine to deliver the proposed outcomes under the auspices of a newly appointed Children's Commissioner and established a common assessment framework, underpinned by two broad aspects of the integrated workforce strategy: 'workforce reform' and 'multi-agency working'. *Removing Barriers to Achievement* (DfES, 2004i: 2) set out the government's ten-year strategy for SEN and in highlighting previous misgivings, established clear targets of where it hoped to be in the future, recognising the challenges for schools 'posed by children with severe behavioural, emotional and social difficulties', and provided a summary of areas in need of development.

In 2005, the *Disability Discrimination Act* (DfES) placed a duty on public bodies to 'promote disability equality' and for schools to have a *Disability Equality Scheme* to bring it in line with existing legislation related to race equality and gender equality. Every Child Matters outcomes are embedded within the second revision to the

---

Reflective task 9.2 **The lives and well-being of children and young people**

Access the following literary sources and compare and contrast their key messages in relation to the Every Child Matters five priority outcomes.

- Gillborn, D. and Mirza, H. (2000) *Educational Inequality: Mapping Race, Class and Gender – A Synthesis of Research and Evidence,* London: Office for Standards in Education.
- UNESCO (1994) *The Salamanca Statement and Framework for Action on Special Educational Needs,* Paris: UNESCO.
- UNICEF (2007) Child poverty in perspective: An overview of child well-being in rich countries, *Innocenti Report Card 7,* Florence, Italy: UNICEF Innocenti Research Centre.

Search policy documents in your school related to equality of opportunity and consider how the Every Child Matters priority outcomes are embedded within them and reflected in school-wide approaches to teaching and learning to safeguard, protect and enhance the lives and well-being of all pupils. Discuss with the SEN Coordinator ways in which the Individual Education Plan for three pupils takes the principles of inclusion into account.

Reflective task 9.3 **A 'big picture' of the National Curriculum**

To recognise how the aims of the National Curriculum are mapped into National Strategies and priorities, download copies of a 'big picture' of the primary curriculum: bigpicture_pri_04_tcm-157420-1.pdf and of the secondary curriculum: bigpicture_sec_05_tcm8-157430.pdf.

These frameworks capture the curriculum as the entire planned learning experience underpinned by a broad set of common values and purposes. Consider how the approaches to learning embedded within these frameworks are reflected in a particular subject/curriculum area in your school.

National Curriculum introduced in 2008 (QCA) which has three statutory aims: to help young people become:

- *successful learners* who enjoy learning, make progress and achieve;
- *confident individuals* who are able to live safe, healthy and fulfilling lives;
- *responsible citizens* who make a positive contribution to society.

Assessment for learning

In a major review of research on assessment and classroom learning, Black and Wiliam (1998) synthesised evidence from more than 250 studies covering nine years of

> *Reflective task 9.4* **Inclusive practice**
>
> Access the following literary sources to compare and contrast examples of effective inclusive practice.
>
> - Dyson, A., Howes, A. and Roberts, B. (2002) A systematic review of the effectiveness of school-level actions for promoting participation by all students, in *Research Evidence in Education Library*, London: EPPI-Centre, Social Science Research Unit, Institute of Education, University of London.
> - Nind, M., Wearmouth, J. with Collins, J., Hall, K., Rix, J. and Sheehy, K. (2004) A systematic review of pedagogical approaches that can effectively include children with special educational needs in mainstream classrooms with a particular focus on peer group interactive approaches, in *Research Evidence in Education Library*, London: EPPI-Centre, Social Science Research Unit, Institute of Education, University of London.
> - Wall, K. (2006) *Synoptic literature review of research relating to SEN and linked to initial teacher training*, London: Training and Development Agency for Schools (TDA).
>
> Select an approach that is new to you and consider how it might be developed with a class you currently teach. Try your ideas out, evaluate their impact and reflect on what next steps you need to take to enhance the learning potential of three pupils with very different learning needs.

international research, which linked assessment and learning. Their findings have been widely recognised and drawn upon by policy makers in England to capture the essence of, and shape how we define and implement, assessment for learning. This research highlights that improving learning through assessment is dependent on five key factors:

- providing effective feedback to pupils;
- actively involving pupils in their own learning;
- adjusting teaching to take account of the results of assessment;
- recognising the influence assessment has on pupils' motivation and self-esteem, both of which are crucial to learning;
- considering the need for pupils to be able to assess themselves and understand how to improve.

A number of risks and inhibiting factors were also found in this research:

- the tendency for teachers to assess presentation and quantity of work rather than the quality of learning;
- focusing more on marking and grading as opposed to providing advice for improvement, which tends to lower pupils' self-esteem;
- demoralising less successful learners when comparing pupils with each other;
- providing feedback to pupils which serves managerial and social purposes rather than helping them learn more effectively;

- teachers not knowing enough about, and working with an insufficient picture of, their pupils' learning needs.

As Black and Wiliam (1998: 6–7) argue, the ultimate user of assessment information elicited to improve learning is the pupil, which can have one negative and one positive aspect. Where the classroom culture focuses on gold stars, grades, place-in-the-class ranking or rewards, pupils look for ways to obtain the best marks rather than the needs of their learning which these marks ought to reflect. One consequence is that where they have any choice, pupils avoid difficult tasks. They also spend time and energy looking for clues to the 'right answer'. Many are reluctant to ask questions out of fear of failure. Pupils who encounter difficulties and poor results are led to believe they lack ability and attribute difficulties to a defect in themselves about which they cannot do a great deal. So they 'retire hurt', avoid investing effort in learning which could only lead to disappointment, and try to build self-esteem in other ways. Whilst high achievers can do well in such a culture, the overall result is to enhance the extent and frequency of under-achievement.

What is needed is a culture of success, backed up by the belief that all can achieve. *Formative assessment* can be powerful if communicated in the right way. Whilst it can help all pupils, it gives particularly good results with low achievers when it concentrates on specific problems with their work, and gives them both a clear understanding of what is wrong and achievable targets for putting it right. Pupils can accept and work with such messages, provided they are not clouded by overtones about ability, competition and comparison with others. Thus, 'feedback to any pupil should be about the particular qualities of his or her work, with advice on what he or she can do to improve, and should avoid comparisons with other pupils' (ibid.: 6).

There is another important dimension. Pupils can only assess themselves when they have a clear picture of the targets their learning is meant to attain. When pupils acquire such an overview, they become more committed and more effective learners: their own assessments become an object of discussion with their teachers and with one another, and this promotes reflection on their own ideas, which is essential to good learning. Where anyone is trying to learn, feedback about their efforts has three elements: the *desired goal*, evidence about their *present position*, and some understanding of the *way to close the gap* between the two. All three elements must be understood before anyone can take action to improve their learning.

Such argument is consistent with general ideas about the way people learn. New understandings are not simply absorbed and stored in isolation – they have to be assimilated in relation to pre-existing ideas. The new and the old may be inconsistent or even in conflict, and disparities need to be resolved by thoughtful actions taken by the learner. Realising there are new goals for learning is an essential part of this process. Thus, 'for formative assessment to be productive, pupils should be trained in self-assessment so that they can understand the main purposes of their learning and thereby grasp what they need to do to achieve' (ibid.: 7).

Further synthesis of this research led Black and Wiliam (2002) to crystallise key messages embedded within their findings into four main areas:

- Questioning
  - More effort has to be spent in framing questions worth asking;

- Wait time has to be increased to several seconds to give pupils time to think, and everyone should be expected to contribute to the discussion;
- Follow-up activities have to provide opportunities to ensure meaningful interventions extend pupils' understanding;
- The only point of asking questions is to raise issues about which the teacher needs information, or about which the pupils need to think.

- Feedback through marking
  - Written tasks, alongside oral questioning, should encourage pupils to develop and show understanding of key features of the subject they have studied;
  - Comments should identify what has been done well, what needs improvement and guidance on how to make that improvement;
  - Opportunities for pupils to follow up comments should be planned as part of the overall learning process;
  - To be effective, feedback should cause thinking to take place.

- Peer and self-assessment
  - The criteria for evaluating any learning achievements must be transparent to enable pupils to have a clear overview of the aims of their work and what it means to complete it successfully;
  - Pupils should be taught the habits and skills of collaboration in peer assessment;
  - Pupils should be encouraged to keep in mind the aims of their work and assess their own progress to meet these aims as they proceed;
  - Peer and self-assessment make unique contributions to the development of pupils' learning and secure aims that cannot be achieved in any other way.

- The formative use of summative tests
  - Pupils should be encouraged in a reflective review of the work they have done to enable them to plan their revision effectively;
  - Pupils should be encouraged to set questions and mark answers to help them understand the assessment process and focus further efforts for improvement;
  - Pupils should be encouraged through peer and self-assessment to apply criteria to help them understand how their work might be improved;
  - Summative tests should be, and should be seen to be, a positive part of the learning process.

From this platform, the Assessment Reform Group (ARG, 2002) identified ten principles of assessment for learning to guide classroom practice, as shown in Table 9.2, and defined assessment for learning as: the process of seeking and interpreting evidence for use by learners and their teachers to decide where the learners are in their learning, where they need to go and how best to get there.

These principles underpin the National Curriculum and provide fertile ground for reflecting upon ways in which to maximise the learning potential of your pupils. The following task invites you to focus on just one of the important strategies you must develop for this purpose, your use of feedback. The active engagement techniques and teaching strategies introduced in Chapter 8, particularly your use of questioning to develop higher order thinking skills, are inextricably linked to assessment for learning.

The *Assessment for Learning Strategy* (DCSF, 2008a) launched in England, builds on the *Making Good Progress* pilot that began in 2007, involving 450 schools trialling new ways to assess, report and stimulate progress at Key Stage 2 and Key Stage 3, to

Table 9.2 Assessment for learning: research-based principles to guide classroom practice

Assessment for learning should be part of effective planning of teaching and learning	A teacher's planning should provide opportunities for both learner and teacher to obtain and use information about progress towards learning goals. It also has to be flexible to respond to initial and emerging ideas and skills. Planning should include strategies to ensure learners understand goals they are pursuing and criteria that will be applied in assessing their work. How learners will receive feedback, take part in assessing their learning and be helped to make further progress should also be planned
Assessment for learning should focus on how students learn	The process of learning has to be in the minds of both learner and teacher when assessment is planned and the evidence interpreted. Learners should become as aware of the 'how' of their learning as they are of the 'what'
Assessment for learning should be recognised as central to classroom practice	Much of what teachers and learners do in classrooms can be described as assessment. That is, tasks and questions prompt learners to demonstrate their knowledge, understanding and skills. What learners say and do is then observed and interpreted, and judgements are made about how learning can be improved. These assessment processes are an essential part of everyday classroom practice and involve teachers and learners in reflection, dialogue and decision making
Assessment for learning should be regarded as a key professional skill for teachers	Teachers require the professional knowledge and skills to: plan for assessment; observe learning; analyse and interpret evidence of learning; give feedback to learners and support learners in self-assessment. Teachers should be supported in developing these skills through continuing professional development
Assessment for learning should be sensitive and constructive because any assessment has an emotional impact	Teachers should be aware of the impact that comments, marks and grades can have on learners' confidence and enthusiasm and be as constructive as possible in the feedback they give. Comments that focus on the work rather than the person are more constructive for learning and motivation
Assessment should take account of the importance of learner motivation	Assessment that encourages learning fosters motivation by emphasising progress and achievement rather than failure. Comparison with others who have been more successful is unlikely to motivate learners. It can also lead to their withdrawing from the learning process in areas where they have been made to feel they are 'no good'. Motivation can be preserved and enhanced by assessment methods which protect the learner's autonomy, provide some choice and constructive feedback, and create opportunity for self-direction
Assessment for learning should promote commitment to learning goals and a shared understanding of the criteria by which they are assessed	For effective learning to take place, learners need to understand what it is they are trying to achieve – and want to achieve it. Understanding and commitment follow when learners have some part in deciding goals and identifying criteria for assessing progress. Communicating assessment criteria involves discussing them with learners using terms they can understand, providing examples of how the criteria can be met in practice and engaging learners in peer- and self-assessment
Learners should receive constructive guidance about how to improve	Learners need information and guidance to plan the next steps in their learning. Teachers should: pinpoint the learner's strengths and advise on how to develop them; be clear and constructive about any weaknesses and how they might be addressed; provide opportunities for learners to improve upon their work
Assessment for learning develops learners' capacity for self-assessment so they can become reflective and self-managing	Independent learners have the ability to seek out and gain new skills, new knowledge and new understandings. They are able to engage in self-reflection and identify the next steps in their learning. Teachers should equip learners with the desire and capacity to take charge of their learning through developing the skills of self-assessment
Assessment for learning should recognise the full range of achievement of all learners	Assessment for learning should be used to enhance all learners' opportunities to learn in all areas of educational activity. It should enable all learners to achieve their best and have their efforts recognised

Adapted from ARG (2002)

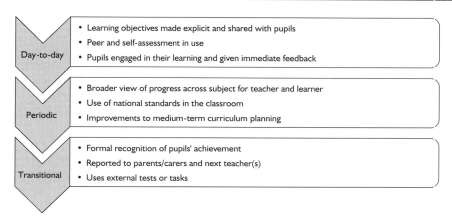

Figure 9.1 Key features of assessment for learning

help every child make good progress. To make assessment for learning more consistent, systematic and widespread, this strategy (ibid.: 4) has four major aims:

• *Every child* knows what they are doing, and understands what they need to do to improve and how to get there. They get the support they need to be motivated, independent learners on an ambitious trajectory of improvement.
• *Every teacher* is equipped to make well-founded judgements about pupils' attainment, understands the concepts and principles of progression, and knows how to use their assessment judgements to forward plan, particularly for pupils who are not fulfilling their potential.
• *Every school* has in place structured and systematic assessment systems for making regular, useful, manageable and accurate assessments of pupils, for tracking their progress.
• *Every parent and carer* knows how well their child is doing, what they need to do to improve, and how they can support the child and their teachers.

Key features of this strategic approach to assessment for learning are presented in Figure 9.1.

Personalised learning

The government in England launched *A National Conversation about Personalised Learning* (DfES, 2004k) in seeking to answer the following questions:

• How can we help every child do even better?
• What teaching practices should we employ to do so?
• How together can we solve the specific challenges faced in each school?

Personalised learning, viewed as the drive to tailor education to individual need, aptitude and interest to fulfil every young person's potential, was described by Milliband (ibid.: 4) as:

Reflective task 9.5 **Oral and written feedback to promote learning**

Oral and written feedback provide opportunities for you to identify pupils' strengths and give constructive guidance and advice on which areas pupils need to improve. Your comments should always be positive and encouraging, recognising pupils' efforts and achievements; and developmental by offering specific details of possible ways forward.

A: The main purposes for using oral feedback (DfES, 2004j: 12) are to:

- acknowledge what pupils have learned and encourage them to reflect on and extend their learning further;
- recognise that pupils need time to reflect on their learning;
- encourage pupils to pose further questions to clarify or further develop their own and each other's thinking;
- encourage pupils to make next steps.

Use a video camera or tape recorder to capture two or three lesson episodes involving oral feedback in your classroom. Use the quadrant in Figure 9.2 to analyse whether your use of oral feedback was mainly positive and specific or negative and non-specific.

Within your analysis, clarify what the feedback related to and to whom it was directed.

In light of your findings, identify aspects you would like to improve and record your next steps.

B: The main purposes for using written feedback (ibid.: 16–17) are to:

- selectively focus on the learning objectives;
- confirm that pupils are on the right track;
- stimulate the correction of errors or improvement of a piece of work;
- scaffold or support pupils' next steps;
- provide opportunities for pupils to think things through for themselves;
- comment on progress over a number of attempts;
- avoid comparisons with other pupils;
- provide pupils with the opportunity to respond.

Select a sample of five pieces of written feedback you have given which represents a range of pupil achievement within a class you teach. Analyse how the purposes identified above for using written feedback are reflected in your own practice (e.g. traffic light your use of feedback: red = rarely, amber = often, green = typically). Within your analysis, clarify what the feedback related to and to whom it was directed.

In light of your findings, identify aspects of written feedback you would like to improve and record your next steps.

C: Access and review: Hattie, P. and Timperley, H. (2007) The Power of Feedback, *Review of Educational Research*, 27 (1): 53–64. Consider how the findings reported in this article relate to your own current practice and identify strategies you can try out to improve future practice.

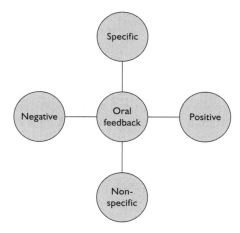

Figure 9.2 Analysing oral feedback

Reflective task 9.6 **The impact of assessment for learning in lessons**

- Download a copy of the *Assessment for Learning Strategy* (DCSF, 2008a) from www.teachernet.gov.uk/publications and review section 2 of Annex A (pages 16–18) which considers assessment for learning practice in lessons and its impact on the quality of learning and teaching.
- In relation to a specific class you teach, gauge the percentage of pupils who are at the *focusing, developing, establishing* or *enhancing* stage for the criteria identified. Undertake this same exercise in relation to criteria aligned to the teacher.
- Write a 1,500-word reflective narrative that explores the extent to which the quality of pupil learning is dependent upon the assessment for learning strategies used by the teacher.
- Discuss the key points of your argument with a critical friend.

High expectations of every child, given practical form by high quality teaching based on a sound knowledge of each child's needs. It is not individualised learning where pupils sit alone. Nor is it pupils left to their own devices – which too often reinforces low aspirations. It means shaping teaching around the way different youngsters learn; it means taking the care to nurture the unique talents of every pupil.

Although personalised learning was not a new initiative and many schools already tailored provision with exemplary outcomes, the drive to make the best practices universal and help all schools and teachers establish their own approaches to personalised learning, is how it was given a more wide-ranging focus and purpose. In setting out its vision of twenty-first-century schools, the Children's Plan recognised that developing personalised learning was critical in working toward a society where a child's chances of success were not limited by their socio-economic background, ethnicity, gender, or disability. Ofsted reports had revealed that children and young people from the most disadvantaged groups were the least likely to achieve well and participate in higher levels of education or training and a key imperative was to work with schools in developing workable strategies to narrow attainment gaps and raise achievement for all. Personalised learning was also an important strand of action in meeting the statutory equalities duties, as personalisation is a matter of both moral purpose and social justice. Five principles of personalised learning were identified (DfES, 2004k: 7) to help guide day-to-day practices, which for:

- *children and young people,* means clear learning pathways through the education system and the motivation to become independent, e-literate, fulfilled, lifelong learners;
- *schools,* means a professional ethos that accepts and assumes every child comes to the classroom with a different knowledge base and skill set, as well as varying aptitudes and aspirations; and as a result, there is a determination for every young person's needs to be assessed and their talents developed through diverse teaching strategies;
- *school governors,* means promoting high standards of educational achievement and well-being for every pupil, ensuring that all aspects of organising and running the school work well together to get the best for all pupils;
- *the DfES and local authorities,* means a responsibility to create the conditions in which teachers and schools have the flexibility and capability to personalise the experience of all their pupils; combined with a system of intelligent accountability so that central intervention is in inverse proportion to success;
- the *system as a whole,* means the shared goals of high quality and high equity.

The rationale behind these principles was to raise standards by focusing teaching and learning on the aptitudes and interests of pupils and removing any barriers to their learning. Based around five key components, a framework was designed for schools and teachers to employ contextually in response to the particular challenges they faced:

- assessment for learning
- effective teaching and learning strategies
- curriculum entitlement and choice
- school organisation
- strong partnership beyond the school.

Since 2004 this framework has been refined, *A Pedagogy of Personalised Learning* (DCSF, 2008b: 7) created and its distinguishing feature expressed as:

the way it expects all children and young people to reach or exceed national expectations, to fulfil their early promise and develop latent potential. Planning for progression and differentiation are fundamental. High expectations of progress apply equally to children and young people working above, at, or below age-related expectations, including those who have been identified as having special educational needs. There is an expectation of participation, fulfilment and success; and teaching and learning is characterised by ambitious objectives, challenging personal targets, rapid intervention to keep pupils on trajectory, and rigorous assessment to check and maintain pupil progress. There are clear plans to support those who are struggling to maintain trajectory.

Reflective task 9.7 **Personalised learning framework**

Access a copy of *A Pedagogy of Personalised Learning* (DCSF, 2008b) from www.teachernet.gov.uk/publications, which presents the following key features:

- High-quality teaching and learning
- Target setting and tracking
- Focused assessment
- Intervention
- Pupil grouping
- The learning environment
- Curriculum organisation
- The extended curriculum
- Supporting children's wider needs.

Consider these features in turn by familiarising yourself with the rationale behind each and examples provided of how to do them well. Investigate how these features are reflected within your own classroom and/or the wider context of your school. Select a class you are familiar with and reflect upon how you secure progression for all pupils over a series of lessons in which you cover a specific topic or unit of work. Identify the differentiated learning strategies you use for this purpose. Make notes of strategies that work effectively with pupils at varying levels of attainment and any barriers to learning experienced by particular pupils. Discuss these barriers with a mentor or professional tutor and consider ways in which they might be overcome. Think of other avenues you could pursue for guidance and advice (e.g. subject associations).

Set SMART targets to remove the barriers to learning experienced by your pupils.

This framework offers nine features that naturally link and overlap and which may provide a focus for school improvement planning and future developmental work.

The day-to-day interactions between you and your pupils provide the bedrock for the effective development of personalised learning. The major challenge for personalisation is in how to cater simultaneously for the different needs of a range of learners within one class.

Summary of key points

This chapter has traced the origins of inclusive education from discriminatory practices that segregated vulnerable children and young people from society on the basis of special educational needs and/or disabilities to the core messages embedded within Every Child Matters and the 2005 Disability Discrimination Act, recognising that all children and young people have a fundamental right to education and equal opportunity to learn. Key milestones in educational reform including the introduction and subsequent revisions to the National Curriculum in England are juxtaposed with major shifts in government policy and legislation for this purpose.

Developments leading to the introduction of the Assessment for Learning Strategy in 2008 have been explored along with their research-based principles to guide classroom practice and help every child make good progress and become an independent learner. A pedagogy of personalised learning, underpinned by the principles of progression, differentiation, relevance and assessment for learning and which aims to narrow the gaps in attainment and raise achievement for pupils by tailoring provision, has also been introduced. The key message is that you must design a range of teaching, learning and assessment experiences in light of the difference and diversity presented by your pupils, to ensure the principles of inclusion are enacted and the learning potential of all your pupils can be fully realised.

Recommended reading

Cheminais, R. (2006) *Every Child Matters: A Practical Guide for Teachers,* London: Fulton.
This text includes: an overview of the Every Child Matters Change for Children programme and its impact on schools and teachers in learning communities; how to access personalised learning opportunities for diverse learners; school self-evaluation, quality assurance and monitoring the Every Child Matters outcomes aligned to the Ofsted Inspection framework.

Office for Standards in Education (Ofsted) (2006a) *Inclusion: Does It Matter Where Pupils are Taught?* HMI Report 2535.
This survey examined factors that promote 'good' outcomes across a range of provision for pupils with learning difficulties and disabilities. It found effective provision was distributed equally between mainstream and special schools when certain factors were securely in place. It also found that more 'good' or 'outstanding' provision existed in resourced mainstream schools.

Zwozdiak-Myers, P. (ed) (2007) *Childhood and Youth Studies,* Exeter: Learning Matters.
This book is presented in four sections – 1: Social and cultural perspectives of childhood and youth; 2: Childhood and youth development (including chapters on the origins of human behaviour, social and emotional development, and cognitive development); 3: Difference, diversity and multidisciplinary perspectives (including chapters on children with special educational needs, and entitlement and potential); 4: Researching childhood and youth.

Chapter 10

Dimension 8

Enhance the quality of your own teaching

Learning objectives

In this chapter you will consider:

- how opportunities created for pupil learning are inextricably linked to the quality of teaching;
- variables and principles associated with effective teaching and learning including the growing impact of ICT;
- some key debates and theoretical positions concerning what constitutes pedagogic expertise and quality teaching from an international perspective;
- how to assess the quality of your own teaching in relation to the new Teachers' Standards (DfE, 2011) and Ofsted's (2008) criteria for 'outstanding' trainee teachers.

Introduction

The multifaceted nature of teaching and complex interrelationships between variables that can influence the quality of teaching to promote pupil learning signal a need to recognise that 'what teachers teach' is as important as 'how they teach' (Shulman, 1987). Not only must teachers acquire a range of knowledge bases (see Chapter 5) and models for teaching but importantly, must explore ways in which they can transform this knowledge into meaningful learning experiences for all their pupils within specific subject areas and across wider aspects of the curriculum in relation to short-, medium- and long-term objectives.

Assessment assumes great significance within this dimension and should provide information aligned to the implementation of specific teaching strategies and approaches about progression in pupil learning, and signpost whether misconceptions or gaps in learning are prevalent. This enables teachers to plan and structure appropriate teaching and learning strategies for subsequent lessons and gives rise to a natural feedback loop. Black, Harrison, Lee, Marshall and Wiliam (2003: 2) suggest an assessment activity can promote learning 'if it provides information to be used as feedback by teachers, and by their students in assessing themselves and each other, to modify the teaching and learning activities in which they are engaged. Such activity becomes formative assessment when the evidence is used to adapt the teaching work to meet learning needs'. Systematically reflecting on the outcomes of each lesson and searching for reasons as to why the learning or lack of learning occurred by examining the minutiae and constituent components of teaching (see Chapter 4) helps teachers to build on their knowledge bases and to make professional judgements from a more informed platform to enhance their pedagogic expertise.

In recent decades, teacher effectiveness research has identified a wealth of teacher behaviours and characteristics associated with the expert pedagogue alongside a range of other factors, which influence the quality of teaching. As Hargreaves (1999: vii) writes:

> We are beginning to recognise that for teachers, what goes on inside the classroom is closely related to what goes on outside it. The quality, range and flexibility of teachers' classroom work are closely tied up with their professional growth – with the way in which they develop as people and as professionals. Teachers teach in the way they do not just because of the skills they have or have not learned. The ways they teach are also rooted in their backgrounds, their biographies, and so in the kinds of teachers they have become. Their careers – their hopes and dreams, their opportunities and aspirations, or the frustrations of these things – are also important for teachers' commitment, enthusiasm and morale. So too are relationships with their colleagues – either as supportive communities who work together in pursuit of common goals and continuous improvement, or as individuals working in isolation, with the insecurities that sometimes brings.

This chapter begins by reviewing research studies on teacher effectiveness to identify variables that either directly or indirectly affect the quality of teaching. Key messages embedded within *Professionalism and Pedagogy* (Pollard, 2010), a timely commentary that aims to build a professional knowledge base concerning what explicitly constitutes effective teaching and learning by combining teacher expertise and research, are then explored. Against this backdrop, you are encouraged to draw on the outcome statements produced by the Department for Education (2011) to assess Teachers' Standards in England and criteria used by Ofsted (2008) to judge 'outstanding' trainee teachers to reflect upon and analyse the quality of your teaching more holistically and identify areas in need of further development.

Effective teaching research

Early research into effective teacher behaviour, effective teaching skills and generic features of effective teaching situated within the *process-product* paradigm, found effective teachers have a strong grasp of subject matter knowledge; high expectations of pupils and themselves; skills to balance pupils' intellectual achievement and interpersonal needs within the classroom; an ability to set high, realistic goals; and present information in an appropriate manner to facilitate pupil learning. They care about and have positive interactions with pupils; possess professional, interpersonal and intrapersonal knowledge; develop strong pupil–teacher relationships; and seek new solutions to problems they encounter through continuous learning (Brophy and Good, 1986; Clark and Peterson, 1986; Kyriacou, 1986; Wittrock, 1986; Wragg, 1984).

Galton's (1987) study involving secondary school teachers found that *class enquirers* generated the greatest gains in mathematics and language but not reading, whereas *individual monitors* made the least progress. More successful class enquirers used quadruple the time in whole-class interactive teaching than individual monitors and a positive (moderate) correlation was found between pupil progress and non-individualised interaction. This study also found whole-class interaction positively related to high levels of pupils' time on task, e.g. on average, class enquirers attracted 10 per cent more time on task for pupils than other teachers. Further analysis revealed not only correlations between high pupil task engagement and high levels of whole-class interaction but also high task engagement during lesson episodes when pupils worked independently (Croll and Moses, 1988).

The primary school study by Mortimore, Sammons, Stoll, Lewis and Ecob (1988) found similar characteristics of effective teachers at the classroom level:

*   a positive classroom atmosphere;
*   high levels of whole-class interaction;
*   teachers addressing one curriculum area at a time;
*   teachers assuming responsibility for ordering pupils activities' during the day, e.g. structured teaching;
*   teachers providing ample, challenging work;
*   pupils having some independence and responsibility for their work within working sessions;
*   high levels of pupil involvement in tasks;
*   teachers showing high levels of praise and encouragement.

In summary, classroom factors contributing to effective pupil outcomes were identified as: intellectually challenging teaching; structured sessions; communication between teachers and pupils; a limited focus within sessions; and a work-orientated environment.

Tizard, Blatchford, Burke, Farquar and Plewis (1988) found low teacher expectations of a sample of inner city pupils (with high expectations on the part of some teachers) correlated with curriculum and learning experiences, e.g. wide variation in curriculum coverage by different teachers affected pupils' progress: 46 per cent of the school day was devoted to classroom-based learning activities, of which only 61 per cent related to pupils' time on task. The ten-year *Louisiana School Effectiveness* study compared low socio-economic and high socio-economic status 'effective' schools and also identified some differences in approach and teaching strategies (Teddlie and Stringfield, 1993). Table 10.1 shows teacher behaviours that Borich (1996) suggests may be necessary to obtain high achievement gains in low as compared with middle socio-economic contexts. It is however important to recognise potential dangers in adopting specific teacher behaviours for different types of pupils based solely on socio-economic factors due, in part, to problems associated with reinforcing stereotypes and low expectations.

The *Mathematics Enhancement Project* (Muijs and Reynolds, 2001) involving 35 primary schools identified almost 60 different classroom teacher behaviours related to improvement in pupil performance across one year and concluded that many small correlations relate to pupil achievement rather than one specific type of teacher behaviour. This indicates that effective teaching is not necessarily equated with the capacity to do a small number of big things right but the capacity to do a large number

Table 10.1 Teacher behaviours in low and middle socio-economic classroom contexts

Low socio-economic context	Middle socio-economic context
Teacher behaviours that: • generate a warm and supportive climate by letting pupils know help is available • elicit a response (any response) before moving on to the next bit of material • present material in small bits, with a chance to practise before moving on • show how pieces fit together before moving on • use individual differentiated material • emphasise knowledge and applications before abstractions (putting the concrete first) • provide immediate help (e.g. use of peers) • generate strong structure and well planned transitions • use the experiences of pupils	Teacher behaviours that: • require extended reasoning • pose questions that require associations and generalisations • give conceptually difficult material • promote rich verbalising • use projects that require independent judgement, discovery, complex problem solving and use of original information • encourage learners to take responsibility for their own learning

of small things very well. This finding has resonance with conclusions drawn by Fraser (1989) in that no single factor is sufficient (or has an impact) on pupil learning by itself but a combination of factors must be optimised for improved learning when measured by cognitive gains.

School effectiveness research has shown significant statistical correlations between such pupil characteristics as age, English as an additional language, ethnicity, gender, socio-economic status and level of attainment (Gillborn and Mirza, 2000; Mortimore *et al.*, 1988; Strand, 2002; Thomas and Mortimore, 1996). This means that pupils from some backgrounds may appear to come to the classroom with an educational advantage or disadvantage. However, these findings do not apply to all children within certain groups (only to average differences) and caution must therefore be exercised to ensure that teachers do not have lower expectations of individual pupils. It is also well documented that children with poor educational attainment and low cognitive outcomes are likely to be at high risk of poor attendance and poor behaviour in school, low motivation and of becoming involved in antisocial or criminal activities later in life (Parsons and Bynner, 1998; Rutter, Maughan, Mortimore and Ousten, 1979). The connection between school effectiveness research and promoting equity in education has been reviewed by Sammons (1999). She argues that, in addition to cognitive measures, affective and social outcomes should also be studied with particular emphasis placed on the equity implications of ethnicity, gender and socio-economic status.

The *Variations in Teachers' Work, Lives and Effectiveness* (VITAE) project (Day, Stobart, Sammons, Kington, Gu, Smees and Mujtaba, 2006) reveals that the intake characteristics of different classes can differ widely, which means it is essential that pupil characteristics that show a statistically significant correlation with attainment are adjusted for before we compare teachers or schools in terms of their contribution to pupils' attainment and progress. In so doing, greater accuracy and a fair comparison of the impact of teachers who teach very different groups of pupils can be realised. Multilevel modelling has been suggested as one way to identify significant factors

> ### Reflective task 10.1 **Pupil characteristics and attainment**
>
> - Select a class of pupils you teach and capture characteristic ways in which they differ (e.g. attainment, ethnicity, gender, socio-economic status).
> - In relation to one specific curriculum or subject area, map out each pupil's level of attainment.
> - Is there a relationship between certain pupil characteristics and attainment level?
> - In what ways do you tailor your teacher behaviours and teaching strategies to help different pupils make progress?
> - Arrange to observe a professional colleague and undertake this same task – with either the same or a different class of pupils. Discuss ways in which your respective approaches to teaching are similar and/or different and which of these result in the greatest learning gains for different types of pupils.

and produce *value added* scores (residual) of teacher effectiveness that have been statistically adjusted to take them into account by controlling for intake influences. The framework of *input–process–output* has commonly been adopted for this purpose, and the importance of context particularly in relation to socio-economic status has been widely recognised (Hill and Rowe, 1996; Muijs, Harris, Chapman, Stoll and Russ, 2004; Sammons, West and Hind, 1997; Scheerens, 1995). The levels involved include: individual pupils, the classroom and the school.

The *Effective Pre-School and Primary Education 3–11 Project* (Sammons, Sylva, Melhuish, Siraj-Blatchford, Taggart, Barreau and Grobbe, 2008) revealed that the overall influence of teacher quality (in mathematics and reading outcomes) was stronger than the net influence of pupil background characteristics such as gender and social disadvantage. A calm, organised and positive climate; a rich variety of teaching methods; sensitivity to pupils; lack of teacher detachment; productive use of teaching time; and feedback to pupils, were found to be important teacher behaviours.

Research undertaken by Gentry, Steenbergen-Hu and Choi (2011) sought to capture pupils' perceptions of the qualities they associated with *exemplary teachers* and found that such teachers received high pupil ratings on the constructs of appeal, challenge, choice, enjoyment, interest, meaningfulness and self-efficacy. Consistent with findings from previous research, a synthesis of the emergent themes from this study shows that exemplary teachers have: a passion for content, pupils and teaching; high expectations of self and pupils; a sense of humour; are patient, impartial, respectful, caring and friendly; a depth of knowledge about and connections with pupils; an ability to engage pupils in meaningful learning and future planning; and a willingness to offer individual pupils help, challenges and choices (Mills, 2003; Roberts, 2006; Robinson, 2008). These findings reinforce the notion that multiple perspectives (see Chapter 7) should be considered when evaluating teacher quality, including pupil voice.

Muijs and Reynolds (2001) identified factors other than teacher behaviour related to pupil achievement, including teachers' subject knowledge, their self-efficacy and beliefs about teaching, which encouraged them to select teaching strategies they perceived as powerful determinants for improving pupils' attainment. A difference

---

Reflective task 10.2 **Pupils' perceptions of exemplary teachers**

Select a class you have been working with for at least 6 weeks and know well. During the last 10 minutes of a lesson, distribute a blank sheet of A5 paper to each pupil and ask them to:

- identify five qualities of a good teacher and explain why they feel each of these qualities is important;
- post their responses into a closed shoe box as they leave the lesson (to secure anonymity).

Analyse your pupils' responses and sort them into themes. Take each theme in turn and think about whether and/or how well these qualities are reflected in your own teaching.

If you teach more than one class, undertake this same exercise with different age groups and classes with diverse pupil characteristics to ascertain whether any similarities and differences or patterns and trends emerge.

Discuss the key points of your findings with a critical friend and consider how they might inform your own future practice.

---

of more than 20 mathematics 'points' resulted from being taught by the most as compared with the least effective teachers.

It is increasingly recognised within the practice of teaching that various knowledge components interact with affective and interpersonal elements; and teacher experience, work contexts and identity play important roles within this process (Acker, 1999; Hegarty, 2000; Woods, Jeffrey and Troman, 1997). It is also evident that events and experiences in the personal lives of teachers are intimately linked to perceptions of performance within their professional role (Ball and Goodson, 1985; Goodson and Hargreaves, 1996). In a study of primary teachers' working lives, Evans (1992) found that the situation-specific variables of headteacher behaviour and staff relationships directly influenced the teachers' morale, job satisfaction and motivation, which related strongly to their professional identities.

The research literature also shows that *commitment* has been found to be a predictor of teachers' attrition, burnout and performance as well as having an important influence on pupils' affective, behavioural, cognitive and social outcomes (Day, Elliot and Kington, 2005; Firestone, 1996; LeCompte and Dworkin, 1991). Teachers committed to their work have an enduring belief that they can make a difference to the achievements and learning lives of pupils (agency and efficacy) through who they are (their identity), what they know (their knowledge, skills, strategies) and how they teach (their attitudes, beliefs, personal and professional values embedded in and expressed through their behaviour in practice settings) (Ashton and Webb, 1986; Rosenholtz, 1989).

Commitment is both a cognitive (intellectual) and affective (emotional) endeavour. To sustain commitment involves the personal and professional investment of emotional labour, emotional understanding and intellectual energy (Denzin, 1984),

---

Reflective task 10.3 **The emotional practice of teaching**

To understand how emotions are located and represented in teachers' relationships with their pupils, Hargreaves (1998: 838) explores four interrelated points:

1   Teaching is an *emotional practice*
2   Teaching and learning involve *emotional understanding*
3   Teaching is a form of *emotional labour*
4   Teachers' emotions are inseparable from their *moral purposes* and their ability to achieve those purposes.

Consider how the key messages in this article are reflected within your own approach to teaching a particular group or class of pupils. Observe other teachers to capture how these same key messages are represented in their practice. Identify whether individual pupils, both in your own practice and that of others, seem to attract heightened frustration or tension in the classroom and consider what possible causes may underpin these reactions.

Write a 2,000-word reflective narrative on the following topic: 'Emotions are at the heart of teaching'.

The following sources provide a useful springboard for researching this area: Hochschild, A. (1993) *The Managed Heart: the commercialisation of human feeling*, Berkeley: University of California Press;Van Manen, M. (1991) *The Tact of Teaching: the meaning of pedagogical thoughtfulness*, Albany, NY: SUNY Press.

---

which requires resilience: the capacity to take a series of purposeful actions over time, 'often accompanied with emotional difficulties' and tremendous stress (Gordon, 1995) – emotional resilience to successfully grow and develop, particularly in the face of adverse circumstances. As Day *et al.* (2006) note, influential factors in teachers' professional life phases and identities may affect their commitment and resilience and in so doing, contribute to their effectiveness.

In response to limited empirically based knowledge concerning ways in which teacher effectiveness in the classroom grows and/or diminishes over the course of a career and within different contexts, the VITAE (Day *et al.*, 2006) project set out to analyse the nature of teacher *effectiveness* in depth by examining two dimensions:

1   perceived effectiveness – defined as the extent to which teachers believed they were able to do the job to the best of their ability – effectiveness was perceived both in cognitive and emotional ways;
2   in terms of pupil attainment, measured by *value added* pupil attainment data.

This research aimed to identify factors which contributed to these variations and why teachers do, or do not, become more effective over time. Core messages (ibid.: vi–vii) arising from this large-scale mixed method research study, involving 300 primary and secondary teachers from 100 schools, drawn from 7 local authorities across England, include the following:

Reflective task 10.4 **Professional identity**

Conduct a desktop search to explore the concept of teachers' professional identity and then respond to the following:

- How is your professional identity influenced and/or shaped by different degrees of tension experienced between your own educational ideals and aspirations, personal life experiences, the leadership and cultures within your school, pupils' behaviour and relationships and the impact of external policies on your work?
- In what ways does emotional resilience enable you to function effectively in adverse situations or circumstances?
- Discuss the major factors arising from searching your own professional identity with a critical friend.

- There are significant variations in both teachers' perceived and relative effectiveness across year groups and sectors. Teachers' capacities to be effective are influenced by variations in their work, lives and identities and their capacities to manage these.
- Teachers' effectiveness is not simply a consequence of age or experience.
- Teachers' sense of identity is a major contributing factor to their commitment and resilience. It is neither intrinsically stable nor unstable, but can be affected positively or negatively by different degrees of tension experienced between their own educational ideals and aspirations, personal life experiences, the leadership and cultures in their schools, pupils' behaviour and relationships and the impact of external policies on their work.
- Teachers who work in schools in more challenging socio-economic contexts are more likely to experience greater challenges to their health, well-being, and thus resilience, than those who work in relatively more advantaged schools.
- There is a statistically significant association between the levels of pupils' progress and attainment at Key Stages 1, 2 and 3 in English and mathematics, and the extent to which teachers sustain their commitment.

Pedagogic expertise

Over the years, a wealth of literature has emerged in the pursuit of trying to capture the essential ingredients of effective teaching. Hopkins (2002) for example identifies these as:

- teaching effects which encompass sets of teaching behaviours and skills;
- acquiring a repertoire of teaching models;
- artistry which is the creative aspect of teaching and involves the capacity to respond appropriately within the teaching situation and to reflect on practice.

Harris (1996) suggests the key dimensions of teaching skills that teachers should consider are:

- knowledge about the subject, curriculum teaching methods, influences on teaching and learning from other factors and knowledge about your own teaching;

- thinking and decision making which occurs before, during and after planning a lesson in relation to how pupils can achieve the intended educational outcomes;
- overt behaviour or action undertaken by teachers to foster and promote pupil learning.

The commentary presented by the Teaching and Learning Research Programme (TLRP) and the General Teaching Council for England (GTCE) in *Professionalism and Pedagogy* (Pollard, 2010: 5) offers a pedagogic rationale and conceptual framework for developing a more precise and holistic understanding of the nature of teacher expertise; and defines pedagogy as:

> the practice of teaching framed and informed by a shared and structured body of knowledge. This knowledge comprises: experience, evidence, understanding moral purpose and shared transparent values. It is by virtue of progressively acquiring such knowledge and mastering the expertise … that teachers are entitled to be treated as professionals.

The proposed construct reflects current national and international initiatives, which aim to build a professional knowledge base about what constitutes effective teaching and learning through combining teacher expertise and research. This framework has been presented to open up debate and support professional thinking and discussion to identify teacher expertise more explicitly and find ways to represent it more clearly. Figure 10.1 illustrates how *pedagogic expertise* (ibid.) has been captured and based around the complementary needs for collectively created knowledge (science), professional skills (craft) and personal capacities (art) grounded in ethical principles and moral commitment.

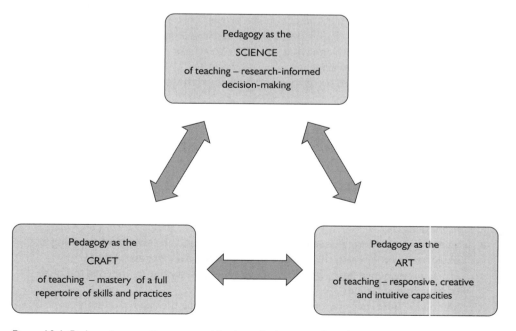

Figure 10.1 Pedagogic expertise as a combination of science, craft and art

The GTCE argues that teaching in the future must be based on the development of a pedagogic discourse, which arises from teachers sharing and scrutinising the practices and kinds of knowledge they build, and the values in which these are rooted. Furlong (2000: 13) explains: 'the theories they espouse ... have been justified and developed by being exposed to the critical scrutiny of other practitioners, whether they are based on a consideration of evidence from research ... whether they have been interrogated in terms of the values and assumptions on which they are based'. The TLRP distilled findings from 22 school-based research projects, consulted widely with practitioners and trawled findings from international research studies to produce *Ten Principles of Effective Teaching and Learning* (James and Pollard, 2006) as shown in Table 10.2. These aim to provide a valid educational rationale based on evidence-informed principles and a holistic view of factors that enhance learning. They are intended to inform professional judgement rather than dictate any particular course of action.

The conceptual framework presented in *Professionalism and Pedagogy* (Pollard, 2010) considers *educational aims, learning contexts, classroom processes* and *learning outcomes* in relation to *curriculum, pedagogy* and *assessment,* which gives rise to a 9 × 4 dimensional construct. Questions are posed within each cell of this construct to exemplify the high levels of reflective expertise that teachers need in order to make evidence-informed judgements.

Reflective task 10.5 **Exploring the principles of effective teaching and learning**

- Take each principle from Table 10.2 in turn and reflect upon the extent to which it is demonstrated in your own practice and/or the context of your school.
- How do these principles reflect those presented by the Assessment Reform Group in Table 9.2 (p. 138) in relation to Assessment for Learning?
- Are there any gaps between what you aspire to achieve with your pupils and what it is possible for you to achieve?
- What new insights have you gained and how could these be developed to improve your future practice?
- Discuss your ideas with a professional colleague and identify SMART targets to take your professional learning forward.

Reflective task 10.6 **Evidence informed judgements**

- Download a copy of *Professionalism and Pedagogy* (Pollard, 2010) from www.tlrp. org/findings.
- Select three 'enduring issues' of particular significance to your own teaching and explore how the research and case studies cited have addressed these.
- From this evidence base, what new ideas could you try out to improve the quality of your own practice?
- Identify SMART targets, try them out and evaluate their subsequent impact on pupil learning.

Table 10.2 Ten principles of effective teaching and learning

1	Equips learners for life in its broadest sense	Learning should aim to help people to develop the intellectual, personal and social resources that will enable them to participate as active citizens and workers and to flourish as individuals in a diverse and changing society. This implies a broad view of learning outcomes and that equity and social justice are taken seriously
2	Engages with valued forms of knowledge	Teaching and learning should engage with the big ideas, facts, processes, language and narratives of subjects so that learners understand what constitutes quality and standards in particular disciplines
3	Recognises the importance of prior experience and learning	Teaching should take account of what learners know already in order to plan their next steps. This means building on prior learning as well as taking account of the personal and cultural experiences of different groups
4	Requires the teacher to scaffold learning	Teachers should provide activities which support learners as they move forward, not just intellectually, but also socially and emotionally, so that once these supports are removed, the learning is secure
5	Needs assessment to be congruent with learning	Assessment should help to advance learning as well as to determine whether learning has taken place. It should be designed and carried out so that it measures learning outcomes in a dependable way and also provides feedback for future learning
6	Promotes the active engagement of the learner	A chief goal of teaching and learning should be the promotion of learners' independence and autonomy. This involves acquiring a repertoire of learning strategies and practices, developing a positive attitude towards learning, and confidence in oneself as a good learner
7	Fosters both individual and social processes and outcomes	Learning is a social activity. Learners should be encouraged to work with others, to share ideas and to build knowledge together. Consulting learners and giving them a voice is both an expectation and a right
8	Recognises the significance of informal learning	Informal learning, such as learning out of school, should be recognised as being at least as significant as formal learning and should be valued and used appropriately in formal processes
9	Depends on teacher learning	The importance of teachers learning continuously in order to develop their knowledge and skills, and adapt and develop their roles, especially through classroom enquiry, should be recognised and supported
10	Demands consistent policy frameworks with support for teaching and learning as their primary focus	Policies at national, local and institutional levels need to recognise the fundamental importance of teaching and learning. They should be designed to make sure everyone has access to learning environments in which they can thrive

---

Reflective task 10.7 **Variables associated with teacher quality**

- Create a mind map to capture the major variables associated with teacher quality and annotate it with examples drawn from your own experience of teaching a particular class or group of pupils – you can build on that shown in Figure 10.2.
- Write a 2,000-word reflective narrative in response to the following claim: 'To measure the quality of teaching solely in terms of pupils' academic attainment presents a narrow view of what we understand by teacher quality and effective teaching'.
- Discuss the main points of your argument with a critical friend.

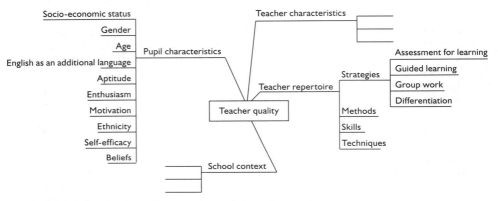

Figure 10.2 Mind map of variables associated with teacher quality

International perspective of quality teaching

The *Teachers Matter: Attracting, Developing and Retaining Effective Teachers* (OECD, 2005) report draws on the results of a major study of teacher policy conducted over the 2002–2004 period in collaboration with 25 countries around the world, including the United Kingdom. This report recognises the professional development of teachers as a key policy lever, as does the McKinsey Report *How the World's Best Performing School Systems Come Out On Top* (Barber and Mourshed, 2007: 13), which has influenced policymakers worldwide and states 'the quality of an education system cannot exceed the quality of its teachers' and the 'only way to improve outcomes is to improve instruction'. These reports recommend countries to have clear and concise statements of what teachers are expected to know and be able to do; and further, that teacher profiles should be embedded throughout the school and teacher education systems. Box 10.1 presents some findings from the OECD's international analysis in relation to quality teaching for improving pupil (student) learning, and Box 10.2 identifies ways in which twenty-first-century teachers' roles and responsibilities are perceived to be changing on four levels.

The overarching message from this report is that the quality of teaching is determined not just by the 'quality' of the teachers, although clearly this is critical, but also by the environment in which they work. Capable teachers are not necessarily going to

Box 10.1 **Quality teaching is vital for improving student learning (OECD, 2005: 2)**

Student learning is influenced by many factors, including: students' skills, expectations, motivation and behaviour; family resources, attitudes and support; peer group skills, attitudes and behaviour; school organisation, resources and climate; curriculum structure and content; and teacher skills, knowledge, attitudes and practices. Schools and classrooms are complex, dynamic environments, and identifying the effects of these varied factors, and how they influence and relate with each other – for different types of students and different types of learning – has been, and continues to be, a major focus of educational research.

Three broad conclusions emerge from research on student learning. The first and most solidly based finding is that the largest source of variation in student learning is attributable to differences in what students bring to school – their abilities and attitudes, and family and community background.

The second broad conclusion is that factors to do with teachers and teaching are the most important influences on student learning; in particular, the broad consensus is that 'teacher quality' is the single most important school variable influencing student achievement.

The third broad conclusion from the research, which is somewhat more contentious, concerns the indicators or correlates of teacher quality. Most of the research has examined the relationship between measures of student performance, most commonly standardised test scores, and readily measurable teacher characteristics such as qualifications, teaching experience, and indicators of academic ability or subject matter knowledge. Such research generally indicates that there is a positive relationship between these measured teacher characteristics and student performance, but perhaps to a lesser extent than may have been expected. A point of agreement among the various studies is that there are many important aspects of teacher quality that are not captured by the commonly used indicators such as qualifications, experience and tests of academic ability. The teacher characteristics that are harder to measure, but which can be vital to student learning, include the ability to convey ideas in clear and convincing ways; to create effective learning environments for different types of students; to foster productive teacher–student relationships; to be enthusiastic and creative; and to work effectively with colleagues and parents.

reach their potential in settings which do not provide appropriate support or sufficient challenge and reward. Although teachers were found to be highly motivated by the intrinsic benefits of teaching, e.g. working with children and young people, helping them to develop and making a contribution to society, system structures and school workplaces must enable teachers to focus on these tasks.

Growing impact of ICT

In building on the OECD (2005) report, the *Teacher Education in Europe Policy Paper* (ETUCE, 2008: 59) notes that Information Communication Technology (ICT) is

Box 10.2 **Teachers' roles are changing (OECD, 2005: 3)**

Teachers are now expected to have much broader roles, taking into account the individual development of children and young people, the management of learning processes in the classroom, the development of the entire school as a 'learning community' and connections with the local community and the wider world. Some examples of areas of broadened teacher responsibility are as follows:

- At the individual student level:
  - Initiating and managing learning processes
  - Responding effectively to the learning needs of individual learners
  - Integrating formative and summative assessment.
- At the classroom level:
  - Teaching in multi-cultural classrooms
  - New cross-curricular emphases
  - Integrating students with special needs.
- At the school level:
  - Working and planning in teams
  - Evaluation and systematic improvement planning
  - ICT use in teaching and administration
  - Management and shared leadership.
- At the level of parents and the wider community:
  - Providing professional advice to parents
  - Building community partnerships for learning.

becoming a major factor in current societies, and is an unavoidable aspect of daily life particularly for children and young people. It stresses the need for teachers to be aware of the growing impact of ICT, to make creative use of the opportunities offered and to be critical of limitations. A European Union survey (Empirica, 2006) reports that over 95 per cent of classroom teachers use computers to prepare lessons and 74 per cent also use them as a teaching aid, although differences between countries ranged from 95 per cent in the United Kingdom to 35 and 36 per cent in Greece and Latvia, respectively. The survey did not however reveal information about the extent to which ICT was used for specific pedagogical purposes.

In England, the government's aspiration to build a twenty-first-century school system based on excellent teaching to raise standards of education across the country, places the role of ICT firmly at the heart of teaching and learning. Byron (2008) not only recognises the advantages of new technologies and the confidence and ease with which children and young people use them, but also notes disadvantages when children and young people do not have the knowledge, skills and understanding necessary to keep themselves safe. She highlights the need for Government to empower children and raise the skills of parents by delivering Internet safety (e-safety) through the curriculum and by providing teachers and the wider children's workforce with the knowledge and skills they need. In their small-scale survey of 35 maintained schools, Ofsted (2010: 7) reports:

Reflective task 10.8 **Improving pedagogical ICT capability**

In a study involving ICT Advanced Skills Teachers, consultants and university lecturers (Zwozdiak-Myers and Audain, 2011) five core principles that underpin effective ICT practice were identified and captured within the acronym to SHARE (e.g. Safety, Harness, Audit, Reflect, Excellence).

- Download a copy of the guidance booklet, which has been designed to support you in developing teaching and learning with and through ICT, from the Training and Development Agency for Schools (TDA) website: www.tda.gov.uk.
- Assess and review your current use of technology against the checklist provided in the Appendix and identify any actions you feel you should be undertaking *more routinely* in your practice and/or actions you feel you *could tackle* with support from a professional colleague or particular resources.
- Set yourself three SMART targets to further develop and improve your capacity to use ICT effectively in your teaching.

New technologies are central to modern life. They enable people across the world to have instant communication with one another. They allow for the rapid retrieval and collation of information from a wide range of sources, and provide a powerful stimulus for creativity. They allow people to discuss sensitive topics which, face to face, they might find difficult. However, these technologies are also potentially damaging. They can give access to harmful and inappropriate materials and, because of the anonymity offered, vulnerable individuals may be harmed or exploited.

All children and young people are unique and, as *digital natives* (Bennett, Maton and Kervin, 2008), bring a vast array of ICT knowledge and skills to the classroom. Teachers who are responsive to a wide range of difference and diversity, and who can support each child and young person to effectively use ICT tools and technologies by personalising provision, are more likely to enable their learners to become independent, self-directed and achieve their full potential in a safe and responsible manner. While the knowledge, skills, understanding and experience each of you brings to your teaching will be different and might well range from: *familiarisation, utilisation, integration, reorientation* to *evolution* on Hooper and Reiber's (1995) scale of *e-maturity*, the rapid advances continually being made in ICT signal the need for each of you to also think of yourselves as a learner.

Criteria to judge teacher quality

Reynolds (1995) suggests the *touchstone* criteria for evaluating different educational policies or practices should be their impact on pupil learning outcomes. The choice of these outcomes is particularly important, as they become the criteria for judging school and teacher effectiveness. He cautions, however, as does the OECD (2005) report, that to focus on a narrow range of outcomes which take no account of pupil and teacher background, individual/collective efficacy, motivation, or cultural, economic, organisational and social contexts, provides only partial indicators of quality teaching.

The new Teachers' Standards (DfE, 2011), which apply to all teachers in England regardless of career stage, take effect from 1 September 2012 and replace the existing standards for Qualified Teacher Status (QTS) and Core professional standards for practising teachers. The government has proposed that teachers' performance will be assessed against the standards as part of new performance management arrangements for schools. The Secretary of State for Education (ibid.: 2–3) explains that these standards set out:

> a basic framework within which all teachers should operate from the point of initial qualification onwards. Appropriate self-evaluation, reflection and professional development activity is critical to improving teachers' practice at all career stages. The standards set out clearly the key areas in which a teacher should be able to assess his or her own practice, and receive feedback from colleagues. As their careers progress, teachers will be expected to extend the depth and breadth of knowledge, skill and understanding that they demonstrate in meeting the standards, as is judged to be appropriate to the role they are fulfilling and the context in which they are working.

These standards are presented in Appendix A: the Preamble summarises the behaviour and values all teachers must demonstrate throughout their career; Part 1 comprises the Standards for Teaching, and Part 2 the Standards for Personal and Professional Conduct (replacing the GTCE's Code of Conduct and Practice for Registered Teachers). To meet the standards, a trainee or teacher must demonstrate their practice is consistent with the

---

Reflective task 10.9 **Assessing the quality of your teaching**

- Take each of the new Teachers' Standards (DfE, 2011) in turn (see Appendix A) and reflect upon the extent to which you are currently able to demonstrate these in your own practice. Gather a range of evidence (three pieces per standard) to exemplify those you have met, are improving or working towards (e.g. interim report or feedback from mentor/colleague following a lesson observation, pupils' perceptions and/or attainment data, video footage of a teaching episode, lesson plan to show differentiated learning objectives, tasks, resources or how to use support staff within the classroom) and collate this evidence into a Best Evidence folder.
- Review the Ofsted descriptors for 'outstanding' trainee teachers (see Appendix B) and assess your progress toward meeting each one of these using the 4-point scale: *not at all, sometimes, often, most of the time.* As above, find a range of evidence to track your progress in relation to each descriptor.
- Identify aspects of your teaching you consider to be particular strengths at this stage of your career and those in need of further development.
- Discuss personal development priorities and opportunities with your mentor and/or professional tutor and devise a plan of action to take your professional learning forward.

definition set out in the Preamble, and that they have met the standards in Parts 1 and 2. The bulleted sub-headings are designed to amplify the scope of each standard and can be used to assess and track progress against each standard, to determine areas where additional development might need to be observed, or areas where excellent practice is already being demonstrated.

For inspection purposes, Ofsted (2008) grade aspects of trainee teachers' performance (as outstanding, good, satisfactory or inadequate) in four key areas: in lessons, their explanations, noticeable characteristics and their files. The criteria aligned to 'outstanding' trainee teachers in each of these areas are presented in Appendix B.

Summary of key points

Teaching is a demanding profession that requires a complex matrix of knowledge, skills and understanding to judge which strategies are most appropriate in accommodating the needs of different groups of learners and each individual learner. Society now expects schools to: deal effectively with different languages and pupil backgrounds; be sensitive to culture and gender issues; promote tolerance and social cohesion; respond effectively to disadvantaged pupils and pupils with learning or behavioural problems; use new technologies; and keep pace with rapidly developing fields of knowledge and approaches to pupil assessment. Teachers need to be capable of preparing pupils for a society and economy in which they are increasingly expected to become self-directed learners, able and motivated to keep learning over a lifetime.

The complex nature of teaching requires teachers to build a range of knowledge bases they can draw upon and relate to their own practice. Building integrated knowledge bases requires an active approach to learning that leads to understanding and linking new to existing knowledge. Moon (1999) presents the view that learners approach their studies with a cognitive structure, a flexible network of ideas and knowledge, shaped by prior learning. This cognitive structure provides the framework within which teachers locate new ideas, and will, if deep learning is to occur, be challenged and modified in the process. The euphemism *transformative learning* describes situations where teachers are prepared to abandon preconceptions and re-examine their fundamental assumptions about themselves, the subject matter and the nature of knowledge.

To that end, this chapter has explored a range of literary sources and research studies to capture the principles and variables associated with effective teaching and learning, including the growing impact of ICT. It has also encouraged you to engage in discourse and debate about what constitutes pedagogic expertise from a research-informed evidence base and what constitutes quality teaching from an international perspective. Two frameworks have been introduced (the new Teachers' Standards (DfE, 2011) and criteria used by Ofsted (2008) for grading 'outstanding' trainee teachers), which enable you to reflect upon aspects of your own teaching you consider to be personal strengths and identify those in need of further development as you enhance the quality of your own teaching.

Recommended reading

European Trade Union Committee for Education (ETUCE) (2008) *Teacher Education in Europe: An ETUCE Policy Paper*, Brussels: ETUCE.

This policy paper presents the ETUCE's vision of teacher education in the twenty-first century. Chapter 7 addresses specific challenges facing teachers in the multicultural and knowledge-based society of today and includes sections on changing family patterns, social factors, economy and technology, equity in learning, interactive education and education for diversity.

Kelchtermans, G. (2009) Who I am in how I teach is the message: self-understanding, vulnerability and reflection, *Teachers and Teaching: Theory and Practice,* 15 (2): 257–272.
Inspired by research into teacher thinking and the narrative-biographical approach to teaching and teacher development, the author argues that the person of the teacher is an essential element in what constitutes professional teaching; and the 'scholarship of teachers' is fundamentally characterised by personal commitment and vulnerability, which have consequences for the kind of reflective attitudes and skills professional teachers should master.

Rodgers, C. and Raider-Roth, M. (2006) Presence in teaching, *Teachers and Teaching: Theory and Practice,* 12 (3): 265–287.
This article articulates a theory of 'presence' in teaching, which has been defined as a state of alert awareness, receptivity, and connectedness to the mental, emotional and physical workings of both the individual and the group in the context of their learning environments, and the ability to respond with a considered and compassionate best next step. The authors seek to address the current educational climate that sees teaching as a checklist of behaviours, dispositions, measures and standards, and to capture the elusive aspect of teaching they call presence.

Timmering, L., Snoek, M. and Dietze, A. (2009) *How do teachers in Europe identify teacher quality?* Paper presented at the Association for Teacher Education in Europe (ATEE) Annual Conference, Mallorca, August.
This paper shares some findings that emerged from a three-year international research project that sought to Identify Teacher Quality (ITQ) characteristics and indicators, and which involved 21 institutions from 12 European countries. A reflective toolbox that emerged from the intensive in-service Socrates programme, Comenius 2.1 Course (NL-2008-171-001) is available online at www.teacherqualitytoolbox.eu.

Chapter 11

Dimension 9

Continue to improve your own teaching

Learning objectives

In this chapter you will consider:

* the key competencies embedded within the *Organisation for Economic Cooperation and Development* (OECD) framework (2003);
* core characteristics of professional learning communities and how communities of practice and online social networks can support teacher learning;
* what research tells us about the essential features of effective CPD;
* how to create a well-structured Professional Development Portfolio to evidence your on-going growth and development as a teacher.

Introduction

There is widespread agreement that initial teacher education cannot provide prospective teachers with all the knowledge, skills and understanding required to handle various tasks and to meet the strong demands of educational reform and social change throughout their professional career (AGQTP, 2008; Barber and Mourshed, 2007). Becoming a teacher is increasingly acknowledged to be a developmental, gradual process, which means that 'teacher education must be seen as a career-long process placed within the context of lifelong learning' (OECD, 2005: 44). The *European Trade Union Committee for Education* (ETUCE, 2008) stresses that the development of new skills, initiatives, teaching methods and ways of working require practice, feedback and training *in situ* as well as time available outside the classroom.

Over the past decade, a number of major trends have taken a central role in the classroom and transformed aspects of the curriculum, e.g. awareness of global issues, living in multi-cultural societies, issues of gender and sexuality, as well as the numerous learning opportunities opened up by rapid advances in Information and Communication Technology. As educators, we need to be able to respond to several fundamental questions including: What demands does today's society place on its citizens? What competencies do individuals need to find and to hold down a job? What kind of adaptive qualities are required to cope with changing technology?

To enable capacity building within the personal, interpersonal and organisational structures of twenty-first-century schools, the *Australian Government Quality Teacher Programme* (2008: 7) reports that teachers 'should be empowered to pursue and apply new knowledge in an environment that supports professional risk taking'. In turn, this has potential to generate knowledge, be transformative and build the capacity of teachers 'to assess progress and effectiveness' (Phillips, 2007: 395). The OECD (2005: 47) reports a growing interest in ways 'to build cumulative knowledge across the profession by strengthening the connections between research and practice and encouraging schools to develop as learning organisations'. Professor Dinham (AGQTP, 2008: 7) notes that encouraging outcomes of the learning communities he witnessed in action were the extent to which 'dialogue and innovation around quality teaching and learning have emerged and reinvigorated jaded mid to late career teachers' and the degree to which 'latent leadership potential has emerged and, in turn, facilitated further change and improvement in the groups, faculties and schools concerned'. Research has also shown that through working collaboratively with peers and experts in *communities of practice* (Wenger, McDermott and Snyder, 2002), professionals can contribute to the co-construction of new knowledge and ideas (Bolam and Weindling, 2006; Leask and Younie, 2001; Pickering, Daly and Pachler, 2007).

These trends illuminate that continuing professional development (CPD), which lies at the core of this dimension needs to be built into a teacher's career trajectory from the outset. In England, the career entry and development profile (CEDP) provides an important bridge between initial teacher education and the newly qualified teacher (NQT) induction year and forms the basis for performance management and the review and appraisal of teachers and headteachers on the basis of an annual cycle.

This chapter presents an international perspective of the key competencies that young people and adults need to develop in order to prepare for life's challenges in the modern world. It explores the core characteristics of a professional learning community and how the policies and practices of professional development in some high-achieving countries have transformed the way in which teachers learn, particularly in terms of communities of practice and online social networks. Informed by research, the key components of effective CPD are then introduced. Against this backdrop, you are encouraged to reflect upon your current priorities and developmental needs and to create a Professional Development Portfolio (PDP) in which you can exemplify progress and accomplishments related to short-, medium- and long-term personal goals and aspirations.

OECD's (2003) perspective on key competencies for the modern world

Globalisation and modernisation are creating an increasingly diverse and interconnected world. To make sense of and function well in this world, individuals need to master changing technologies and make sense of large amounts of available information. They also face collective challenges as societies, such as balancing economic growth with environmental sustainability, and prosperity with social equity. Within these contexts, the competencies individuals need to meet their goals have become more complex and require more than the mastery of certain narrowly defined skills. A competence involves the ability to meet complex demands by drawing on and mobilising psychosocial resources (including skills and attitudes) within a particular context. The ability to communicate effectively for example is a competence that may draw on an individual's knowledge of language, practical ICT skills and attitudes toward those with whom he is communicating. Individuals need to draw on a range of appropriate competencies, which enable them to adapt to a world characterised by change, complexity and interdependence as:

- Technology is changing rapidly and continuously, and learning to deal with it requires not just one-off mastery of processes but also adaptability.
- Societies are becoming more diverse and compartmentalised, with interpersonal relationships therefore requiring more contact with those who are different from oneself.
- Globalisation is creating new forms of interdependence, and actions are subject both to influences (such as economic competition) and consequences (such as pollution) that stretch well beyond an individual's local or national community.

(OECD, 2003: 7)

In recent decades, international surveys have been measuring the degree to which young people and adults have the knowledge and skills they need to face life's challenges, e.g. the Programme for International Student Assessment (PISA) and the Adult Literacy and Life Skills Survey (ALL) allow the outcomes of learning to be compared across national cultures. In 1997, OECD member countries launched the PISA with the aim of monitoring the extent to which pupils near the end of compulsory schooling have acquired the knowledge and skills essential for full participation in society. Many scholars and experts agree that coping with today's challenges calls for better development of individuals' abilities to tackle complex mental tasks, going well beyond the basic reproduction of accumulated knowledge. PISA assessments began with comparing pupils' knowledge and skills in the subject areas of reading, mathematics, science and problem solving with the caveat that pupils' success in life depends on a much wider range of competencies.

The OECD's Definition and Selection of Competencies (DeSeCo) Project, which spanned 1997 through 2003 (Rychen and Salganik, 2003), was designed to bring a wide range of existing research and expert opinion together to produce a coherent and widely shared analysis of which key competencies are necessary for the modern world. In so doing, it sought to improve the assessments of how well prepared young people and adults are for life's challenges, as well as identify overarching goals for education systems and lifelong learning.

The competencies identified by the DeSeCo Project are presented in three broad categories, as illustrated in Figure 11.1, which are interrelated and collectively form a basis for identifying and mapping key competencies. The need for individuals to think and act reflectively is central to this framework and involves not only the ability to apply a formula or method for confronting a situation routinely, but also importantly the ability to deal with change, learn from experience and to think and act with a critical stance.

1: Use tools interactively

a   *The ability to use language, symbols and text interactively* concerns the effective use of spoken and written language skills, computation and other mathematical skills,

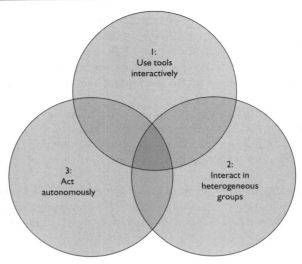

Figure 11.1 Conceptual framework for key competencies

in multiple situations. It is an essential tool for functioning well in society and the workplace and participating in effective dialogue with others. Terms such as 'communication competence' or 'literacies' are associated with this key competence.

b   *The ability to use knowledge and information interactively* requires critical reflection on the nature of the information itself – its technical infrastructure and social, cultural and ideological context and impact. Information competence is necessary as a basis for understanding options, forming opinions, making decisions, and carrying out informed and responsible actions, which requires individuals to:
 – recognise and determine what is not known;
 – identify, locate and access appropriate information sources (e.g. assembling knowledge and information in cyberspace);
 – evaluate the quality, appropriateness and value of that information, as well as its sources;
 – organise knowledge and information.

c   *The ability to use technology interactively* requires an awareness of new ways in which individuals can use technologies in their daily lives. ICT has the potential to transform the way people work together (reducing the importance of location), access information (making vast amounts of information sources instantly available) and interact with others (facilitating relationships and networks of people from around the world on a regular basis). To harness such potential, individuals need to go beyond the basic technical skills needed to simply use the Internet or send emails and relate the possibilities embedded within technological tools to their personal circumstances and goals.

2: Interact in heterogeneous groups

a   *The ability to relate well to others* assumes that individuals are able to respect and appreciate the values, beliefs, cultures and histories of others in order to create an environment where they feel welcome, are included and thrive, which requires:

- empathy – taking the role of the other person and imagining the situation from his perspective. This leads to self-reflection, when, upon considering a wide range of opinions and beliefs, individuals recognise that what they take for granted in a situation is not necessarily shared by others;
- effective management of emotions – being self-aware and able to effectively interpret one's underlying emotional and motivational states and those of others.

b *The ability to cooperate* – individuals must be able to balance commitment to the group and its goals with their own priorities, share leadership and support others, which requires:
- the ability to present ideas and listen to those of others;
- an understanding of the dynamics of debate and following an agenda;
- the ability to construct tactical and sustainable alliances;
- the ability to negotiate;
- the capacity to make decisions that allow for different shades of opinion.

c *The ability to manage and resolve conflicts* – conflict occurs in all aspects of life and is an inherent part of human relationships. The key to approaching conflict in a constructive manner is to recognise that it is a process to be managed rather than seeking to negate it, which requires consideration of the interests and needs of others and solutions wherein both sides gain. To take an active part in conflict management and resolution, individuals must be able to:
- analyse the issues and interests at stake (e.g. power, recognition of merit, division of work, equity), the origins of the conflict and the reasoning of all sides, recognising there are different possible positions;
- identify areas of agreement and disagreement;
- reframe the problem;
- prioritise needs and goals, deciding what they are willing to give up and under what circumstances.

3: Act autonomously

a *The ability to act within the big picture* requires individuals to understand and consider the wider context of their actions and decisions; to take account of how they relate, for example, to society's norms, social and economic institutions and what has happened in the past, which requires individuals to:
- understand patterns;
- have an idea of the system in which they exist (e.g. understand its structure, culture, practices, formal and informal rules and expectations, and the roles they play within it) including understanding laws and regulations; and unwritten social norms, moral codes, manners and protocol;
- identify the direct and indirect consequences of their actions;
- choose between different courses of action by reflecting on their potential consequences in relation to individual and shared norms and goals.

b *The ability to form and conduct life plans and personal projects* applies the concept of project management to individuals and requires them to interpret life as an organised narrative, to give it meaning and purpose in a changing environment where life is often fragmented. It assumes an orientation toward the future, implying both optimism and potential; and also a firm grounding within the realm of what is feasible, which requires individuals to:

- define a project and set a goal;
- identify and evaluate the resources to which they have access and those they need (e.g. time and money);
- prioritise and refine goals;
- balance the resources needed to meet multiple goals;
- learn from past actions, projecting future outcomes;
- monitor progress, making necessary adjustments as a project unfolds.

c *The ability to assert rights, interests, limits and needs* – on the one hand, this competence relates to self-orientated rights and needs; and on the other, to the rights and needs of the individual as a member of the collective (e.g. actively participating in democratic institutions and in local and national processes), which implies the ability to:

- understand one's own interests;
- know written rules and principles on which to base a case;
- construct arguments in order to have needs and rights recognised;
- suggest arrangements or alternative solutions.

The framework described here relates to individual competencies, rather than to the collective capacities of organisations or groups. However, as illustrated in Figure 11.2, the sum of individual competencies also affects the ability to achieve shared goals.

Insofar as competencies are needed to help accomplish collective goals, the selection of key competencies needs to be informed by an understanding of shared values. This framework is anchored in such values at a general level as all OECD societies agree on the importance of democratic values and achieving sustainable development. These values imply that individuals should both be able to achieve their potential, and respect

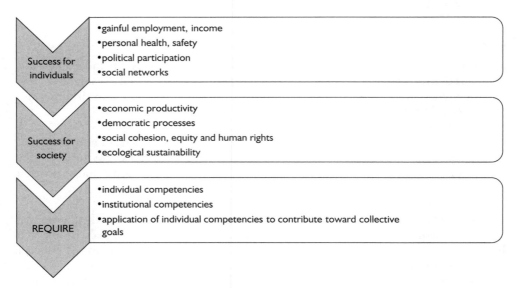

Figure 11.2 Individual and collective goals and competencies

others and contribute to producing an equitable society. In most OECD countries, value is placed on flexibility, entrepreneurship and personal responsibility. Individuals are expected not only to be adaptive, but also innovative, creative, self-directed and self-motivated. These demands place varied requirements on individuals in different places and different situations.

At the centre of the framework is the ability of individuals to think for themselves as an expression of moral and intellectual maturity, and to take responsibility for their learning and for their actions. Human capital not only plays a critical role in economic performance but also brings important individual and social benefits such as better health, improved well-being, and increased social and political engagement.

The framework applies equally to the competencies that need to be nurtured at school and those that can be developed throughout the course of life. Central to the concept of *lifelong learning* is the assertion that not all of life-relevant competencies can be provided by initial education, and an evolutionary model of human development provides a theoretical foundation for the purpose of adult education, as:

- Developmental psychology shows that competence development does not end at adolescence but continues through the adult years. In particular, the ability to think and act reflectively, central to the framework, grows with maturity;
- Competencies develop and change throughout the lifespan, with the possibility of acquiring or losing competence as one grows older;
- The demands on individuals can be expected to change throughout their adult lives as a result of transformations in technology and in social and economic structures.

Reflective task 11.1 **Improving personal competencies**

- Select three key competencies from the DeSeCo framework (above) of significance to your own professional development and interrogate ways in which you currently demonstrate each competence.
- Examine the ways in which three of your peers or colleagues demonstrate each of these competencies (e.g. this might involve discussion and/or peer observation followed by discussion).
- Seek out and engage in professional development opportunities that will enable you to learn more about each of these competencies.
- Consider ways in which you can incorporate new ideas associated with each competence to improve your teaching, try them out and critically evaluate their impact on pupil learning (both intended and unintended outcomes).

Reflective task 11.2 **Critical review of the DeSeCo framework**

- Write a 2,000-word reflective narrative on the extent to which you believe the DeSeCo framework of key competencies are appropriate in preparing you for the challenges of working within the context of twenty-first-century schools.
- Discuss the main points of your argument with a critical friend.

Professional learning communities

A professional learning community can be viewed as an extended learning opportunity that aims to promote collaborative learning amongst colleagues working within a particular field of study or environment. It is commonly used in schools to integrate people from the community with those in school to enhance curriculum planning and pupil learning or to organise teachers into specific working groups. A professional learning community has been described as: 'a shared vision or running a school in which everyone can make a contribution, and staff are encouraged to collectively undertake activities and reflection in order to constantly improve their students' performance' (Ministry of Education, 2005). Dufour (2004) attributes a number of core characteristics to effective professional learning communities including:

- Shared vision and shared values lead to the collective commitment of school staff as expressed within their day-to-day practices;
- Teams work collaboratively and cooperatively to achieve common goals;
- Experimentation is actively encouraged and viewed as an opportunity to learn;
- As solutions are sought, school staff are receptive to new ideas;
- The status quo is questioned which leads to the on-going pursuit of improvement and professional learning;
- Improvement is based on evaluating the impact of outcomes;
- Reflective activity underpins both individual and community growth.

In commenting on the practice of shared vision, Senge (1990: 9) suggests this incorporates such skills as 'unearthing shared "pictures of the future" that foster genuine commitment and enrolment rather than compliance. In mastering this discipline, leaders learn the counter-productiveness of trying to dictate a vision, no matter how heartfelt', which reinforces Fullan's (1999) argument that 'top-down mandates' and 'bottom-up energies' need each other. This requires a shift from the more traditional leadership role to one of shared or distributed leadership where head teachers 'lead from the centre rather than the top' (Dufour and Eaker, 1998).

The benefits to educators and pupils derived from working as professional learning communities include: reduced isolation of teachers; academic gains for pupils; more committed and better informed teachers (Hord, 1997). As teachers improve and experience success they come to recognise the collective capability of the community as a site of learning: 'where one person's knowledge ends and another begins is not always clear ... Thus we tend to think of knowledge less as an assembly of discrete parts and more like a watercolor painting. As each new color is added, it blends with the others' (Brown and Duguid, 2000: 16). Much knowledge within a professional learning community is tacit, created by doing, and distributed throughout the community. One individual may, for example, be able to do much that the community needs yet not be able to articulate this, and no one individual will know what the community knows as a whole. Knowing, in the form of expectations and dispositions, information, skills and rules, is an emergent property of the community, which is 'partly explicit and partly outside consciousness' (Knight, 2002: 232). Professional learning communities can help to convert theory into practice by bridging the gap between knowing *how* (tacit knowledge) and knowing *what* (explicit knowledge) (Duguid, 2005).

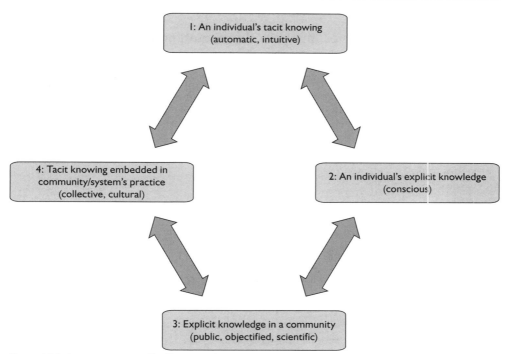

Figure 11.3 Learning as social/collective achievement

Figure 11.3 illustrates that an individual's explicit knowledge (2) of how to teach is linked to tacit knowing (1), which comes from many things including personal biography, beliefs, experiences of schooling and very often informal and subliminal sources (Eraut, 2000). It can be observed through an individual's intuitive actions and judgements, and in part captured through reflection or metacognition. Tacit knowledge is also considered to be those valuable context-based experiences that cannot easily be captured, codified and stored (Davenport and Prusak, 2000). An individual's explicit knowledge can also come from apprenticeship, books, focused observations, the Internet and through networking.

Figure 11.3 also illustrates the interplay between the tacit knowing (4) and explicit knowledge (3) embedded within a community. In addition to the variables associated with each individual, other sources of tacit knowing and explicit knowledge within a community include its history and folk memory. The links between an individual and community suggest that people learn both as individuals within groups, and reciprocally groups can learn from individuals. Thus, each new teacher brings tacit knowing and explicit knowledge into the school context which not only undergoes modification as he becomes socialised into the established ways of working but can also influence the community's tacit knowing and explicit knowledge. The quality of the community and emphasis placed on *knowledge management* through such means as encouraging collegiality, informal interaction, formal and non-formal learning opportunities contribute significantly to a teacher's professional learning.

A community of practice is a particular type of professional learning community and refers to a group of people who share an interest, craft and/or profession. The

Reflective task 11.3 **Professional learning communities in school**

Within the context of your own school, identify the range of groups you are currently attached to, e.g. curriculum area, subject department, year group, special working group, whole-school staff.

For each of these groups, use the Wenger et al. (2002) defining characteristics of a community of practice to describe how it is structured in relation to:

- domain of knowledge
- community
- practice.

Now consider ways in which each of these groups exemplify the seven attributes of effective professional learning communities identified by Dufour (2004).

Reflect upon the following:

- Which groups enhance your own professional learning? How and why?
- Which groups do you contribute toward the most? How and why?

Write a 2,000-word reflective narrative to critically analyse and evaluate the personal benefits and frustrations (if appropriate) of working in professional learning communities within the context of your own school over the past year.

group evolves naturally due to the members' common interest in a particular area or it can be created with the specific goal of gaining knowledge relevant to their field. Through sharing information and experiences within the group, members learn from one another and have the opportunity to develop both personally and professionally (Lave and Wenger, 1991). Wenger (1998: 72–73) explains how the community of practice is structured around three fundamental principles:

- *Mutual engagement*: through participation within the community, members establish norms and build collaborative relationships, which bind the members of the community together as a social entity;
- *Joint enterprise*: through their interactions group members create a shared understanding of what binds them together, which can be (re)negotiated by its members and is often referred to as the 'domain' of the community;
- *Shared repertoire*: as part of its practice the community produces a set of communal resources that are used in the pursuit of their joint enterprise, which can include literal and symbolic meanings.

This structure was refined further by Wenger *et al.* (2002) to capture the notion that learning is central to the formation of identity, e.g. the individual as an active participant in the practice of social communities constructs her identity through these communities. Thus, structural characteristics of a community of practice were revised and based around:

- *A domain of knowledge*: which creates common ground, inspires members to participate, guides their learning and gives meaning to their actions;
- *A community*: which creates the social fabric for learning – a strong community fosters interactions, encourages a willingness to share ideas and gain social capital;
- *Practice*: while the domain defines the general area of interest for the community, the practice is the specific focus around which the community develops, shares and maintains its core of knowledge.

Communities of practice have become associated with finding, sharing, transferring and archiving knowledge as well as making tacit knowledge and expertise more 'explicit'. Individually and collectively the community of practice is considered a rich potential source of helpful information in the form of actual experiences and best practices. Thus, for knowledge management and its principle concern to 'capture, organise and retrieve information', a community of practice is one source of content and context that when codified, documented and archived can be accessed for later use.

Reflective task 11.4 **New technologies for teacher learning**

1   Access the following two literary sources to explore ways in which new media tools and social networking web resources are being used for teacher learning:
    - Lieberman, A. and Mace, D. (2010) Making practice public: teacher learning in the twenty-first century, *Journal of Teacher Education*, 61 (1–2): 77–88.
    - Australian Government Quality Teacher Programme (AGQTP) (2008) *Innovative and Effective Professional Learning*, Department of Education, Employment and Work Relations: Commonwealth of Australia.
2   Search the Advanced Skills Teachers website (www.advancedskillsteachers.com), Future Lab (www.futurelab.org.uk) and/or the Teacher Training Resource Bank (www.ttrb.ac.uk) to find additional examples related to your own curriculum or subject area.
3   Within your own school, explore the ways in which new media tools and social networking web resources are being used by five teachers in different curriculum or subject areas.
4   Identify up to three ways in which other teachers, by making their own practice with new media tools and social networking web resources public, could enhance your own teaching. Plan to develop these in your future teaching and seek the necessary guidance and support well in advance.
5   If you yourself are a 'digital native' and confident in this area, consider ways in which you can support teacher learning within your own school.

Continuing professional development

As a teacher you have a professional responsibility (see Chapter 1) to engage in continuing professional development (CPD) to ensure you stay abreast of new developments across the professional landscape of education, which is in a constant state of flux, so that you can draw upon the most up-to-date knowledge and best practice available to inform your own teaching. In light of Dewey's (1958) principle of the *continuity of experience*, which views education as the continual pursuit of becoming (a central tenet of adult learning theory (Tusting and Barton, 2003) inextricably linked to the development of personal and professional identity), it is also important to be mindful that: 'Learning can change and/or reinforce that which is learned, and can change and/or reinforce the *habitus* of the learner. In these ways, a person is constantly learning through becoming, and becoming through learning' (Hodkinson, Biesta and James, 2008: 41). This lends considerable support to the argument that each new learning experience should not only build upon former experiences but also build capacity for further learning and on-going professional growth and development.

Over the past decade, a significant amount of research has been undertaken to investigate the nature of professional development required by teachers at different stages of their career, and of ways in which it can be structured and organised to ensure, within the limited amount of time teachers have available when juxtaposed against competing priorities and pressures, that it leads to the best possible outcomes for teachers and supports career-long professional learning to improve educational practice. Many traditional forms of CPD including one-off, one-day sporadic provision often undertaken away from the school site have been found 'woefully inadequate' (Borko, 2004: 3), fragmented and disconnected from any prior teacher learning or indeed to the context within which such learning was to be applied (Day *et al.*, 2006; Lieberman and Miller, 2008; Muijs and Lindsay, 2008).

In 2006, the Training and Development Agency for Schools (TDA) developed a national strategy for teachers' CPD in England, part of which developed guidance for schools to develop a CPD policy. In this strategy, CPD is described as a 'reflective activity designed to improve an individual's attributes, knowledge, understanding and skills. It supports individual needs and improves professional practice' (TDA, 2008: 4); and as shown in Figure 11.4, three main sources of CPD have been identified.

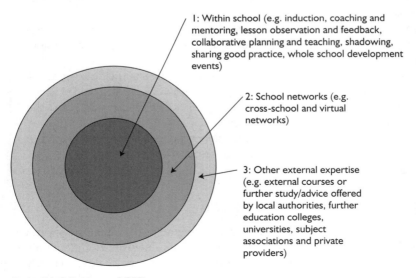

1: Within school (e.g. induction, coaching and mentoring, lesson observation and feedback, collaborative planning and teaching, shadowing, sharing good practice, whole school development events)

2: School networks (e.g. cross-school and virtual networks)

3: Other external expertise (e.g. external courses or further study/advice offered by local authorities, further education colleges, universities, subject associations and private providers)

Figure 11.4 Sources of CPD

Informed by substantive research studies and government reports, particularly those of Bolam and Weindling (2006); Cordingley, Bell, Isham, Evans and Firth (2007); Cordingley, Bell, Evans and Firth (2005); and Ofsted's (2006b) report entitled *The Logical Chain: CPD in Effective Schools*, the TDA identified eleven key features of effective CPD, as detailed in Table 11.1.

A strong theme permeating through these features is evaluating the impact of professional development in a way that has resonance with Guskey's (2000) five-stage hierarchical approach to effectively evaluate CPD by gathering robust evidence of: participant support, participant learning, organisational support, participant behaviour and pupil learning outcomes. This can be viewed as a positive step forward as Muijs and Lindsay (2008: 196) note that the hitherto use of post-event 'opinionnaires' so often failed to take account of how any professional learning might subsequently be applied in practice and was 'rarely undertaken in a systematic and focused manner'. Another important theme is the focus on customising CPD to suit the needs of each individual participant, as the VITAE project (Day *et al.*, 2006: xv) has revealed, one source of dissatisfaction relating to the range of CPD in-service courses and events provided, was the focus on 'classroom knowledge and skill updating, the implementation of policy and other organisation related matters' rather than the developmental needs of individual teachers' professional life phases.

The TDA (2008: 19) suggest participants need to consider the following questions *before* any professional development event is undertaken:

1   Who have you discussed the potential impact of your intended learning outcomes with?
2   What specific outcomes will result from this professional development activity? How will your practice be changed? How will the professional development benefit you?
3   How will the professional development benefit the wider school, your colleagues, and children and young people?
4   When would it be appropriate to evaluate the evidence of outcomes (e.g. short-, medium- or long-term staged reviews)?
5   How will the evidence base for evaluating the impact of the professional development be collected? How will children and young people contribute to this? What will be the form of evidence?
6   What would be appropriate criteria to judge the intended impact?

The TDA (ibid.: 20) also suggest participants need to consider the following questions *after* the professional development event has been completed and that this dialogue should take place within the context of revised performance management arrangements:

1   What is your evidence of impact? Is there more evidence to be reviewed? If so, when will it be available for review?
2   Does the evidence suggest that the professional development had the intended impact on you, your colleagues, your school and your students, when judged against the agreed criteria? If not, why might this be the case?
3   Were there any unexpected outcomes for you, for your colleagues, your school, or your students?

Table 11.1 Key features of effective CPD (adapted from TDA, 2008: 6)

Each activity is part of a coherent long-term plan that gives the participants opportunities to apply what they have learned, evaluate the effect on their practice, and develop their practice	Research shows that CPD is most effective when it is sustained, as part of a deliberately planned process
It is planned with a clear vision of the effective or improved practice being sought. This vision is shared by those undertaking the development and by the people leading or supporting it	The plan needs to show precisely what expertise, understanding or technique the CPD is intended to deliver. Sharply defined outcomes are also the starting point for evaluating the impact of CPD
It enables the participants to develop skills, knowledge and understanding which will be practical, relevant and applicable to their current role or career aspiration, e.g. in curriculum or subject content, teaching and learning strategies and the uses of technology	CPD is only effective when it is directly relevant to each participant. Where CPD is provided for large groups, or for the whole staff, it may be useful to separate the participants into smaller groups so the CPD can be customised to suit each type of participant
It is provided by people with the necessary experience, expertise and skills	These providers may sometimes be colleagues and peers. Other times they may be specialists from inside or outside the school
It is based on the best available evidence about teaching and learning	The evidence needs to include current research and inspection evidence. Research shows that pupils learn best when staff are motivated, developed and updated. Research also indicates positive links between pupils' learning and sustained CPD
It takes account of the participant's previous knowledge and experience	Professional learning needs to be tailored to the individual so that it provides experience and insights which build on their existing level of expertise. Professional learning journals and various forms of accreditation can be useful in ensuring a person's existing expertise is properly taken into account
It is supported by coaching and mentoring from experienced colleagues, either from within the school or from outside	Coaching is most effective when a staff member with a clearly identified need is paired with a colleague who has acknowledged expertise in that area
It uses lesson observation as a basis for discussion about the focus of CPD and its impact	Conducted in a collaborative and supportive manner, observations of teaching can be particularly useful for identifying areas for development
It models effective learning and teaching strategies, e.g. active learning	To be effective, CPD needs to go beyond theory and exposition. Ideally, it demonstrates techniques and strategies and gives the participant opportunities to try them out in a supportive setting
It promotes continuous enquiry and problem-solving embedded in the daily life of schools	A hallmark of effective CPD is an ethos in the school of lifelong learning and development. If the staff exemplify learning as an instinctive and continual activity, they will also act as role models for the pupils
Its impact on teaching and learning is evaluated, and this evaluation guides subsequent professional development activities	The ultimate purpose of all CPD in a school is to maintain the highest possible standards of education and care for children and young people. CPD needs to be vigorously evaluated to ensure it is making the maximum contribution to this objective. The most effective evaluations are planned from the outset as an integral part of the CPD

Reflective task 11.5 **CPD and performance management**

- Access a copy of the CPD policy in your school and find out how opportunities available to you at your particular career stage are situated within the wider context of whole-school CPD provision.
- If you are a newly qualified teacher (NQT), find out how the induction period, induction programme and appeals process operate by visiting the TDA induction website at www.tda.gov.uk/teacher/nqt-induction.aspx.
- If you have successfully completed your NQT induction period, find out how the revised arrangements for performance management and the review and appraisal of teachers and head teachers (effective from September 2007) operate by visiting one of the following links:
  - *The Education (School Teacher Performance Management) (England) Regulations 2006*: www.legislation.gov.uk/uksi/2006/2661/contents/made.
  - DfES (2006) *Performance Management for Teachers and Headteachers: Guidance:* www.education.gov.uk/publications (search for DFES-03984-2006).
- Arrange a meeting with your line manager (or designated mentor/coach) to discuss professional development opportunities in relation to your short-, medium- and long-term goals and aspirations.
- Prioritise three short-term goals and using the TDA guidelines set out above devise a professional development plan to realise these goals and to gather evidence of their impact on you, your pupils, colleagues and your school.

Professional Development Portfolio

To capture evidence of your professional growth and development as a teacher, which begins during your initial teacher education course and continues as you progress through each stage of your teaching career, you should create a Professional Development Portfolio (PDP). From the available literature on portfolios, the Wolf and Dietz (1998) model aptly portrays the professional development portfolio as a learning portfolio, as shown in Table 11.2. This shows that learning can be very effective when it occurs in the real-life contexts and situations within which teachers work to: collaboratively solve problems; work as 'critical friends' by observing one another teach and providing constructive, focused feedback on that teaching; rigorously investigate their own practice;

Table 11.2 Portfolio model (Wolf and Dietz, 1998)

Portfolio model	Professional growth and development
Purpose	To explore, extend, showcase and reflect on teachers' own learning (e.g. portfolios prepared for teacher education programmes or for individual growth plans)
Process	Teachers identify own goals and build portfolios that reflect these goals, self-assessment with assistance from peers or mentors
Audiences	Teacher/colleagues
Structure	Open-ended, teacher determined
Content	Wide variety of teacher selected work and records relating to self-selected goals

and construct a teaching portfolio to capture evidence of their learning. The reflective tasks embedded within each chapter of this book have been designed to provide a wealth of source material you can draw upon to evidence your professional growth and development as a teacher.

The principle purpose of a PDP is to advance teacher learning by enabling teachers to critically reflect on the development of their own work and to set goals for themselves as learners (Wolf and Dietz, 1998). The PDP thus becomes a highly personalised *collection* and *selection* of your work, with an emphasis on *reflection* and self-evaluation to exemplify your accomplishments and progress by target setting and on-going review. Box 11.1 provides an example of the reflective statement made by a primary post-graduate student teacher in response to the questions asked at Transition Point 1 of the Career Entry and Development Profile (CEDP). In addition to the evidence gathered during initial teacher education, particularly that selected to demonstrate achievement related to the Professional Standards for QTS, this statement is an important stepping stone for the NQT induction period, during which time similar reviews will be undertaken with a *professional tutor* at Transition Points 2 and 3 (http://www.tda.gov.uk/induction).

This statement highlights aspects of teaching in which the student teacher would value further experience; others will very likely surface during the induction period, particularly when working alongside colleagues toward the school improvement plan; and still others as her career trajectory unfurls and she prepares for the additional roles and responsibilities toward which she aspires. It is always important to prioritise personal goals and targets to ensure you do not take on too much in any given timeframe otherwise you may become overwhelmed and unable to accomplish them all.

In building your PDP, try to create a system that is easy to use and where you can readily access and store evidence. You might decide to organise your PDP chronologically, divide it by class, level or create specific sections, e.g. categories, themes or topics of interest. The structure will very much depend on the purpose of your PDP and the teaching context. You will need to be selective about what you decide to include and be prepared to exercise some flexibility in modifying the content by building in regular reviews and a basis for reflection. Think of it as a *work in progress,* which aims to help you evidence your knowledge, skills, accomplishments, expertise, goals and aspirations over time to demonstrate professional growth and development as your career progresses. It can be used for multiple purposes including when applying for jobs, career progression and as part of a formal inspection or school evaluation process. Ultimately, what goes into your PDP is for you to decide – it should be representative of you, your experience and on-going professional development. Artefacts you might select to evidence your on-going professional development include:

- qualifications and curriculum vitae;
- syllabi, units of work, lesson plans, reviews of lesson plans and activities;
- professional development plans and subsequent reviews;
- feedback from peers, mentors, supervisors;
- observation and appraisal reports with personal reflections following such events;
- reflections on aspects of your teaching;
- reflective log or learning diary;
- information, handouts, programmes from conferences, seminars and workshops you have participated in and reflections on sessions you have attended;

> *Reflective task 11.6* **Creating a Professional Development Portfolio**
>
> - Familiarise yourself with templates available in your institution or school for recording evidence of on-going progress and development, e.g. career profile, professional development plans (action plans), self-evaluation checklists, subject knowledge audits, lesson observation and feedback proformas, course attendance and evaluation forms.
> - Conduct a web search to find any alternative models, templates and ideas you could use and ask colleagues to share ideas and examples of their own PDP with you.
> - Select a range of evidence to represent your knowledge, skills, accomplishments, expertise, personal goals and aspirations at this moment in time.
> - Decide how you would like to present this evidence logically and coherently.
> - Create a well-structured and clearly indexed PDP, which enables you to build in regular reviews, modify and update content periodically and provides a sound basis for reflection.

- plans for training sessions you have delivered along with participants' evaluations of those sessions;
- support and guidance given to colleagues;
- samples of pupils' work and your feedback to them;
- records of assessing pupils and tracking their progress;
- notes and letters from parents/carers/ pupils;
- personal reflections on source material you have read and research undertaken.

Summary of key points

This chapter has explored key competencies embedded within the OECD (2003) framework that young people and adults need to develop in order to prepare for life's challenges in the modern world, and which situates teacher education as a career-long profession within the context of lifelong learning. To exemplify capacity building in the personal, interpersonal and organisational structures of twenty-first-century schools, the core characteristics of effective professional learning communities and communities of practice have been introduced. This enables you to recognise how the collective capability of the community as a site of learning through mutual engagement, joint enterprise and shared repertoire can significantly contribute toward your professional growth and development as a teacher.

The key features of effective CPD underpinned by evidence-based research have been introduced; of particular significance is the need to evaluate the impact of professional development and for opportunities to be tailored to meet the developmental needs of individual teachers at different career stages. To conclude, this chapter has considered the main purposes of the Professional Development Portfolio and provided guidance on how you might go about creating a PDP to evidence your knowledge, skills, accomplishments, expertise, goals and aspirations as you progress throughout your teaching career.

Box 11.1 **Reflective statement at Transition Point 1**

1   At this stage, which aspect(s) of teaching do you find most interesting and rewarding?
There are so many aspects of teaching that I feel are interesting and rewarding. I find the process of assessing the achievements of children and my teaching highly rewarding because it allows me to reflect on my teaching to identify areas of particular strength as well as any weaknesses that may have arisen. This then allows me to plan for follow-up lessons where I am confident I can address the needs of the whole class as well as any individuals that may need additional support, while at the same time eliminate the flaws in my teaching practice.

I find it extremely rewarding when I have taught the children a new skill or new knowledge and take immense pride when children show full understanding of a concept. My positive approach to mathematics was certainly transmitted to my pupils. A particular child had such anxiety about mathematics that it was having a detrimental effect on what she was capable of. My 'can do' approach made a real difference to her mathematics; she now loves fractions and percentages!

I also enjoy the positive impact I can have on shaping a child toward becoming a more valued citizen through teaching subjects such as PSHE and geography that supports the child's pastoral development. I particularly enjoyed working in an economically deprived school where I felt the children were eager to learn and I was making a real difference to their lives. I enjoyed hearing about the children's lives out of school and using this information to inform my academic planning to keep the children motivated and interested.

2   As you approach the award of QTS, what do you consider to be your main strengths and achievements as a teacher?
I consider my main strengths and achievements as a teacher are that I am able to reflect on my teaching in a purposeful way and then improve my practice in the lessons that follow. I have been able to take advice and suggestions on board and improve my teaching style. This was highlighted by both of my mentors who commented on my impressive evaluations. I believe this to be a vital attribute of a good teacher.

I am also aware of my professional duties as a teacher as well as the policies and practices of the workplace. I work collaboratively with other members of staff. Some of my best work is achieved when I cooperate with others and I can participate effectively as part of a team. I have listened to and contributed to discussion concerning planning and general classroom issues and concerns. I believe it is vital to be able to work as part of a team when working in a school environment.

I have an ability to form warm relationships with the children I teach and the staff I work with. I am approachable, which I feel is a valuable attribute to have when working with children. This will help me to form strong bonds with the children that I teach and allow me to establish a welcoming and safe teaching environment for the children to learn in.

I strongly believe in approaching lessons through a multi-sensory approach which assists all styles of learners and encourages variety in the lesson where children are active participants which promotes inclusion and positive behaviour in the lesson.

I have kept very detailed assessment records and used different forms of formative assessment including peer- and self-assessment. I have discovered that I have a potential strength in APP, as I found the assessment grids and highlighting AF statements a very good way to assess the progress of focus children throughout my school experiences. I feel that APP will help me to become more secure with accurately levelling the children's work.

I am a confident user of ICT to enhance children's learning and I feel that it is not only computer based, but also uses other sources like tape recorders, CD players and digital cameras which help children in learning about different topics. I have found opportunities for the children to develop their own ICT skills as well as making good use of the interactive whiteboard.

3   In which aspects of teaching would you value further experience?
One area I would value further experience with is the use of support staff within the classroom. I had a little experience with the use of Learning Support Assistants during my second teaching

placement working in Key Stage 2, but they had specific duties relating to two individual children with disabilities and so they were not used in the same way that a Teaching Assistant would be used in a school without disabled children. As I know that I will have a full-time Teaching Assistant during my induction year, I would value developing my skills to effectively use her to help support, develop and assess children's learning.

Another area that I feel is very important to further develop is differentiating activities so that children of all abilities can achieve their potential. I feel that I am able to do this already but there is room for improvement. For example, I would like to plan a lesson and be able to differentiate activities so that all children can work to their full potential; however, I feel that I need to develop my capacity to challenge and extend the gifted and talented children much more.

Although I have some experience in working with children who have English as an additional language, it is very limited. I would like to observe more experienced teachers so that I can see how they approach teaching in various subjects across the curriculum. I would like to develop my use of visual aids, although I am aware of demonstrations, sometimes children just need the props there for them to be able to focus and understand.

In my Key Stage 2 placement, I did not get to teach very much science beyond revision sessions in preparation for the optional QCA tests. This means that I have limited experience of providing interesting and practical science lessons at Key Stage 2, including science experiments. I am very keen to plan and teach stimulating science lessons in this phase as I had a very positive experience doing so in Key Stage 1.

I was limited in opportunities to develop my skills in phonics and feel this is an area I am less confident in and so I aim to further develop this area during my NQT year and will take the opportunity to observe experienced teachers in school before I start teaching.

I would also like to develop my subject knowledge in some of the Foundation subjects, e.g. Physical Education, Geography and Music.

Another area I am keen to develop is behaviour management. I have encountered and observed different strategies; some were effective and others were not so effective. During my induction period I would like to further develop my strategies and competence in this very important area because it has a domino effect in all other areas of the classroom environment and the attainment of pupils both academically and socially.

I feel I need to increase my experience of communicating to parents about their child's progress. I took every possible opportunity at both school placements to talk to parents/carers, however neither of the schools had parent consultations whilst I was there. This will naturally occur when I have my own class and I would like to be as prepared as I can be.

4   Do you have any thoughts about how you would like to see your career develop?
My main priority at this time is to focus my energies on becoming an 'outstanding' teacher and I am willing to do whatever I need to, to get there. I would hope to use my NQT year to really cement everything I have learnt throughout my year in university and put into practice anything I may not as yet have had the opportunity to experience. Also, I would like to spend the first two years of my career becoming more confident in my own teaching style as well as becoming more familiar with the day-to-day running of school life.

I would be interested in researching certain topics and further down the line engaging in the rest of my Masters Level qualifications.

My aspiration as a teaching professional is to become an art co-ordinator as this is an area of particular interest. I would like to improve the way in which art is taught and help teachers who may feel a little restricted in teaching art as a subject to feel more confident and get the most out of their children. I feel art is very important to teach well as it allows children to think outside the box and have the freedom to show their ideas and thought processes, seeing them develop in a visual way.

I would eventually like to become a year leader and then head of Key Stage 2.

Recommended reading

Borko, H. (2004) Professional development and teacher learning: mapping the terrain, *Educational Researcher*, 33 (8): 3–15.
This article maps the terrain of research on teacher professional development and provides an overview of what we have learned about effective professional development programmes and their impact on teacher learning. It suggests some important directions and strategies for extending our knowledge into some areas yet to be explored.

Facer, K. (2009) *Educational, Social and Technological Futures: A report from the Beyond Current Horizons Programme*, Beyond Current Horizons: Technology, Children, Schools and Families, Bristol: Futurelab.
This report explores social and technological change and considers the potential challenges and opportunities these provide for education. A number of socio-technical developments likely to occur in the next few decades are identified, which include: individuals in perpetual contact within networks and communities; growing sense of together apart; weakening institutional boundaries; machines assuming more traditional human roles; and widening inequality.

Kimble, C., Hildreth, P. and Bourdon, I. (eds) (2008) *Communities of Practice: Creating Learning Environments for Educators*, Information Age Publishing, ISBN 1593118635.
This book combines current academic research in education with practitioner-based experience to provide an eclectic mix of different perspectives on communities of practice in education from around the world. In Chapter 18 of volume 2 for example, Leonie Ramondt describes work from ULTRALAB and her experiences of facilitating virtual communities of practice at the National College of School Leadership in England. She presents a practical, step-by-step methodology for establishing online communities of practice, illustrated by case studies and observations, and explores how such communities can leverage the 'next generation' of technology.

Appendix A

Standards for teachers
(DfE, 2011: 5–8)

Preamble

Teachers make the education of their pupils their first concern, and are accountable for achieving the highest possible standards in work and conduct. Teachers act with honesty and integrity; have strong subject knowledge; keep their knowledge and skills as teachers up-to-date and are self-critical; forge positive professional relationships; and work with parents in the best interests of their pupils.

Part 1: Teaching

A teacher must:

1   Set high expectations which inspire, motivate and challenge pupils
    - establish a safe and stimulating environment for pupils, rooted in mutual respect
    - set goals that stretch and challenge pupils of all backgrounds, abilities and dispositions
    - demonstrate consistently the positive attitudes, values and behaviour which are expected of pupils.
2   Promote good progress and outcomes by pupils
    - be accountable for pupils' attainment, progress and outcomes
    - plan teaching to build on pupils' capabilities and prior knowledge
    - guide pupils to reflect on the progress they have made and their emerging needs
    - demonstrate knowledge and understanding of how pupils learn and how this impacts on teaching
    - encourage pupils to take a responsible and conscientious attitude to their own work and study.
3   Demonstrate good subject and curriculum knowledge
    - have a secure knowledge of the relevant subject(s) and curriculum areas, foster and maintain pupils' interest in the subject, and address misunderstandings
    - demonstrate a critical understanding of developments in the subject and curriculum areas, and promote the value of scholarship
    - demonstrate an understanding of and take responsibility for promoting high standards of literacy, articulacy and the correct use of standard English, whatever the teacher's specialist subject

    – if teaching early reading, demonstrate a clear understanding of systematic synthetic phonics

    – if teaching early mathematics, demonstrate a clear understanding of appropriate teaching strategies.

4   Plan and teach well-structured lessons

    – impart knowledge and develop understanding through effective use of lesson time; promote a love of learning and children's intellectual curiosity; set homework and plan other out-of-class activities to consolidate and extend the knowledge and understanding pupils have acquired

    – reflect systematically on the effectiveness of lessons and approaches to teaching; contribute to the design and provision of an engaging curriculum within the relevant subject area(s).

5   Adapt teaching to respond to the strengths and needs of all pupils

    – know when and how to differentiate appropriately, using approaches which enable pupils to be taught effectively; have a secure understanding of how a range of factors can inhibit pupils' ability to learn, and how best to overcome these

    – demonstrate an awareness of the physical, social and intellectual development of children, and know how to adapt teaching to support pupils' education at different stages of development; have a clear understanding of the needs of all pupils, including those with special educational needs, those of high ability, those with English as an additional language, those with disabilities, and be able to use and evaluate distinctive teaching approaches to engage and support them.

6   Make accurate and productive use of assessment

    – know and understand how to assess the relevant subject and curriculum areas, including statutory assessment requirements; make use of formative and summative assessment to secure pupils' progress; use relevant data to monitor progress, set targets, and plan subsequent lessons; give pupils regular feedback, both orally and through accurate marking, and encourage pupils to respond to the feedback.

7   Manage behaviour effectively to ensure a good and safe learning environment

    – have clear rules and routines for behaviour in classrooms, and take responsibility for promoting good and courteous behaviour both in classrooms and around the school, in accordance with the school's behaviour policy

    – have high expectations of behaviour, and establish a framework for discipline with a range of strategies, using praise, sanctions and rewards consistently and fairly; manage classes effectively, using approaches which are appropriate to pupils' needs in order to involve and motivate them

    – maintain good relationships with pupils, exercise appropriate authority, and act decisively when necessary.

8   Fulfil wider professional responsibilities

    – make a positive contribution to the wider life and ethos of the school; develop effective professional relationships with colleagues, knowing how and when to draw on advice and specialist support; deploy support staff effectively

    – take responsibility for improving teaching through appropriate professional development, responding to advice and feedback from colleagues; communicate effectively with parents with regard to pupils' achievements and well-being.

Part 2: Personal and professional conduct

A teacher is expected to demonstrate consistently high standards of personal and professional conduct. The following statements define the behaviour and attitudes which set the required standard for conduct throughout a teacher's career.

- Teachers uphold public trust in the profession and maintain high standards of ethics and behaviour, within and outside school, by:
    - treating pupils with dignity, building relationships rooted in mutual respect, and at all times observing proper boundaries appropriate to a teacher's professional position
    - having regard for the need to safeguard pupils' well-being, in accordance with statutory provisions
    - showing tolerance of and respect for the rights of others
    - not undermining fundamental British values, including democracy, the rule of law, individual liberty and mutual respect, and tolerance of those with different faiths and beliefs
    - ensuring that personal beliefs are not expressed in ways which exploit pupils' vulnerability or might lead them to break the law.
- Teachers must have proper and professional regard for the ethos, policies and practices of the school in which they teach, and maintain high standards in their own attendance and punctuality.
- Teachers must have an understanding of, and always act within, the statutory frameworks which set out their professional duties and responsibilities.

Appendix B

Criteria to determine 'outstanding' trainee teachers

(Ofsted, 2008)

In lessons, outstanding trainees:

- teach lessons that are mostly good, and often show characteristics of outstanding lessons
- ensure that all learners make good progress so that they fully achieve the challenging intended learning outcomes
- teach learners to be able to explain how the teaching helped them to make progress
- teach lessons that invariably capture the interest of learners, are inclusive of all learners, and feature debate between learners and the teacher
- have a rapport with learners – high-quality dialogue and questioning, guiding learning, with attention to individuals and groups
- monitor learners' progress to evaluate quickly how well they are learning so that they can change the approach during the lesson if necessary, and provide detailed feedback and targets to individual learners that are focused well to ensure further progress
- demonstrate the ability to apply their own depth of subject knowledge to support learners in acquiring understanding and skills, often showing understanding, through application of a range of different approaches to ensure that all learners make the expected progress
- demonstrate flexibility and adaptability by changing pace, approach and teaching method in a lesson in response to what learners say and do
- make links with other aspects of learners' development and understanding (for example, linking to work in other subjects)
- fully exploit possibilities to promote learners' understanding and appreciation of social and cultural diversity.

Outstanding trainees' explanations:

- describe the stages in progress through a topic/set of ideas and concepts/sequence of teaching – explaining what they would look for in learners
- can give examples of lessons, and individual/groups of learners, to illustrate this – including the identification of barriers to learning and how these were/can be overcome
- are able to discuss in detail individual learners' progress as well as attainment/ achievement

- are able to use their depth of subject-specific pedagogical understanding to explain in detail why they use particular teaching approaches and why these are likely to be more successful than others
- demonstrate an understanding of the range of professionals that contribute to learners' overall development and their place in the 'bigger picture' – well-informed discussion about individual/groups of learners and particular needs
- show a depth of understanding of the implications of Every Child Matters across a wide range of work and how to promote learners' understanding and exploit the potential provided by social and cultural diversity.

Noticeable characteristics of outstanding trainees. They:

- take risks when trying to make teaching interesting, are able to deal with the unexpected and 'grab the moment'
- inspire and communicate their enthusiasm to learners
- have an intrinsic passion for learning
- show innovative and creative thinking – lateral thinkers
- have the ability to reflect critically and rigorously on their own practice to inform their professional development, and to take and evaluate appropriate actions – they are able to learn from their mistakes
- take full responsibility for their own professional development
- are highly respected by learners and colleagues and, where appropriate, parents/ carers and employers
- have the clear capacity to become outstanding teachers
- demonstrate, or show the capacity to develop leadership and management skills.

Outstanding trainees' files:

- demonstrate a clear and deep understanding of how to plan for progression – stages in learning, different rates of progress, identifying clear 'strands of progression' and the use of these to plan 'steps in learning', their teaching, dealing with barriers to learning, and through this demonstrate depth of subject knowledge and subject pedagogy
- provide evidence of monitoring and recording learners' progress and how the outcomes are used in subsequent planning, with a clear focus on groups and individual learners
- demonstrate the clarity of links between learning objectives, teaching approaches and assessment strategies – 'what I want learners to learn, how they will learn, and how I know that they have, what I will do next'
- show innovation within the constraints of a scheme of work/curriculum
- maintain working documents – annotated as part of self-evaluation
- show high-quality self-evaluation with clear focus on learners and setting challenging targets for their own professional development – including, for example, future career progression with evidence of implementation and further review, and critical analysis and reflection, taking full account of feedback from trainers and other professionals they work with
- demonstrate innovative approaches to the integration of Every Child Matters, and social and cultural diversity.

References

Aaronson, C., Carter, J. and Howel, M. (1995) Preparing monocultural teachers for a multicultural world: attitudes toward inner-city schools, *Equity and Excellence in Education*, 28 (1): 5–9.

Abbey, D., Hunt, D. and Weiser, J. (1985) Variations on a theme by Kolb: a new perspective for understanding counseling and supervision, *The Counseling Psychologist*, 13 (3): 477–501.

Acker, S. (1999) *The Realities of Teachers' Work: Never A Dull Moment*, London: Cassell.

Adams, C. and Forsyth, P. (2006) Proximate sources of collective teacher efficacy, *Journal of Educational Administration*, 44, 625–642.

Allard, A. and Cooper, M. (1997) *Too much talk, not enough action: An investigation of fourth year teacher education students' responses to issues of gender in the teacher education curriculum*, Paper presented at the Annual Meeting of the American Educational Research Association, Chicago, March.

Argyris, C. and Schon, D. (1974) *Theory into Practice: Increasing Professional Effectiveness*, San Francisco, CA: Jossey-Bass.

Ashton, P. and Webb, R. (1986) *Making a Difference: Teachers' Sense of Efficacy and Student Achievement*, New York: Longman.

Askew, M. and Wiliam, D. (1995) *Recent research in mathematics education 5–16*, Office for Standards in Education, ISBN: 0113500491.

Assessment Reform Group (ARG) (2002) *Assessment for Learning: 10 research-based principles to guide classroom practice*, Online: http://www.assessment-reform-group.org.uk

Australian Government Quality Teacher Programme (AGQTP) (2008) *Innovative and Effective Professional Learning*, Department of Education, Employment and Workplace Relations: Commonwealth of Australia.

Ball, S. and Goodson, I. (1985) *Teachers' Lives and Careers*, Lewes: Falmer Press.

Bandura, A. (1986) *Social Foundations of Thought and Action: A Social Cognitive Theory*, Englewood Cliffs, NJ: Prentice-Hall.

Bandura, A. (1997) *Self-efficacy: The Exercise of Control*, New York: Freeman.

Bandura, A. (2006) Guide for constructing self-efficacy scales, in F. Pajares and T. Urdan (eds) *Self-efficacy Beliefs of Adolescents*, Greenwich, CT: Information Age.

Banks, F., Leach, J. and Moon, B. (1999) New understandings of teachers' pedagogic knowledge, in J. Leach and B. Moon (eds) *Learners and Pedagogy*, pp. 89–110, London: Paul Chapman.

Barber, M. and Mourshed, M. (2007) *How the World's Best-performing School Systems Come Out on Top*, London: McKinsey and Company.

Barnett, R. (1997) *Higher Education: A Critical Business*, Buckingham: Open University Press.

Bassey, M. (1998) Action research for improving practice, in R. Halsall (ed) *Teacher Research and School Improvement: Opening Doors from the Inside*, Buckingham: Open University Press.

Baxter Magolda, M. (1999) *Creating Contexts for Learning and Self-authorship*, San Francisco: Jossey-Bass.

Beattie, M. (2000) Narratives of professional learning: Becoming a teacher and learning to teach, *Journal of Educational Enquiry*, 1 (2), 1–22.

Bell, J. (2005) *Doing your Research Project: A Guide for First Time Researchers in Education and Social Sciences*, 4th edition, Maidenhead: Open University Press.

Bennett, S., Maton, K. and Kervin, L. (2008) The 'digital natives' debate: a critical review of the evidence, *British Journal of Educational Technology*, 29 (5): 775–786.

Ben Peretz, M. (1995) Curriculum of teacher education programs, in L. Anderson (ed) *International Encyclopaedia of Teaching and Teacher Education* (pp. 543–547), Oxford: Elsevier Science/Pergamon.

Betoret, F. (2006) Stressors, self-efficacy, coping resources and burnout among secondary school teachers in Spain, *Educational Psychology*, 26, 519–539.

Beynon, J. and Toohey, K. (1995) Access and aspirations: careers in teaching as seen by Canadian university students of Chinese and Punjabi-Sikh ancestry, *Alberta Journal of Educational Research*, 41 (4): 435–461.

Bird, T., Anderson, L., Sullivan, B. and Swidler, S. (1993) Pedagogical balancing acts: attempts to influence prospective teachers' beliefs, *Teaching and Teacher Education*, 9 (3): 253–267.

Black, P. and Wiliam, D. (1998) *Inside the Black Box: Raising Standards through Classroom Assessment*, London: King's College.

Black, P. and Wiliam, D. (2002) *Working Inside the Black Box: Assessment for Learning in the Classroom*, London: King's College.

Black, P., Harrison, C., Lee, C., Marshall, B. and Wiliam, D. (2003) *Assessment for Learning: Putting It into Practice*, Maidenhead: Open University Press.

Block, J. and Hazelip, K. (1995) Teachers' beliefs and belief systems, in L. Anderson (ed) *International Encyclopedia of Teaching and Teacher Education*, 2nd edition, New York: Pergamon Press.

Bloom, B. (1956) *Taxonomy of Educational Objectives, Handbook 1: Cognitive Domain*, London: Longman.

Bolam, R. and Weindling, D. (2006) Synthesis of research and evaluation projects concerned with capacity building through teachers' professional development, Online: http://www.gtce.org.uk/networks/personal_cpd/news/think_tank/

Borich, G. (1996) *Effective Teaching Methods*, 3rd edition, New York: Macmillan.

Borko, H. (2004) Professional development and teacher learning: mapping the terrain, *Educational Researcher*, 33 (8): 3–15.

Borko, H. and Mayfield, V. (1995) The roles of the cooperating teacher and university supervisor in learning to teach, *Teaching and Teacher Education*, 11 (5): 501–518.

Boshuizen, H. (2003) Expertise development: how to bridge the gap between school and work, Inaugural address, Heerlen: Open Universiteit Nederland.

Boud, D. (1999) Avoiding the traps: seeking good practice in the use of self assessment and reflection in professional courses, *Social Work Education*, 18, 121–132.

Boud, D. and Miller, N. (1996) *Working with Experience: Animating Learning*, London: Routledge.

Boud, D., Keogh, R. and Walker, D. (1985) Promoting reflection in learning: a model, in D. Boud, R. Keogh and D. Walker (eds) *Reflection: Turning Experience into Learning*, London: Kogan Page.

Boyatzis, R., Goleman, D. and Rhee, K. (2000) Clustering competence in emotional intelligence: insights from the Emotional Competence Inventory [ECI], in R. Bar-On and J. Parker (eds) *Handbook of Emotional Intelligence*, San Francisco: Jossey-Bass. Online: www.eiconsortium.org

British Educational Research Association (BERA) (2004) *Revised Ethical Guidelines for Ethical Research*, Southwell: BERA.

Bronfrenbrenner, U. (1979) *The Ecology of Human Development,* Cambridge, MA: Harvard University Press.

Brookfield, S. (1995) *Developing Critical Thinkers: Challenging Adults to Explore Alternative Ways of Thinking and Acting,* San Francisco: Jossey-Bass.

Brophy, J. and Good, T. (1986) Teacher behaviour and student achievement, In M. Wittrock (ed) *Handbook of Research on Teaching,* 3rd edition, New York: Macmillan.

Brouwer, C. (1989) *Geintegreerde lerarenopleiding, principes en effecten* (Integrated teacher education, principles and effects), Amsterdam: Brouwer.

Brown, J. and Duguid, P. (2000) *The Social Life of Information,* Cambridge, MA: Harvard University Press.

Brown, J., Collins, A. and Duguid, P. (1989) Situated cognition and the culture of learning, *Educational Researcher,* 18, 32–42.

Bruce, C. and Ross, J. (2008) A model for increasing reform implementation and teacher efficacy: teacher peer coaching in grades 3 and 6 mathematics, *Canadian Journal of Education,* 31, 346–370.

Bruner, J. (1996) *The Culture of Education,* Cambridge, MA: Harvard University Press.

Bullough, R. (1997) Practicing theory and theorising practice in teacher education, in J. Russell (ed) *Purpose, Passion and Pedagogy in Teacher Education,* London: Falmer Press.

Busher, H. (2002) Ethics of research in education, in M. Coleman and A. Briggs (eds) *Research Methods in Educational Leadership and Management,* London: Paul Chapman.

Butler, R. (1944) *Education Act 1944,* London: House of Commons, Online: www.legislation. gov.uk

Byron, T. (2008) *Safer children in a digital world: the report of the Byron Review,* DCSF and DCMS, Online: www.dcsf.gov.uk/byronreview/

Calderhead, J. (1989) Reflective teaching and teacher education, *Teaching and Teacher Education,* 5 (1): 43–51.

Calderhead, J. (1996) Teachers: beliefs and knowledge, in D. Berliner and R. Calfee (eds) *Handbook of Educational Psychology,* New York: Macmillan.

Calderhead, J. and Robson, M. (1991) Images of teaching: Student teachers' early conceptions of classroom practice, *Teaching and Teacher Education,* 7, 1–8.

Campbell, S., Freedman, E., Boulter, C. and Kirkwood, M. (2003) *Issues and Principles in Educational Research for Teachers,* Southwell: British Educational Research Association.

Carr, W. (1992) Practical enquiry, values and the problem of educational theory, *Oxford Review of Education,* 18 (3): 241–251.

Carr, W. and Kemmis, S. (1986) *Becoming Critical: Education, Knowledge and Action Research,* Lewes, Sussex: Falmer Press.

Centre for Studies on Inclusion in Education (CSIE) (1989) *The Inclusion Charter,* Online: www.csie.org.uk

Centre for Studies on Inclusion in Education (CSIE) (2000) *Index for Inclusion: Developing Learning and Participation in Schools,* Bristol: SSIE with University of Manchester and Christ Church University College, Canterbury.

Centre for the Use of Research and Evidence in Education (CUREE) (2005) *Mentoring and Coaching CPD Capacity Building Project 2004–2005; National Framework for Mentoring and Coaching,* CUREE/DfES.

Cheminais, R. (2006) *Every Child Matters: A Practical Guide for Teachers,* London: Fulton.

Chetcuti, K. (2002) Becoming a reflective practitioner, in C. Bezzina, A. Grima, D. Purchase and R. Sultana (eds) *Inside Secondary Schools: A Maltese Reader,* Malta: Indigo Books.

Clandinin, D. and Connelly, M. (eds) (1995) *Teachers' Professional Knowledge Landscapes,* New York: Teachers' College Press.

Clark, C. (1988) Asking the right questions about teacher preparation: contributions of research on teacher thinking, *Educational Researcher,* 17 (2), 5–12.

Clark, C. and Peterson, P. (1986) Teachers' thought processes, in M. Wittrock (ed) *Handbook of Research on Teaching*, 3rd edition, New York: Macmillan.

Cohen, L. and Manion, L. (1994) *Research Methods in Education*, London: Routledge.

Cohen, L., Manion, L. and Morrison, K. (2007) *Research Methods in Education*, 6th edition, London: RoutledgeFalmer.

Connelly, F. and Clandinin, D. (1990) Stories of experience and narrative inquiry, *Educational Researcher*, 19 (5), 2–14.

Cordingley, P., Bell, M., Evans, D. and Firth, A. (2005) The impact of collaborative CPD on classroom teaching and learning. Review: What do teacher impact data tell us about collaborative CPD? Report, in *Research Evidence in Education Library*, London: EPPI-Centre, Social Science Research Unit, Institute of Education, University of London.

Cordingley, P., Bell, M., Isham, C., Evans, D. and Firth, A. (2007) What do specialists do in CPD programmes for which there is evidence of positive outcomes for pupils and teachers? Report, in *Research Evidence in Education Library*, London: EPPI-Centre, Social Science Research Unit, Institute of Education, University of London.

Corporaal, B. (1988) *Bouwstenen voor een opleidingsdidactiek* (Building blocks for a pedagogy in teacher education), De Lier: Academisch Boeken Centrum.

Cowan, J. (1998) *On Becoming an Innovative University Teacher: Reflection in Action*, Buckingham: Open University Press.

Croll, P. and Moses, D. (1988) Teaching methods and time on task in junior classrooms, *Educational Researcher*, 30 (2): 90–97.

Davenport, T. and Prusak, L. (2000) *Working Knowledge: How Organisations Manage What They Know*, 2nd edition, Cambridge, MA: Harvard Business School Press.

Day, C. (1999) *Developing Teachers: The Challenges of Lifelong Learning*, London: Falmer Press.

Day, C., Elliot, B. and Kington, A. (2005) Reforms, standards and teacher identity: challenges of sustaining commitment, *Teaching and Teacher Education*, 21, 563–577.

Day, C., Kington, A., Stobart, G. and Sammons, P. (2006) The personal and professional selves of teachers: stable and unstable identities, *British Educational Research Journal*, 32, (4): 601–616.

Day, C., Stobart, G., Sammons, P., Kington, A., Gu, Q., Smees, R. and Mujtaba, T. (2006) *Variations in Teachers' Work, Lives and Effectiveness (VITAE)*, Research Report RR743: Department for Education and Skills.

Denzin, N. (1984) *On Understanding Emotion*, San Francisco: Jossey-Bass.

Denzin, N. and Lincoln, Y. (eds) (1998) *Strategies of Qualitative Inquiry*, Thousand Oaks, CA: Sage.

Department for Children, Schools and Families (DCSF) (2008a) *The Assessment for Learning Strategy*, Nottingham: DCSF.

Department for Children, Schools and Families (DCSF) (2008b) *Personalised Learning – A Practical Guide*, Nottingham: DCSF.

Department for Education (DfE) (1994) *Code of Practice on the Identification and Assessment of Pupils with Special Educational Needs*, London: DfE.

Department for Education (DfE) (2011) Teachers' Standards, Online: www.education.gov.uk

Department for Education and Employment (DfEE) (1995) *Disability Discrimination Act (1995): A Consultation on the Employment Code of Practice Guidance on the Definition of Disability and Related Regulations*, London: DfEE.

Department for Education and Employment (DfEE) (1997) *Excellence for All*, London: DfEE.

Department for Education and Employment/Qualifications and Curriculum Authority (DfEE/QCA) (1999) *The National Curriculum for England*, London: The Stationery Office.

Department for Education and Skills (DfES) (2001) *Special Educational Needs Code of Practice*, Nottingham: DfES.

Department for Education and Skills (DfES) (2003) *Summary of the Green Paper, Every Child Matters*, Norwich: The Stationery Office.

Department for Education and Skills (DfES) (2004a) *Five Year Strategy for Children and Learners,* London: DfES.

Department for Education and Skills (DfES) (2004b) *Pedagogy and Practice: Teaching and Learning in Secondary Schools, Unit 7: Questioning,* London: DfES.

Department for Education and Skills (DfES) (2004c) *Pedagogy and Practice: Teaching and Learning in Secondary Schools, Unit 11: Active engagement techniques,* London: DfES.

Department for Education and Skills (DfES) (2004d) *Pedagogy and Practice: Teaching and Learning in Secondary Schools, Unit 6: Modelling,* London: DfES.

Department for Education and Skills (DfES) (2004e) *Pedagogy and Practice: Teaching and Learning in Secondary Schools, Unit 8: Explaining,* London: DfES.

Department for Education and Skills (DfES) (2004f) *Pedagogy and Practice: Teaching and Learning in Secondary Schools, Unit 10: Group work,* London: DfES.

Department for Education and Skills (DfES) (2004g) *Every Child Matters: Change for Children in Schools,* Nottingham: DfES.

Department for Education and Skills (DfES) (2004h) *Children Act 2004,* Nottingham: DfES.

Department for Education and Skills (DfES) (2004i) *Removing Barriers to Achievement: The Government's SEN Strategy,* Nottingham: DfES.

Department for Education and Skills (DfES) (2004j) *Pedagogy and Practice: Teaching and Learning in Secondary Schools, Unit 12: Assessment for learning,* London: DfES.

Department for Education and Skills (DfES) (2004k) *A National Conversation about Personalised Learning,* Nottingham: DfES.

Department for Education and Skills (DfES) (2005) *Implementing the Disability Discrimination Act in Schools and Early Years Settings,* Nottingham: DfES.

Department for Education and Skills (DfES) (2006) *Performance Management for Teachers and Headteachers,* London: DfES.

Department for Education and Skills (DfES) (2007) *Pedagogy and Personalisation,* London: DfES.

Department of Education and Science and the Welsh Office (DES/WO) (1988) *National Curriculum Task Group on Assessment and Testing* (the TGAT Report), London: DES/WO.

Dewey, J. (1910) *How We Think,* New York: Promethius.

Dewey, J. (1933) *How We Think: A Restatement of the Relation of Reflective Thinking to the Educative Process,* Boston: DC Heath and Company.

Dewey, J. (1958) *Education and Experience,* New York: Macmillan.

Dillon, J. and Maguire, M. (eds) (2001) *Becoming a Teacher: Issues in Secondary Teaching,* 3rd edition, Buckingham: Open University Press.

Dolk, M. (1997) *Onmiddellijk onderwijsgedrag* (Immediate teaching behavior), Utrecht: WCC.

Dreyfus, H. and Dreyfus, S. (1986) *Mind Over Machine,* Oxford: Blackwell.

Druskat, V., Sala, F. and Mount, G. (eds) (2006) *Linking Emotional Intelligence and Performance at Work: Current Research Evidence with Individuals and Groups,* Mahwah, NJ: Lawrence Erlbaum.

Dufour, R. (2004) Schools as learning communities, *Educational Leadership,* 61 (8): 6–11.

Dufour, R. and Eaker, R. (1998) *Professional Learning Communities at Work: Best Practices for Enhancing Student Achievement,* Bloomington, IN: National Educational Service.

Duguid, P. (2005) The art of knowing: social and tacit dimensions of knowledge and the limits of communities of practice, in *The Information Society,* Taylor and Francis, 109–118.

Dweck, C. (2000) *Self-theories: Their Role in Motivation, Personality and Development,* Psychology Press, ISBN: 1841690244.

Dyson, A., Howes, A. and Roberts, B. (2002) A systematic review of the effectiveness of school-level actions for promoting participation by all students, in *Research Evidence in Education Library,* London: EPPI-Centre, Social Science Research Unit, Institute of Education, University of London.

Eisner, E. (1998) *The Enlightened Eye: Qualitative Inquiry and the Enhancement of Educational Practice*, Upper Saddle River, NJ: Prentice Hall.

Elliott, J. (1991) *Action Research for Educational Change*, Milton Keynes: Open University Press.

Elliott, J. (1998) *The Curriculum Equipment: Meeting the Challenge of Social Change*, Buckingham: Open University Press.

Elliott, J. (2005a) Becoming critical: the failure to connect, *Educational Action Research*, 13 (3): 359–373.

Elliott, J. (2005b) *Using Narrative in Social Research: Qualitative and Quantitative Approaches*, London: Sage.

Elliott, J. (2006) *Reflecting Where the Action Is*, London: Routledge.

Ellis, C. and Bochner, A. (2000) Autoethnography, personal narrative, reflexivity: researcher as subject, in N. Denzin and Y. Lincoln (eds) *Handbook of Qualitative Research*, London: Sage.

Empirica (2006) Benchmarking access and use of ICT in European schools 2006, European Commission Staff Working Document, *Progress towards the Lisbon objectives in education and training, indicators and Benchmarks* (2007), p. 95.

Eraut, M. (1994) *Developing Professional Knowledge and Competence*, Lewes: Falmer Press.

Eraut, M. (2000) Non-formal learning and tacit knowledge in professional work, *British Journal of Educational Psychology*, 70, 113–136.

Eraut, M. (2007) Learning from other people in the workplace, *Oxford Review of Education*, 33 (4): 403–422.

European Trade Union Committee for Education (ETUCE) (2008) *Teacher Education in Europe: An ETUCE Policy Paper*, Brussels: ETUCE.

Evans, R. (1992) The state of the union in industrial, technical and technology teacher education, *Journal of Industrial Teacher Education*, 29 (2): 7–14.

Facer, K. (2009) *Educational, Social and Technological Futures: A Report from the Beyond Current Horizons Programme*, Beyond Current Horizons: Technology, Children, Schools and Families, Bristol: Futurelab.

Fairclough, N. (1998) *Discourse and Social Change*, Cambridge: Polity Press.

Fenstermacher, G. (1986) Philosophy of research on teaching: three aspects, in M. Wittrock (ed) *Handbook of Research on Teaching*, 3rd edition, New York: Macmillan.

Firestone, W. (1996) Images of teaching and proposals for reform: a comparison of ideas from cognitive and organisational research, *Educational Administration Quarterly*, 32 (2): 209–235.

Fishbein, M. and Ajzen, I. (1975) *Belief, Attitude, Intention and Behavior*, Reading, MA: Addison-Wesley.

Fontana, A. and Frey, J. (2000) *The Interview: From Structured Questions to Negotiated Text*, 2nd edition, Thousand Oaks, CA: Sage.

Fosnot, C. (1996) Teachers construct constructivism: The Center for Constructivist Teaching/ Teacher Preparatino Project, in C. Fosnot (ed) *Constructivism: Theory, Perspectives and Practice*, New York: Teachers' College Press.

Franz, N. (2005) Transformative learning in intra organization partnerships: facilitating personal, joint and organizational change, *Journal of Transformative Education*, 3 (3): 254–270.

Fraser, B. (1989) Research syntheses on school and instructional effectiveness, in B. Creemers and J. Scheerens (eds) *International Journal of Educational Research*, 13 (7): 707–719.

Freire, P. (1972) *Pedagogy of the Oppressed*, Harmondsworth: Penguin.

Fullan, M. (1999) *Change Forces: The Sequel*, London: Falmer Press.

Furlong, J. (2000) *Higher Education and the New Professionalism of Teachers: Realising the Potential of Partnership*, A discussion paper, London: SCOP/CVCP.

Furlong, J. and Maynard, T. (1995) *Mentoring Student Teachers: The Growth of Professional Knowledge*, London: Routledge.

Furlong, J., Barton, L., Miles, S., Whiting, C. and Whitty, G. (2000) *Teacher Education in Transition: Re-forming Professionalism*, Buckingham: Open University Press.

Gabriele, A. and Joram, E. (2007) Teachers' reflections on their reform-based teaching in mathematics: implications for the development of teacher self-efficacy, *Action in Teacher Education*, 29, 60–74.

Galton, M. (1987) An ORACLE chronicle: a decade of classroom research, *Teaching and Teacher Education*, 3 (4): 299–313.

Garner, I. (2000) Problems and inconsistencies with Kolb's learning styles, *Educational Psychology*, 20: 341–349.

General Teaching Council for England (GTCE) (2006a) *The Statement of Professional Values and Practice for Teachers*, Online: www.gtce.org.uk. Accessed 12.09.08.

General Teaching Council for England (GTCE) (2006b) *Peer Observation*, London: GTC, Code: P-TP02-0906.

Gentry, M., Steenbergen-Hu, S. and Choi, B. (2011) Student-identified exemplary teachers: insights from talented teachers, *Gifted Child Quarterly*, 55 (2) 111–125.

Ghaye, A. and Ghaye, K. (1998) *Teaching and Learning through Critical Reflective Practice*, London: David Fulton.

Gillborn, D. and Mirza, H. (2000) *Educational Inequality: Mapping Race, Class and Gender – A synthesis of Research and Evidence*, London: Office for Standards in Education.

Glaser, B. and Strauss, A. (1967) *The Discovery of Grounded Theory: Strategies for Qualitative Research*, Chicago: Aldine.

Goddard, R., Hoy, W. and Woolfolk Hoy, A. (2004) Collective efficacy beliefs: theoretical developments, empirical evidence and future directions, *Educational Researcher*, 33 (3): 3–13.

Gomez, M. (1994) Teacher education reform and prospective teachers' perspectives on teaching 'other people's' children, *Teaching and Teacher Education*, 10 (3): 319–334.

Good, T. and Brophy, J. (2000) *Looking in Classrooms*, 8th edition, New York: Addison-Wesley Longman.

Goodman, J. (1988) Constructing a practical philosophy of teaching: a study of pre service teachers' professional perspectives, *Teaching and Teacher Education*, 4, 121–137.

Goodson, I. and Hargreaves, A. (eds) (1996) *Teachers' Professional Lives*, London: Falmer Press.

Gordon, K. (1995) The self-concept and motivational patterns of resilient African American high school students, *Journal of Black Psychology*, 21: 239–255.

Gore, J. (1993) *The Struggle for Pedagogies*, London: Routledge.

Graber, K. (1996) Influencing student beliefs: the design of a 'high impact' teacher education program, *Teaching and Teacher Education*, 12 (5): 451–466.

Grimmett, P., Mackinnon, A., Erickson, G. and Riechen, T. (1990) Reflective practice in teacher education, in R. Clift, W. Houston and M. Pugach (eds) *Encouraging Reflective Practice in Education: An Analysis of Issues and Programs*, New York: Teachers' College Press.

Grossman, P. (1990) *The Making of a Teacher: Teacher Knowledge and Teacher Education*, New York: Teachers' College Press.

Guskey, T. (2000) *Evaluating Professional Development*, Thousand Oaks, CA: Corwin Press.

Habermas, J. (1971) *Knowledge and Human Interests* (trans. J. Shapiro), London: Heinemann.

Hargreaves, A. (1998) The emotional practice of teaching, *Teaching and Teacher Education*, 14 (8): 835–854.

Hargreaves, A. (1999) Series Editor's Forward, in S. Acker, *The Realities of Teachers' Work: Never a Dull Moment*, London: Cassell.

Hargreaves, D. (2003) *Teaching in the Knowledge Society: Education in the Age of Insecurity*, Maidenhead: Open University Press.

Harris, A. (1996) Effective teaching, *School Improvement Network Bulletin*, London: Institute of Education.

Hattie, P. and Timperley, H. (2007) The power of feedback, *Review of Educational Research*, 27 (1): 53–64.

Hatton, N. and Smith, D. (1995) Reflection in teacher education: towards definition and implementation, *Teaching and Teacher Education,* 11 (1): 33–49.

Haydon, G. (1997) *Teaching About Values: A New Approach,* London: Cassell.

Hegarty, S. (2000) Teaching as a knowledge-based activity, Special Issue: The Relevance of Educational Research, *Oxford Review of Education,* 26 (3 and 4): 451–465.

Hill, P. and Rowe, K. (1996) Modelling student progress in studies of educational effectiveness, *School Effectiveness and School Improvement,* 9 (3): 310–333.

Hine, A. (2000) Mirroring effective education through mentoring, metacognition and self reflection, Paper presented at the Australian Association for Research in Education Conference, Sydney.

Hochschild, A. (1993) *The Managed Heart: The Commercialisation of Human Feeling,* Berkeley: University of California Press.

Hodkinson, P., Biesta, G. and James, D. (2008) Understanding learning culturally: overcoming the dualism between social and individual views of learning, *Vocations and Learning,* 1, 27–47.

Hollingsworth, S. (1989) Prior beliefs and cognitive change in learning to teach, *American Educational Research Journal,* 26, 160–189.

Holmes, L. (2004) Underactive area of brain implicated in children with ADHD. Belmont, Massachusetts: Ascribe News. 9th June 2004. Available at: http://mentalhealth.about.com/library/archives/0300/blmriadd300.htm.

Holt-Reynolds, D. (1992) Personal history-based beliefs as relevant prior knowledge in coursework: can we practice what we teach? *American Educational Research Journal,* 29, 325–349.

Hooper, S. and Reiber, L. (1995) Teaching with technology, in A. Ornstein (ed) *Teaching: Theory into Practice,* Neeham Heights: Allyn and Bacon.

Hopkins, J. (2002) *A Teachers' Guide to Classroom Research,* 3rd edition, Buckingham: Open University Press.

Hord, S. (1997) *Professional Learning Communities: Communities of Continuous Inquiry and Improvement,* Austin, TX: Southwest Educational Development Laboratory.

Hoyle, E. (1974) Professionality, professionalism and control in teaching, *London Education Review,* 3 (2), 13–19.

Hoyle, E. and John, P. (1995) *Professional Knowledge and Professional Practice,* London: Cassell.

Humes, W. (2001) Conditions for professional development, *Scottish Educational Review,* 33 (1), 6–17.

Hunt, D. (1987) *Beginning With Ourselves in Practice, Theory and Human Affairs,* Cambridge, MA: Brookline Books.

James, M. and Pollard, A. (2006) *Improving Teaching and Learning in Schools: A TLRP Commentary,* London: TLRP.

Jay, J. and Johnson, K. (2002) Capturing complexity: a typology of reflective practice for teacher education, *Teaching and Teacher Education,* 18, 73–85.

Johnson, D. and Johnson, R. (1994) *Joining Together: Group Theory and Group Skills,* Prentice Hall, ISBN: 0205158463.

Johnson, D. and Johnson, R. (1999) *Learning Together and Alone: Cooperative, Competitive and Individualistic Learning,* Allyn and Bacon, ISBN: 0205287719.

Joyce, B., Weil, M. and Calhoun, E. (2009) *Models of Teaching,* 8th edition, Boston, MA: Allyn and Bacon.

Kagan, D. (1990) Ways of evaluating teacher cognition: inferences concerning the Goldilocks principle, *Review of Educational Research,* 60, 419–469.

Kagan, D. (1992) Professional growth among pre service and beginning teachers, *Review of Educational Research,* 62, 129–169.

Kayes, D. (2002) Experiential learning and its critics: preserving the role of experience in management education, *Academy of Management Learning and Education,* 1 (2): 137–149.

Kelchtermans, G. (2009) Who I am in how I teach is the message: self-understanding, vulnerability and reflection, *Teachers and Teaching: Theory and Practice,* 15 (2): 257–272.

Kemmis, S. (1988) Action research in retrospect and prospect, in Deakin University, *The Action Research Reader,* Victoria: Deakin University Press.

Kemmis, S. and McTaggart, R. (2005) Participatory action research: communicative action and the public sphere, in N. Denzin and Y. Lincoln (eds) *Handbook of Qualitative Research,* 3rd edition, London: Sage.

Kennedy, M. (2004) Reform ideals and teachers' practical intentions, *Education Policy Analysis Archives,* 12 (13). Retrieved 20 April 2011 from http://epaa.asu.edu/epaa/v12n13/

Kimble, C., Hildreth, P. and Bourdon, I. (eds) (2008) *Communities of Practice: Creating Learning Environments for Educators,* Information Age Publishing, ISBN 1593118635.

King, P. and Kitchener, K. (1994) *Developing Reflective Judgement,* San Francisco, CA: Jossey-Bass.

Knight, P. (2002) A systemic approach to professional development: learning as practice, *Teaching and Teacher Education,* 18 (3), 229–241.

Kolb, D. (1971) *Individual Learning Styles and the Learning Process,* Working Paper #535-71, Sloan School of Management, Massachusetts Institute of Technology.

Kolb, D. (1984) *Experiential Learning: Experience as the Source of Learning and Development,* Englewood Cliffs, NJ: Prentice Hall.

Kolb, D. (1999) *Learning Style Inventory, Version 3,* Boston, MA: Training Resources Group Hay/McBer, Boston, MA. Retrieved from trg_mcber@haygroup.com

Kolb, A. and Kolb, D. (2005) Learning styles and learning spaces: enhancing experiential learning in higher education, *Academy of Management Learning and Education,* 4 (2): 193–212.

Korthagen, F. (1993) Two modes of reflection, *Teaching and Teacher Education,* 9 (3): 317–326.

Korthagen, F. and Kessels, J. (1999) Linking theory and practice, *Educational Researcher,* 28 (4): 4–17.

Korthagen, F. and Lagerwerf, B. (1996) Reframing the relationship between teacher thinking and teacher behaviour: levels in learning about teaching, *Teachers and Teaching: Theory and Practice,* 2 (2): 161–190.

Korthagen, F. and Vasalos, A. (2005) Levels in reflection: core reflection as a means to enhance professional growth, *Teachers and Teaching: Theory and Practice,* 11 (1), 47–71.

Korthagen, F. (in cooperation with) Kessels, J., Koster, B., Lagerwerf, B. and Wubbels, T. (2001) *Linking Practice and Theory: The Pedagogy of Realistic Teacher Education,* London: Routledge.

Koshy, V. (2005) *Action Research for Improving Practice: A Practical Guide,* London: Paul Chapman.

Kounin, J. (1970) *Discipline and Group Management in Classrooms,* New York: Holt, Rinehart and Winston.

Kyriacou, C. (1986) *Effective Teaching in Schools,* Cheltenham: Stanley Thorne.

LaBoskey, V. (1993) A conceptual framework for reflection in preservice teacher education, in J. Calderhead and P. Gates (eds) *Conceptualizing Reflection in Teacher Development,* Lewes: Falmer Press.

Lave, J. and Wenger, E. (1991) *Situated Learning: Legitimate Peripheral Participation,* Cambridge: Cambridge University Press.

Leask, M. and Younie, S. (2001) Communal constructivist theory: information and communications technology pedagogy and internationalisation of the curriculum, *Journal of Information Technology for Teacher Education,* 10 (1–2): 117–134.

LeCompte, M. and Dworkin, A. (1991) *Giving Up on School: Student Dropouts and Teacher Burnouts,* Newbury Park, CA: Corwin Press.

Lee, H. (2005) Understanding and assessing preservice teachers reflective thinking, *Teaching and Teacher Education*, 21, 699–715.

Leinhardt, G. (1990) Capturing craft knowledge in teaching, *Educational Researcher*, 19 (2): 18–25.

Levin, B. and Ye He (2008) Investigating the content and sources of teacher candidates' personal practical theories (PPTs), *Journal of Teacher Education*, 59 (1) 55–68.

Lewin, K. (1946) Action research and minority problems, *Journal of Social Issues*, 2, 34–46.

Lewin, K. (1952) Group decision and social change, in G. Swanson, T. Newcomb and L. Hartley (eds) *Readings in Social Psychology*, New York: Holt.

Lieberman, A. and Mace, D. (2010) Making practice public: teacher learning in the twenty-first century, *Journal of Teacher Education*, 61 (1–2): 77–88.

Lieberman, A. and Miller, L. (eds) (2008) *Teachers in Professional Communities: Improving Teaching and Learning*, New York: Teachers' College Press.

Lomax, P. (2002) Action research, in M. Coleman and A. Briggs (eds) *Research Methods in Educational Leadership and Management*, London: Paul Chapman.

Lortie, D. (1975) *School Teacher: A Sociological Study*, Chicago: University of Chicago Press.

Loughran, J. (1996) *Developing Reflective Practice: Learning about Teaching and Learning Through Modelling*, London: Falmer Press.

MacFarlane, J. (1985) The Education Act 1981, *British Medical Journal*, Vol 290, 22 June.

Macintyre, C. (2000) *The Art of Action Research in the Classroom*, London: David Fulton.

MacKinnon, A. (1989) *Reflection in a science teaching practicum*, Paper presented at the annual conference, AERA, San Francisco.

Mainemelis, C., Boyatzis, R. and Kolb, D. (2002) Learning styles and adaptive flexibility: testing experiential learning theory, *Management Learning*, 33 (1): 5–33.

Mayer, J. and Salovey, P. (1997) What is emotional intelligence? In P. Salovey and D. Sluyter (eds) *Emotional Development and Emotional Intelligence: Implications for Educators*, New York: Basic Books.

McCall, A. (1995) Constructing conceptions of multicultural teaching: pre service teachers' life experiences and teacher education, *Journal of Teacher Education*, 46 (5): 340–350.

McIntyre, D. (1993) Theory, theorising and reflection in initial teacher education, in J. Calderhead and P. Gates (eds) *Conceptualising Reflection in Teacher Education*, London: Falmer Press.

McIntyre, D. (2005) Bridging the gap between research and practice, *Cambridge Journal of Education*, 35 (3), 357–382.

McKernan, J. (1996) *Curriculum Action Research: A Handbook of Methods and Resources for the Reflective Practitioner*, 2nd edition, London: Kogan Page.

Mertz, N. and McNeely, S. (1992) *Pre-existing teaching constructs: how students 'see' teaching prior to training*, Paper presented at the Annual Meeting of the American Educational Research Association, San Francisco, April.

Mezirow, J. (1990) *Fostering Critical Reflection in Adulthood: A Guide to Transformative and Emancipatory Learning*, San Francisco: Jossey-Bass.

Mills, C. (2003) Characteristics of effective teachers of gifted students: teacher background and personality styles of students, *Gifted Child Quarterly*, 47 (4): 272–281.

Milner, H. and Woolfolk Hoy, A. (2003) A case study of an African American teacher's self-efficacy, stereotype threat, and persistence, *Teaching and Teacher Education*, 19, 263–276.

Ministry of Education (2005) *Education For All: the report of the expert panel on literacy and numeracy instruction for students with special education needs, kindergarten to grade 6*, Ontario Education, ISBN 0779480600.

Moon, J. (1999) *Reflection in Learning and Professional Development*, London: Kogan Page.

Moon, J. (2005) *We Seek It Here: A new perspective on the elusive activity of critical thinking: A theoretical and practical approach*, Higher Education Academy: University of Bristol.

Moore, A. (2000) *Teaching and Learning Pedagogy: Curriculum and Culture,* London: Routledge Falmer.

Moran, A. and Dallart, J. (1995) Promoting reflective practice in initial teacher training, *International Journal of Educational Management,* 9 (5): 20–26.

Mortimore, P., Sammons, P., Stoll, L., Lewis, D. and Ecob, R. (1988) *School Matters,* Wells, Somerset: Open Books.

Moshman, D. (1999) *Adolescent Psychological Development,* Mahwah, NJ: Lawrence Erlbaum Associates.

Mosston, M. and Ashworth, S. (2002) *Teaching Physical Education,* 5th edition, San Francisco: Benjamin Cummings.

Muijs, D. and Lindsay, G. (2008) Where are we at? An empirical study of levels and methods of evaluating continuing professional development, *British Educational Research Journal,* 34 (2): 195–212.

Muijs, D. and Reynolds, D. (2001) *Student Background and Teacher Effects on Achievement and Attainment in Mathematics: A Longitudinal Study,* Presentation at the International Congress for School Effectiveness and School Improvement, Toronto, January.

Muijs, D. and Reynolds, D. (2011) *Effective Teaching: Evidence and Practice,* 3rd edition, London: Paul Chapman (Sage).

Muijs, D., Harris, A., Chapman, C., Stoll, L. and Russ, J. (2004) Improving schools in socio-economically disadvantaged areas: an overview of research, *School Effectiveness and School Improvement,* 15 (2): 149–176.

National Curriculum Council and the National Oracy Project (1997) *Teaching, Talking and Learning in Key Stage 3,* National Curriculum Council titles, ISBN: 1872676278.

Nespor, J. (1987) The role of beliefs in the practice of teaching, *Journal of Curriculum Studies,* 19, 317–328.

Nind, M., Wearmouth, J. with Collins, J., Hall, K., Rix, J. and Sheehy, K. (2004) A systematic review of pedagogical approaches that can effectively include children with special educational needs in mainstream classrooms with a particular focus on peer group interactive approaches, in *Research Evidence in Education Library,* London: EPPI-Centre, Social Science Research Unit, Institute of Education, University of London.

Nixon, J. (1995) Teaching as a profession of values, in J. Smyth (ed) *Critical Discourses in Teacher Development,* London: Routledge.

Nonaka, I. and Konno, N. (1998) The concept of 'ba': building a foundation for knowledge creation, *California Management Review,* 40 (3): 40–54.

Nosich, G. (2005) *Learning to Think Things Through: A Guide to Critical Thinking Across the Disciplines,* 2nd edition, New Jersey: Pearson-Prentice Hall.

Office for Standards in Education (Ofsted) (2000) *Improving Schools: The Framework,* London: Ofsted.

Office for Standards in Education (Ofsted) (2006a) *Inclusion: Does It Matter Where Pupils Are Taught?* HMI Report 2535.

Office for Standards in Education (Ofsted) (2006b) *The Logical Chain: CPD in Effective Schools,* London: Ofsted.

Office for Standards in Education (Ofsted) (2008) Grade criteria for the inspection of initial teacher education 2008–2011, Online: www.ofsted.gov.uk

Office for Standards in Education (Ofsted) (2010) *The Safe Use of Technologies,* London: Crown, Online: www.ofsted.gov.uk/publications/090231

O'Leary, Z. (2004) *The Essential Guide to Doing Research,* London: Sage.

Oppenheim, A. (1992) *Questionnaire Design, Interviews and Attitude Measurement,* London: Cassell.

Organisation for Economic Cooperation and Development (OECD) (2003) *The Definition and Selection of Key Competencies: Executive Summary,* Paris: OECD.

Organisation for Economic Cooperation and Development (OECD) (2005) *Teachers Matter: Attracting, Developing and Retaining Effective Teachers, An Overview,* Paris: OECD, Online: www.oecd.org (April 2010).

Pajares, M. (1992) Teachers' beliefs and educational research: cleaning up a messy construct, *Review of Educational Research,* 62 (3), 307–332.

Pajares, M. (1996) Self-efficacy beliefs in academic settings, *Review of Educational Research,* 66 (4): 543–578.

Palincsar, A. and Brown, A. (1984) Reciprocal teaching and comprehension fostering and comprehension monitoring activities, *Cognition and Instruction,* 1: 117–175.

Palmer, J. (1998) *The Courage to Teach: Exploring the Inner Landscape of a Teacher's Life,* San Francisco: Jossey-Bass.

Parker, S. (1997) *Reflective Teaching in the Postmodern World: A Manifesto for Education in Postmodernity,* Buckingham: Open University Press.

Parsons, S. and Bynner, J. (1998) *Influences on Adult Basic Skills Factors Affecting the Development of Literacy and Numeracy from Birth to 37,* London: Basic Skills Unit.

Paul, R. and Elder, L. (2006) *The Miniature Guide to Critical Thinking Concepts and Tools,* 4th edition, Dillon Beach, CA: Foundation for Critical Thinking.

Pendlebury, S. (1995) Reason and story in wise practice, in H. McEwan and K. Egan (eds) *Narrative in Teaching, Learning and Research,* New York: Teachers' College Press.

Perry, W. (1970) *Forms of Intellectual and Ethical Developments in the College Years,* New York: Holt, Rhinehart and Winston.

Petrie, H. (1986) *The Liberal Arts and Sciences in the Teacher Education Curriculum,* Paper presented at the Conference on Excellence in Teacher Preparation through the Liberal Arts, May, Muhlenberg College, Allentown, PA.

Phillips, D. (2007) Adding complexity: philosophical perspectives on the relationship between evidence and policy, in P. Moss (ed) *Evidence and Decision Making,* the 106th yearbook of the National Society for the Study of Education (376–402), Malden, MA: Blackwell.

Piaget, J. (1967) *Six Psychological Studies,* New York: Random House.

Pickering, J., Daly, C. and Pachler, N. (eds) (2007) New designs for teachers' professional learning, *Bedford Way Papers,* London: Institute of Education.

Pintrich, P. and Schunk, D. (2002) *Motivation in Education: Theory, Research and Applications,* 2nd edition, Columbus, OH: Merrill Prentice Hall.

Polkinghorne, D. (1995) Narrative configuration in qualitative analysis, in J. Hatch and R. Wisniewski (eds) *Life History and Narrative,* London: Falmer Press.

Pollard, A. (2002) *Reflective Teaching: Effective and Evidence-informed Professional Practice,* London: Continuum.

Pollard, A. (ed) (2010) *Professionalism and Pedagogy: A Contemporary Opportunity.* Commentary by TLRP and GTCE. London: TLRP.

Pollard, A., Collins, S., Maddock, M., Simco, S., Swaffield, S., Warin, J. and Warnick, P. (2005) *Reflective Teaching,* 2nd edition, London: Continuum.

Qualifications and Curriculum Authority (QCA) (2008) *National Curriculum for England,* London: Crown, Online: http://curriculum.qcda.org.uk

Qualifications and Curriculum Development Agency (QCDA) (2010a) *A Big Picture of the Primary Curriculum,* London: Crown, Online: bigpicture_pri_04_tcm-157420–1.pdf

Qualifications and Curriculum Development Agency (QCDA) (2010b) *A Big Picture of the Secondary Curriculum,* London: Crown, Online: bigpicture_sec_05_tcm8–157430.pdf

Reason, P. and Bradbury, H. (2001) *Handbook of Action Research: Participative Enquiry and Practice,* London: Sage.

Resnick, L. (1987) Learning in school and out, *Educational Researcher,* 16, 13–20.

Reynolds, A. (1995) The knowledge base for beginning teachers: education professionals' expectation versus research findings on learning to teach, *Elementary School Journal,* 95 (3): 199–221.

Richardson, V. (1996) The role of attitudes and beliefs in learning to teach, in J. Sikula, T. Buttery and E. Guyton (eds) *Handbook of Research on Teacher Education*, 2nd edition, New York: Macmillan.

Roberts, J. (2006) Teachers of secondary gifted students, in F. Dixon and S. Moon *The Handbook of Secondary Gifted Education*, Waco, TX: Prufrock.

Robinson, A. (2008) Teacher characteristics, in J. Plucker and S. Callahan (eds) *Critical Issues and Practices in Gifted Education*, Waco, TX: Prufrock.

Robson, C. (2002) *Real World Research*, Oxford: Blackwell.

Rodgers, C. (2002) Defining reflection: another look at John Dewey and reflective thinking, *Teachers College Record*, 104 (4), 842–866.

Rodgers, C. and Raider-Roth, M. (2006) Presence in teaching, *Teachers and Teaching: Theory and Practice*, 12 (3): 265–287.

Rogers, B. (2011) *Classroom Behaviour: A Practical Guide to Effective Teaching, Behaviour Management and Colleague Support*, 3rd edition, London: Sage.

Rogers, C. (1983) *Freedom to Learn for the 80s*, Columbia, OH: Charles E. Merrill.

Rokeach, M. (1972) *Beliefs, Attitudes and Values: A Theory of Organisation and Change*, San Francisco: Jossey-Bass.

Rosenholtz, S. (1989) *Teachers' Workplace: The Social Organisation of Schools*, New York: Longman.

Ruddock, J. and McIntyre, D. (2007) *Improving Learning through Consulting Pupils*, London: Routledge.

Russell, T. and Munby, H. (2002) *Teachers and Teaching: From Classroom to Reflection*, 3rd edition, London: Falmer Press.

Rust, F. (1994) The first year of teaching: it's not what they expected, *Teaching and Teacher Education*, 10 (2): 205–217.

Rutter, M., Maughan, B., Mortimore, R. and Ousten, J. (1979) *Fifteen Thousand Hours: Secondary Schools and their Effects on Children*, London: Open Books.

Rychen, K. and Salganik, L. (eds) (2003) *Key Competencies for a Successful Life and a Well-functioning Society*, Gottingen: Hogrefe and Huber.

Sammons, P. (1999) *School Effectiveness: Coming of Age in the Twenty-First Century*, Lisse, PA: Swets and Zeitlinger.

Sammons, P., West, A., and Hind, A. (1997) Accounting for variations in pupil attainment at the end of Key Stage 1, *British Educational Research Journal*, 23: 489–511.

Sammons, P., Sylva, K., Melhuish, E., Siraj-Blatchford, I., Taggart, B., Barreau, S. and Grobbe, S. (2008) *Effective Pre-School and Primary Education 3–11 Project (EPPE): The Influence of School and Teacher Quality on Children's Progress in Primary School*, Nottingham: DCSF.

Scheerens, J. (1995) *Measuring the Quality of Schools*, Washington DC: OECD Information and Publications Centre.

Schon, D. (1983) *The Reflective Practitioner: How Professionals Think in Action*, New York: Basic Books.

Schon, D. (1987) *Educating the Reflective Practitioner*, San Francisco: Jossey-Bass.

Schon, D. (ed) (1991) *The Reflective Turn: Case Studies in and on Educational Practice*, New York: Teachers' College Press.

Schunk, D. and Zimmerman, B. (1997) Social origins of self-regulatory competence, *Educational Psychologist*, 32 (4): 195–208.

Schwab, J. (1978) *Science, Curriculum and Liberal Education*, Chicago: University of Chicago Press.

Senge, P. (1990) *The Fifth Discipline: The Art and Practice of the Learning Organisation*, New York: Currency Doubleday.

Shapiro, B. (1991) A collaborative approach to help novice science teachers reflect on changes in their construction of the role of science teacher, *Alberta Journal of Educational Research*, 37 (2): 119–132.

Shulman, L. (1986) Those who understand: knowledge growth in teaching, *Educational Researcher,* February, 4–14.

Shulman, L. (1987) Knowledge and teaching: foundations of the new reform, *Harvard Educational Review,* 57, 1–22.

Slavin, R. (1996) *Education For All,* Swets and Zeitlinger, ISBN: 9026514735.

Smyth, J. (1992) Teachers' work and the politics of reflection, *American Educational Research Journal,* 29 (2): 267–300.

Sparks-Langer, G. (1992) In the eye of the beholder: cognitive, critical and narrative approaches to teacher reflection, in L. Valli (ed) *Reflective Teacher Education: Cases and Critiques,* New York: SUNY Press.

Stenhouse, L. (1975) *An Introduction to Curriculum Research and Development,* London: Heinemann Education.

Stenhouse, L. (1983) Curriculum, research and the art of the teacher, in L. Stenhouse (ed) *Authority, Education and Emancipation: A Collection of Papers,* London: Heinemann Education.

Stevens, R. (1996) Introduction: making sense of the person in the social world, in R. Stevens (ed) *Understanding the Self,* Milton Keynes: Open University Press.

Stoddart, T., Stofflett, R. and Gomez, M. (1992) *Breaking the Didactic Teaching–Learning–Teaching Cycle: Reconstructing Teacher's Knowledge,* Paper presented at the Annual Meeting of the American Educational Research Association, San Francisco, April.

Stooksberry, L., Schussler, D. and Bercaw, L. (2009) Conceptualising dispositions: intellectual, cultural and moral domains of teaching, *Teachers and Teaching: Theory and Practice,* 15 (6): 719–736.

Strand, S. (2002) Pupil mobility, attainment and progress during Key Stage 1: a study in cautious interpretation, *British Education Research Journal,* 28: 63–78.

Stringer, E. (1996) *Action Research: A Handbook for Practitioners,* London: Sage.

Sugrue, C. (1996) Student teachers' lay theories: Implications for professional development, in F. Goodson and A. Hargreaves (eds) *Teachers' Professional Lives,* Washington DC: Falmer Press.

Tatto, M. (1996) Examining values and beliefs about teaching diverse students: understanding the challenge for teacher education, *Educational Evaluation and Policy Analysis,* 18 (2), 155–180.

Teddlie, C. and Stringfield, S. (1993) *Schools Make a Difference: Lessons Learned from a 10-Year Study of School Effects,* New York: Teachers' College Press.

Thomas, S. and Mortimore, P. (1996) Comparison of value-added models for secondary-school effectiveness, *Research Papers in Education,* 11 (1): 5–33.

Thompson, A. (1992) Teachers' beliefs and conceptions: a synthesis of the research, in D. Grouws (ed) *Handbook of Research on Mathematics Teaching and Learning,* New York: Macmillan.

Tickle, L. (2000) *Teacher Induction: The Way Ahead,* Buckingham: Open University Press.

Timmering, L., Snoek, M. and Dietze, A. (2009) *How Do Teachers in Europe Identify Teacher Quality?* Paper presented at the Association for Teacher Education in Europe (ATEE) Annual Conference, Mallorca, August.

Tizard, B., Blatchford, P., Burke, J., Farquar, C. and Plewis, I. (1988) *Young Children at School in the Inner City,* Hove: Lawrence Erlbaum.

Training and Development Agency for Schools (TDA) (2007a) *Professional Standards for Teachers: Qualified Teacher Status,* Online at: www.tda.gov.uk. Accessed 06.08.08.

Training and Development Agency for Schools (TDA) (2007b) *Supporting the Induction Process: TDA Guidance for Newly Qualified Teachers,* Online at: www.tda.gov.uk. Accessed 20.10.08.

Training and Development Agency for Schools (TDA) (2008) *Continuing Professional Development Guidance,* London: TDA.

Trumbull, D. (1990) Evolving conceptions of teaching: reflections of one teacher, *Curriculum Enquiry,* 20, 161–182.

Tschannen-Moran, M., Woolfolk Hoy, A. and Hoy, W. (1998) Teacher efficacy: its meaning and measure, *Review of Educational Research*, 68, 202–248.

Tusting, K. and Barton, D. (2003) *Models of Adult Learning: A Literature Review*, Leicester: NRDC for ALN.

UNESCO (1994) *The Salamanca Statement and Framework for Action on Special Educational Needs*, Paris: UNESCO.

UNICEF (2007) Child poverty in perspective: an overview of child well being in rich countries, *Innocenti Report Card 7*, Florence, Italy: UNICEF Innocenti Research Centre.

Valli, L. (ed) (1992) *Reflective Teacher Education: Cases and Critiques*, Albany, NY: SUNY Press.

Valli, L. (1995) The dilemma of race: Learning to be color blind and color conscious, *Journal of Teacher Education*, 46 (2): 120–129.

Van Hiele, P. (1986) *Structure and Insight: A Theory of Mathematics Education*, Orlando, FL: Academic Press.

Van Manen, M. (1977) Linking ways of knowing with ways of being practical, *Curriculum Inquiry*, 6 (3): 205–228.

Van Manen, M. (1990) *Researching Lived Experience: Human Science for an Action Sensitive Pedagogy*, Albany: State University of New York Press.

Van Manen, M. (1991) *The Tact of Teaching: The Meaning of Pedagogical Thoughtfulness*, Albany, NY: SUNY Press.

Vygotsky, L. (1986) *Thought and Language*, tr. and ed. A. Kozulin, London: MIT Press.

Wall, K. (2006) *Synoptic Literature Review of Research Relating to SEN and Linked to Initial Teacher Training*, London: Training and Development Agency for Schools (TDA).

Wallace, M. (1987) A historical review of action research: some implications for the education of teachers in their management role, *Journal of Education for Teaching*, 13 (2): 97–115.

Warnock, H. (1978) *Special Educational Needs: Report of the Committee of Enquiry into the Education of Handicapped Children and Young People* (The Warnock Report), London: HMSO, Online: www.sen.ttrb.ac.uk

Webb, N. (1991) Task-related verbal interaction and mathematics learning in small groups, *Journal for Research in Mathematics Education*, 22: 366–389.

Weber, S. and Mitchell, C. (1996) Drawing ourselves into teaching: studying the images that shape and distort teacher education, *Teaching and Teacher Education*, 12 (3): 303–313.

Weinstein, C. (1990) Prospective elementary teachers' beliefs about teaching: implications for teacher education, *Teaching and Teacher Education*, 6 (3): 279–290.

Wenger, E. (1998) *Communities of Practice: Learning, Meaning and Identity*, Cambridge: Cambridge University Press.

Wenger, E., McDermott, R. and Snyder, W. (2002) *Cultivating Communities of Practice: A Guide to Managing Knowledge*, Cambridge, MA: Harvard Business School Press.

Whitehead, J. (1993) *The Growth of Educational Knowledge: Creating Your Own Living Educational Theories*, Bournemouth: Hyde Publications.

Whitehead, J. (2009) Generating living theory and understanding in action research studies, *Action Research*, 7 (1): 85–99, Online: http://arj.sagepub.com/cgi/content/abstract/7/1/85

Whitehead, J. and Fitzgerald, B. (2006) Professional learning through a generative approach to mentoring: lessons from a training school partnership and their wider implications, *Journal of Education for Teaching*, 32 (1): 37–52.

Wilson, E. (2009) *School-based Research: A Guide for Education Students*, London: Sage.

Witherall, C. and Noddings, N. (1991) *Stories Lives Tell: Narrative and Dialogue in Education*, New York: Teachers' College Press.

Wittrock, M. (1986) (ed) *Handbook of Research on Teaching*, 3rd edition, New York: Macmillan.

Wolf, K. and Dietz, M. (1998) Teaching portfolios: purposes and possibilities, *Teacher Education Quarterly*, Winter, 9–23.

Woods, P., Jeffrey, B. and Troman, G. (1997) *Restructuring Schools, Reconstructing Teachers*, Buckingham: Open University Press.

Woolfolk, A. and Hoy, W. (1990) Prospective teachers' sense of efficacy and beliefs about control, *Journal of Educational Psychology*, 82, 81–91.

Wragg, E. (1984) Conducting and analysing interviews, in J. Bell, T. Bush, A. Fox, J. Goodey and S. Goulding (eds) *Conducting Small-Scale Investigations in Educational Management*, London: Harper Row.

Wragg, E. and Brown, G. (2001a) *Questioning in the Secondary School*, London: RoutledgeFalmer.

Wragg, E. and Brown, G. (2001b) *Explaining in the Secondary School*, London: RoutledgeFalmer.

Yinger, R. (1990) The convention of practice, in R. Clift, W. Houston and M. Pugach (eds) *Encouraging Reflective Practice in Education*, New York: Teachers' College Press.

Zeichner, K. and Liston, D. (1987) Teaching student teachers to reflect, *Harvard Educational Review*, 57 (1): 23–48.

Zeichner, K. and Liston, D. (1996) *Reflective Teaching: An Introduction*, Mahwah, NJ: Lawrence Erlbaum Associates.

Zulich, J., Bean, T. and Herrick, J. (1992) Charting stages of pre service teacher development and reflection in a multicultural community through dialogue journal analysis, *Teaching and Teacher Education*, 8 (4): 345–360.

Zull, J. (2002) *The Art of Changing the Brain: Enriching Teaching by Exploring the Biology of Learning*, Sterling, VA: Stylus.

Zwozdiak-Myers, P. (ed) (2007) *Childhood and Youth Studies*, Exeter: Learning Matters.

Zwozdiak-Myers, P. (2010) *An analysis of the concept reflective practice and an investigation into the development of student teachers' reflective practice within the context of action research*, London: Brunel University. PhD thesis.

Zwozdiak-Myers, P. and Audain, J. (2011) *Links between ICT Advanced Skills Teachers and Initial Teacher Education*, Guidance material for the TDA, London: Brunel University.

Zwozdiak-Myers, P., Cameron, K., Mustard, C., Leask, M. and Green, A. (2010) *Literature Review: analysis of current research, theory and practice in partnership working to identify constituent components of effective ITT partnerships*, Report for the TDA, London: Brunel University.

Index